Doing contextual theology

Christian theology, like all forms of knowledge, thinking and practice, arises from and in influenced by the context in which it is done. In *Doing Contextual Theology* Angie Pears demonstrates the radically contextual nature of Christian theology by focusing on different forms of liberation theology:

- Latin American liberation theologies
- Feminist informed theologies
- Black theologies
- Body, sexual, queer and indecent theologies
- Postcolonial theologies.

Pears analyses how each of these asserts a clear and persistent link to the Christian tradition whilst employing often radical approaches to many aspects of Christian belief, practice and organization. This book explores the relationship between local, contextual, experiential-based theologies and the Christian tradition.

Doing Contextual Theology offers students a clear and up-to-date survey of the field of contemporary liberation theology and provides them with a sound understanding of how contextual theology works in practice.

Angie Pears is Learning and Development Officer in Equality and Diversity at Nottingham Trent University.

Doing Contextual Theology

Angie Pears

Routledge
Taylor & Francis Group

LONDON AND NEW YORK

First published 2010
by Routledge
2 Park Square, Milton Park, Abingdon, Oxon OX14 4RN

Simultaneously published in the USA and Canada by Routledge
711 Third Avenue, New York, NY 10017

Routledge is an imprint of the Taylor & Francis Group, an informa business

© 2010 Angie Pears

Typeset in Sabon by Taylor & Francis Books

British Library Cataloguing in Publication Data
A catalogue record for this book is available from the British Library

Library of Congress Cataloging in Publication Data
Pears, Angie.
Doing contextual theology / Angie Pears.
    p. cm.
Includes bibliographical references and index.
1. Modernism (Christian theology) 2. Theology, Doctrinal – History – 20th century. 3. Christianity and culture. I. Title.
    BT82.P43 2009
    230 – dc22
                      2009009370

ISBN10:0-415-41704-X (hbk)
ISBN10:0-415-41705-8 (pbk)
ISBN10:0-203-87782-9 (ebk)

ISBN13: 978-0-415-41704-4 (hbk)
ISBN13: 978-0-415-41705-1 (pbk)
ISBN13: 978-0-203-87782-1 (ebk)

For Stan and June Boby

Contents

Acknowledgements

Writing a book such as this is an adventure. Many people have either shared part of this adventure or supported me during the course of it.

I began writing this book whilst in post as Senior Lecturer in Religion, Theology and Culture at Oxford Brookes University. Working with both undergraduate and postgraduate students on various theology and religion courses, and in particular students on the MA in Practical and Contextual Theology, provided engaging debate and so many rich opportunities to explore and probe questions of context and Christian theology.

My thanks and deep appreciation go to Graeme Smith whose critical reading of the complete manuscript of this book was enormously helpful and, as always, challenging.

I have been sustained over the last few years by the support of friends, family and colleagues. Robert Bastes is a friend whose gentle strength and wisdom is inspiring and much cherished. Other friends and colleagues at Oxford Brookes whose support I have appreciated include Brian Marshall, Dominic Corrywright, Bob Langridge and Ailsa Clarke. To Jan Pegram, Ella Boby, Maddi Ginn, Joan Turner, Tracey Adams and Tony Gowlett – thank you.

The editorial team at Routledge, especially Lesley Riddle and Amy Grant, have been outstanding.

Finally, and most of all, to Deb – just thank you.

Introduction

Christianity is a religion in transition. As part of a constantly changing world that progresses, develops, renews and reinvents itself, Christianity is subject to the changes of human cultural and social existence. In the last half of the twentieth century and into the twenty-first century Christianity has been influenced by a number of cultural shifts. One of these is the shift from a perspective which views truths and human knowledge as universal to a perspective which views them as shaped, determined and even validated by specific cultural, social and political contexts. This shift is informed by the insights and criticisms of post-structuralism and postmodernism and whilst it is not always played out or followed through to its full conclusions it is nevertheless having a profound impact on the place of Christian theology and the Christian Church in the world today. It has also given rise to an explicit critical awareness that is influencing the shape of contemporary theology – that Christian theology is and has always been contextual. This claim, its implications and outworkings, are the focus of this book, which is concerned in particular with investigating the ways in which the theologian's or the theological community's own context influences Christian theology.

The term 'contextual theology' is in some ways an evasive and fluid term to which a number of meanings, some contrasting, could and do attach themselves. As a general rule 'contextual theology' is used here to refer to that theology which *explicitly* places the recognition of the contextual nature of theology at the forefront of the theological process. Such theology understands all Christian theology as being influenced and indeed determined by the context of those engaged in the theological enterprise, but recognizes that not all Christian theologies explicitly acknowledge or signify this in their theologies. 'Contextual theology' is used very clearly here to refer to Christian theology which is explicitly shaped, if not driven, by the recognition of the contextual nature of theology with all of its potentially controversial and problematic implications. This is different from the claim that all theology is contextual. One is a theological stance which places and celebrates context at the centre of the theological enterprise, and the other an epistemological claim about the contextual nature of all theology.

This book will engage in an analysis of the relationship between context and the theologian or the theological community. It is interested to explore the ways in which the specificity of a particular contextual theology interacts with the traditions of Christianity through the engaged reflection of the theologian and the theological community. It raises the question of the distinction between theological content and context, asking if such a distinction is really possible. It recognizes that both context and human experiences along with other more traditional theological sources are significant components of contemporary Christian theologies. In doing this it will probe the relationship between different components of contextual theology and very importantly between the different expressions and instances of contextual theology. Given that context is so important to understanding these types of Christian theology and given that context is so varied and that there are many, many different Christian theologies then the question arises of what exactly all of these theologies have got in common, as is claimed, if they have emerged from a particular situation or in response to a particular situation. An approach that takes a very radical inter-pretation of Christian theology as contextual sees that theology as inextricably tied to its context. One of the aims of this book is to examine the implications of a reading of Christian theology as radically contextual. Such a reading sees Christian theology as not only arising out of a specific context but also as in some senses bound to the very context from which it arises because of its specificity and because of its particularly embedded relationship to that context. This then gives rise to questions such as is Christian theology in this sense really bound by context or does it somehow transcend context? Also, what is the relationship between the many different theologies that exist? Does there in fact need to be a relationship between them in terms of Christian identity? In the face of the great pluralism that is Christian theologies is there a Christian 'orthodoxy' or a Christian 'core' that can be identified within these different theologies, regardless of context? Within a pool of such questions it is persistently the place and significance of context in contemporary theology which is the concern of this book.

Whilst the study of contextual theology could be said to be in its relative infancy there are nevertheless a number of existing texts that are significant for the ways in which contextual theology is being understood and studied as a contemporary Christian theological enterprise. These texts will be examined in order to understand the way in which thinking about the relationship between human context and Christian theology has developed so far and for how con-textual theology has been understood. Most significant here is Stephan Bevans' *Models of Contextual Theology*, published in 1992, which engages with the key elements and typologies of contextual theology as interpreted by Bevans. Its significance in terms of the understanding of contextual theology lies with its fundamental and persistent stress on the nature of Christian theology as con-textual. As will be seen in Chapter 1, in many ways Bevans' text despite being written nearly 20 years ago holds its position as the main study in this field. Other texts to be examined include Robert Schreiter's 1985 *Constructing Local Theologies*, *The Blackwell Reader in Pastoral and Practical Theology* which was published in 2000 and edited by James Woodward and Stephen Pattison and also Sigurd Bergmann's *God in Context: A Survey of Contextual Theology* published in 2003. *Doing Contextual Theology* differs in its approach and concerns from those texts that will be examined in Chapter 1. In that, rather than arguing that theology should be contextual, it takes forward the claim that Christian theology is necessarily contextual and explores this identity and raises questions about the limits of this identity. Beyond Chapter 1 the approach that will be taken to the study of contextual theology will be through the study of liberation theologies as clear and conscious examples of contextual theologies. A number of liberation theologies will be studied in depth to determine how it is exactly in relation to this particular group of theologies that context impacts Christian theology. The nature of contextual theology, then, is explored in relation to specific theologies, rather than in the abstract. A grounded theology such as contextual theology demands of any study of it an appropriately grounded approach.

Why is it that liberation theologies are being used as the focus for this study of contextual theology rather than any other theologies? Justice-seeking theologies or liberation theologies, as they are now widely known, have emerged within Western Christianity since the 1960s and provide a diverse and theologically rich resource through which the study of the nature of Christian theology as contextual can be made. In one sense this is an easy choice, as these theologies make explicit their political, cultural and social standpoints. An alternative might have been to take key theologians whose influence on Christianity and Christian theology can be clearly demonstrated and explore how their theologies might be said to be shaped and determined by their own specific contexts. This may be the focus of another book. The tapestry that is the spectrum of liberation theologies demands contextual analysis. Liberation theologies have embedded in them the critical insight that all Christian theology is contextual but that theology has traditionally failed to make its interests explicit. With liberation theologies we see the implications of a sometimes radical reading of all Christian theology as contextual played out in fascinating and sometimes painful detail. Specific, focused and local theologies have developed in response to the needs of particular contexts.

Liberation theologies will be explored for the ways in which they uncover in their critique of 'traditional' theologies the bias of all Christian theology with the claim that all theologies are informed and influenced by their context and shaped, if not driven, by particular concerns. From this the mechanisms by which liberation theologies weave their contexts and contextual awareness into the very fabric of their theologies can then be explored. Having explored the ways in which context impacts on Christian theology this study of contextual theology will also include an analysis of liberation theologies as contextual theologies and raise the crucial question of whether a radical contextual reading of Christian theologies necessarily leads to a relativist understanding of Christianity. It will ask if contextual theologies are bound in relevance and meaning by the very contexts that inspire them. It will also ask if all theologies are not only necessarily limited and local but also dynamically fluid because just as different aspects of the contexts out of which they emerge change so these theologies must also change.

The first chapter will introduce the claim, deemed variously as controversial, inerrant or without need of exploration, that all Christian theology is contextual. It will define the understanding of the intrinsically contextual nature of Christian theology that lies at the heart of this study in considerable detail to enable the reader to approach the book with a clear understanding of what is meant by the claim that Christian theology is contextual. It will then engage in a detailed exploration of the claim that Christian theology is intrinsically contextual and offer an introductory outline of the potentially radical implications of this claim for Christian theology, practice and organization. These are implications that need to be highlighted in this foundational chapter before progressing the study through the exploration of specific contextual theologies. Any and all of the implications suggested in this chapter as outcomes of the claim that Christian theology is necessarily contextual will be returned to and examined in depth for their accuracy and full working out for Christian theology and for Christianity in Chapter 6.

In Chapter 1 the strand of theological publications which focuses specifically on an analysis of the methodological and theological implications of the contextual nature of Christian will be examined. Key texts relating to understandings of contextual theology will be engaged critically in order to gain some insight and understanding into how the field of theological studies that we might refer to as contextual theology has developed, and what progress has actually been made in examining the finer details and complexities of this field. Chapter 2 moves on from the exploration of key literature in the developing field of contextual theology to a more situated and specific critical theological study of this theology itself. It will base itself in a historical and theological understanding of the religious, political, social and cultural contexts out of which Latin American liberation theologies arose. It will argue that the emergence of Latin American liberation theologies in the 1960s and 1970s marks the beginnings of the distinctive, but increasingly diverse, group of theologies that we today refer to as liberation theologies. It will engage with the factors that seemingly shaped the formation and clarification of this early liberation theology by analysing key formative texts and individuals as well as looking at key historical Church gatherings and conferences. Texts to be examined here will include Gustavo Gutiérrez's groundbreaking *A Theology of Liberation*, and key figures in the development of liberation theology that will be focused on include, Gustavo Gutiérrez, Juan Luis Segundo, Leonardo Boff, José Miguez Bonino, Hélder Câmara and Oscar Romero. Given the significance of Gutiérrez's *A Theology of Liberation* within the history, and especially within the textual history, of Latin American liberation theology this particular text will be focused on in considerable depth. Finally, influential events that will be examined include the Medellín conference of 1968 and the Second Vatican Council. From this, a historical and theological overview of the emergence of liberation theology in Latin America will be established. The study will then move to an analysis of the theological motivations and implications of early Latin American liberation theology. This will engage with important issues and theological proposals such as the hermeneutical privilege of the oppressed, Base Ecclesial Communities and the place of Marxism and politics in general in Christian theology. It will begin to ask of the implications of these radical contextual and local theologies for the wider Christian community and Church structures.

Chapter 3 will move on from the geographically based liberation theology of Latin America and focus on that liberation theology that has emerged out of an awareness of the significance of gender for Christian theology. It will engage with the theological implications, controversies and complications that have arisen from the introduction of gender as a problematized but fundamental aspect of human existence which necessarily needs to be addressed by Christian theology. The chapter will explore the emergence of feminist informed theologies and the great diversity of such theologies that exist today. It will explore and question the ways in which feminist informed theologies might be said, and indeed at times has claimed, to be radically contextual. In particular it will examine the critique that some feminist informed theologies, despite their claimed commitment to the contextual and experiential nature of Christian theology, have in fact universalized certain aspects of women's experiences to the detriment of feminist informed theologies as a whole. This, then, brings into question the genuinely contextual nature of such feminist informed theologies, or at least raises the question as to how and why such a development could have taken place given that one of the key foundational insights of feminist informed theologies is that traditional Christian theologies (including liberation theologies such as Latin American liberation theologies and black theologies) have given precedence if not complete authority to their own essentially male perspective and failed to hear, reflect and utilize the experiences of women. Here, the critiques and unique contributions to the range of feminist informed theologies by mujerista, womanist, Latino, African, Asian and Asian American theologies will be explored and engaged as discourses which not only challenge and question Western feminist theologies but which widen the important spectrum that is feminist informed theologies in its great and important diversity and seemingly endless depth. A more critical approach is taken in this chapter, then, than in previous chapters, to the claims and methodologies of contextual theologies (here feminist informed theologies). This is because the purpose of this chapter is in part to illustrate the problems and complexities surrounding contextual theologies and not because feminist informed theologies are intrinsically more problematic than other contextual theologies such as Latin American liberation theologies.

Chapter 4 glimpses the multiplicity of justice-seeking contextual theologies and probes further the contextual nature of liberation theologies. It explores the theological outworkings of contextuality in black theologies, body theologies, sexual theologies, queer theologies and indecent theology.

Having explored some of the criticisms and counterclaims of a number of liberation theologies in Chapter 4, and having begun to engage in depth with the question of what really constitutes the contextual nature of Christian theology, Chapter 5 focuses on a relatively new but increasingly significant group of theologies, postcolonial theologies, which may justifiably, but with some qualification, also be called liberation theologies. In this chapter the underlying claims, methodologies and shapes of postcolonial theologies will be explored. Postcolonial theologies are diverse, complex, subversive, and in a twenty-first century seemingly lost in a maze of the promises and sometimes apparent failures of liberation theologies, they are a fascinating development in contemporary Christian theology. Postcolonial theologies are united by their context as either one of having a history of colonialism, being the subject of neo-colonialism or still struggling under the oppressive regimes of imperialism. Postcolonial theologies offer glimpses of hope for many Christians around the world, and claim, like other liberation theologies, to be contextual in nature. What is interesting for this study, and what differentiates them as a point of focus here, is that they often draw on the problems and apparent failures experienced by liberation theologies such as feminist theologies, Latin American theologies, black theologies and lesbian and gay theologies. As such, potentially they offer glimpses of lessons learnt harshly by other liberation theologies and suggest new ways of doing contextual theology that draw on postmodern and poststructuralist thinking, as well as a wealth of other critical tools. This is not to impose or imply a hierarchy of supersession of contextual liberation theologies but it does raise important questions about the ongoing development of justice-seeking contextual theologies. The postcolonial theologies of R.S. Sugirtharajah, Kwok Pui-lan, Wai Ching Wong, Justin Upkong and Musa W. Dube Shomanah will be explored and critiqued as contextual theologies.

Chapter 6 of this study brings together the findings about the nature of liberation theologies and their claims to be contextual in nature and directly addresses the question of, what is contextual theology?

At the heart of this study, and indeed at the heart of contextual theology, is the recognition that there has been a significant shift in the way in which claims to truth are understood. In an apparently post-enlightenment age, characterized by postmodernist thinking, the idea that there are universally valid claims to truth that can be developed in one particular place and transported to any context is thoroughly rejected by such theologies. The implications of this for Christianity, with its central belief system and the enduring place of tradition within Christian faith, are very challenging. Contextual theology responds to this challenge.

1   The contextual nature of theology

There are a number of different ways in which the task of exploring and probing claims about the contextual nature of Christian theology might be approached. One possible approach would be to map out a broad chronological spectrum of Christian theological history and examine the ways in which different theologies have responded to specific contextual circumstances and have been shaped by these circumstances. Here different theologians could be focused on for the ways in which their own contexts might be seen to have influenced their theologies. Bearing in mind that the focus here is Western Christian theology candidates for just such a project must be the key influential theologians who have determined the shape of Western Christian history, theology and practice with their specific theologies. Theologians here include Paul, Tertullian, Athanasius, Augustine, Thomas Aquinas, Martin Luther, John Calvin, Friedrich Schleiermacher, Karl Barth, Dietrich Bonhoeffer, Karl Rahner, Rudolf Bultmann, Paul Tillich, Jürgen Moltmann, Gustavo Gutiérrez, James Cone, Rosemary Radford Ruether, Elisabeth Schüssler Fiorenza and many others. Certain theologians, groups or theologies might be identified as, in effect, case studies for the analysis of the relationship between the lives of theologians and the situation, cultural context and the theologies that they develop. Any list would of course vary depending on the person choosing such a list and on the geographical and religious context being studied. Wide variation in the selection of theologians must be expected to be seen, especially post-reformation. This methodology might well be one to be used at another time. Here, one particular group of theologies has been chosen, that of Christian liberation theologies, as the way into understanding both the nature of explicitly contextual theology as well as exploring the fundamental claim that all Christian theologies are necessarily contextual.

This first chapter aims to provide a general introduction to the concept of contextual theology. It will trace the emergence of contextual theology as a theological discipline that is now a focus of study in its own right. As it is possible to argue that Christian theology has always been contextual, why then attempt to identify any particular group of theologies to demonstrate the nature of Christian theology as contextual? This is an important question and brings to light a significant distinction that lies at the heart of this book – between the claim that *all* theology is contextual and the claim that *some* Christian theologians and Christian theological communities are explicitly and fundamentally incorporating their own context into their theologies. This latter theological claim stresses that specific situations, concerns, cultures, socioeconomic situations and political experiences are explicitly and purposefully incorporated into some Christian theologies. Both the claim that *all* theology is contextual and the claim that *some* Christian theologians and Christian theological communities are explicitly incorporating context into their theologies will be explored here but the distinction between these will be maintained. In this first chapter the arguments and claims of those texts that have acknowledged and explored this emerging consciousness that is a key characteristic of contextual theology, and indeed of Christian theology generally, will be examined. These texts will form a significant base for critical interrogation and reflection in this chapter. These texts are those which are influencing the way in which contextual theology is being understood and as such they are not so much examples of 'doing contextual theology' as texts which have contributed to the understanding of the ways in which contextual theologies operate, their methodologies, presuppositions and key arguments.

What does it mean to speak of Christian theology as contextual?

To speak of Christian theology as contextual, and in particular as radically contextual, proposes a shift in the way in which Christian theology is often understood. Such a shift in understanding in relation to Christian theology is influenced and supported by the insights of poststructuralist thinking which stresses the fluid, shifting nature of human knowledge and concepts. Traditionally Christian theology has been understood by many as being beyond the critical interrogation and questioning that other disciplines or sources of knowledge might and should be subjected to. Whilst critical debates about Christian theology can certainly be found within Christian theological history largely these debates were constrained or situated within defined, accepted and even regulated parameters. Christian theology has often been seen as inspired and so, in effect, as true and as beyond critical questioning. More than this it has been seen as universally true, as objective and valid regardless of the particular location, time or circumstances out of which it emerged. This kind of status was accorded to Christian theology because of the sources from which it was understood to have emerged, those of scripture and tradition. Both of these were seen as unchanging and non-specific in cultural or experiential terms. As a result Christian theologies have often remained unexplored for the influences and factors that have given particular shape to and determined their content. In terms of the development and spread of Christianity as a religion this approach to its validity and authority has had telling consequences. It has meant that essentially Western Christianity has been transported and imposed on contexts and cultures very different to those out of which it emerged. The Christian missionary movement has, for example, been depicted as being responsible for imposing Western Christianity and Western understandings of civilization, morality and humanity on many different cultures around the world in the process of evangelization and through the transplantation of Christianity from a Western setting. The implications of this understanding of the imposition of Western Christianity on diverse cultures globally and the development of alternative possible approaches to the witnessing and development of Christianity are the complex and challenging concerns of contemporary missiology.

Theologians have always been influenced by their context and to varying degrees some have demonstrated an awareness of the influence that their own specific context and experiences have had on the theologies they develop. Such a claim about the influence of context on theology cannot be selectively applied. However, theologians who explicitly demonstrate an awareness of the influence of context on theology are few when viewed against the vastness that is Christian theological history. Concern with the contextual nature of theology is an emerging area for contemporary Christian theological concern and can be seen to be influencing a developing area of discussion, and raising questions about many areas of Christian practice, faith and understanding. To talk of Christian theology as contextual cannot be said to be completely new although the language being used today may be different. Stephen Bevans argues that in some ways the term 'indigenous theology' has been replaced by the term 'contextual theology' (2002:80). Contextual theology as a distinct theology is so much more than a perspective or approach to theology. We see debate about the contextual nature of Christian theology and the explicit incorporation of context into some Christian theologies in the writings of a number of theologians and in a number of key texts that are influencing and shaping this growing discourse. This list is limited not only by time and space that can be given over to analysis here but also by the actual number of texts that have so far emerged. However, four texts stand out as key texts in need of detailed consideration when assessing the emergence of an understanding of contextual theology as a methodology and as a distinct theology, contemporary and effective in its own right. The four texts are:

(1) Robert Schreiter (2007) [1985] *Constructing Local Theologies*, Maryknoll, New York: Orbis Books.
(2) Stephen Bevans (2002) [1992] *Models of Contextual Theology* (Revised and Expanded Edition), Maryknoll, New York: Orbis Books.
(3) James Woodward and Stephen Pattison (2000) *The Blackwell Reader in Pastoral and Practical Theology*, Oxford: Blackwell Publishers Ltd.
(4) Sigurd Bergmann (2003) *God in Context: A Survey of Contextual Theology*, Aldershot: Ashgate.

There are of course other texts which could also be said to be indicators of the emergence of explicitly contextual theology. Such texts here might be located in the writings of Dietrich Bonhoeffer, Paulo Freire, Kenneth Leech and Duncan Forrester. Beyond these is the challenging but highly relevant issue of theology and culture, and here the writings of Gordon Lynch, Paul Heelas, Clive Marsh and, in their own if often challenging ways, the writings of the radical orthodox theologians such as John Milbank, Catherine Pickstock and Graham Ward are all of interest.

As already pointed out, important to any study of contextual theology is the question of the role that mission and the study of mission, missiology, has played in the emergence of contextual theology. On the one level it could be said that consciously and radical contextual theologies such as liberation theologies emerged out of a negative experience and in response to traditional Christian mission. Such an approach sees the Christian mission movement as responsible for the imposition of global, Western-based understandings of Christianity on different communities around the world regardless of the contexts and particular needs and contours of these communities. Refutation of such a reading of Christian history is a challenging task. So, some discussion will be needed in this study of the place of mission and the ongoing relationship that it inevitably maintains with contextual theologies as the Christian missionary movement inspired, in spite of itself, a ground swelling of local theologies. The missiological terms which have progressively been contested, controlled and challenged by contextual theology need to be acknowledged. Key terms to be discussed for their significance and often complex relationship to contextual theology include 'inculturation' and 'practical theology'.

Whilst this book is clearly not a history of the Western Christian mission movement in exploring the emergence of liberation theologies, we will see why Christian mission has proved to be problematic. Christian mission will be revisited throughout this book but many competent and comprehensive books on mission have already been written and are a rich resource to complement the study of contextual theology. Specifically Chapter 4 will consider the ways in which the presence of Christianity in many different geographical and cultural contexts has influenced the ways in which Christianity is now perceived on a local level by practising Christians and the problems that the institutional churches face in dealing with the history by which Christianity was brought to, and often imposed upon, indigenous cultures. This was imposed in a way that was often at the expense of traditional beliefs and practices, cultural heritage and indeed the very wellbeing and health of indigenous people.

Robert Schreiter: *Constructing Local Theologies*

Rather than simply briefly outlining the content of the four texts identified as key to any literature review pertinent to a book of this nature, the approach that will be adopted here will be to analyse and assess the contribution that each text has made to the development of the argument that all Christian theology is necessarily contextual. The four texts will be examined for their different contributions and will be studied in the chronological order of publication. In-depth analysis will be given in particular to Stephen Bevans' *Models of Contextual Theology*, first published in 1992, as it incorporates many of the questions that are raised when we begin to ask questions about the contextual nature of Christian theology. Bevans' text itself was a reflection on theology and cultural context, examining the way in which we might be able to speak in a meaningful way about the interaction between culture and Christianity, or the Gospel and culture.

Constructing Local Theologies was written by Robert Schreiter and first published by Orbis Books in 1985. Such was its importance and popularity that by 2007 it had reached its fourteenth printing. It is not only the ideas contained in *Constructing Local Theologies* which make it such a significant text but also the ongoing impact that it has had on subsequent Christian theologians, students of theology and missionaries. Schreiter has held key academic positions around the world including Associate Professor of Theology of the Catholic Theological Union in Chicago and Professor of Theology and Culture at the University of Nijmegen. In *Constructing Local Theologies* Schreiter was concerned with the concept of theological bias. Like others around him he was beginning to take on board the claim that all Christian theology has a standpoint and is influenced by the context from which it arose. He became part of the theological movement that is questioning the viability of universal theological concepts, universal theologies or even universal Christianity in the sense of one Christian theology valid and true for all people at all times. Edward Schillebeeckx in the foreword to Schreiter's *Constructing Local Theologies* sums up the task of the book and describes well the development of discernible and conscious contextual theology as a whole:

> Previously, one almost took for granted that the theology of the Western churches was supraregional and was, precisely in its Western form, universal and therefore directly accessible for persons from other cultures. But especially with the emergence of liberation theology, as in Latin America for example, Western theologians came to the realization that their own theology has just as much sociological bias as any other. That theology, too, is a 'local' theology that, although in this (particular Western) social and contextual context, nonetheless wants to bring *the Gospel* to expression. How can this selfsame Gospel, which is given only in a societal and cultural context (even in the New Testament, for that matter) and can never be wholly extricated from any culture, to be allowed to speak the language of an entirely different culture? That is the chief concern of this book.
>
> (Schillebeeckx, E., in Schreiter, 2007:ix)

Of particular significance here is Schillebeeckx's claim that 'Western theologians came to the realization that their own theology has just as much sociological bias as any other'. He points out the significance of this for missiologists and the persistent question of inculturation for all of Christian theology. Schillebeeckx then goes on to note that 'This then raises the question about Christian identity in the polycentric and yet one Catholica' (Schillebeeckx, E., in Schreiter, 2007:ix).

Schreiter begins his argument in *Constructing Local Theologies* with the claim that Christians around the world are no longer content to simply receive and incorporate into their own cultures and contexts the prevailing universal, or 'supraregional' theology as Schillebeeckx refers to it. In the face of such dynamism and activity Schreiter highlights the central problem that arises from this:

> In the midst of this tremendous vitality that today's Christians are showing, one set of problems emerges over and over again: how to be faithful both to the contemporary experience of the gospel and to the tradition of Christian life that has been received. How is a community to go about bringing to expression its own experience of Christ in its concrete situation? And how is this to be related to a tradition that is often expressed in language and concepts vastly different from anything in the current situation.
>
> (Schreiter, 2007:xi)

It is precisely this potential problematic or exciting dynamic (depending on the way the issue is approached) that is of persistent interest here. Specifically, what is the relationship between local, contextual, experiential-based theologies and Christian tradition? Or is this question fundamentally misconstrued in relation to the nature of Christianity as a religion and in relation to Christian theology? Such questions will no doubt be revisited and reconfigured throughout this book because as will become apparent they will simply not go away when discussing contextual theology or contemporary theology in general. Schreiter noted in 1985, when *Constructing Local Theologies* was originally written, that this question and related questions were very new in the sense of being genuinely and fully articulated, and understanding the relationship between theology and context was very much in its infancy. Indeed at the time of writing this book, 2008, these questions still remain in many cases without satisfactory responses and persistently challenging, which they may well always be.

In exploring what he meant by the term 'local theology' (as opposed to contextual theology) Schreiter points out the significance of understanding terms such as 'inculturation', 'localization', 'contextualization', and 'indigenization' in terms of what theologians mean by them and differentiating between them. Schreiter gives an interesting analysis of these terms and their usage. He argues that all of these terms refer to the same basic issue, expressed in different ways and used in different contexts. They are all part of the same theological issue: 'Despite slightly different nuances in meaning, all of these terms point to the need for and responsibility of Christians to make their response to the gospel as concrete and lively as possible' (Schreiter, 2007:1).

Schreiter begins his own study of Christian theology in *Constructing Local Theologies* with the important question of why such a shift was apparently taking place at the time of his writing. He locates the origins of this shift in the 1950s and geographically in Africa and Asia with the indigenous peoples to whom Christianity had been 'introduced' beginning to question the validity and relevance of essentially Western theologies from a cultural perspective (Schreiter, 2007:1). He argues that official Church responses evident in such as the Vatican II decree on the Church's Missionary Activity *Ad Gentes* ('To the Nations'), promulgated in 1965 by Pope Paul VI, indicates awareness among the Church hierarchies as well as missionaries on the ground that the way in which Christianity was being taken to developing countries was at least open to question and possibly ineffective and damaging. Missionaries and theologians writing about mission were beginning to question and explore the relationship between culture and the gospel. Schreiter argues that from the early 1970s the words that have come to be so central in the debate about the relationship between culture and Christianity, and about contextual theology as a whole, such as '"contextualization", "indigenization", "inculturation", and "adaptation"' (Schreiter, 2007:2) began to be used on a regular basis by both Protestants and Catholics. For him this was a sign of a significant shift in the way in which Christian theology and its development and existence on a global level was coming to understand, reflect upon and no doubt be influenced by the development of Latin American liberation theology. There developed a significant focus on the local situation and a concern that local customs, cultural practices and beliefs might not cohere with or may even be in conflict with what we might call imported Western Christianity.

For Schreiter the 'traditional frameworks of theology' (Schreiter, 2007:3) were simply unable to respond to the questions and issues that were arising from the apparent clash between universal Christianity and the local cultural situation. This was also bound up with issues of Christianity's relationship with colonialism. It became increasingly clear, claims Schreiter, that the concerns of the Western Church were different in priority and interest to those of the Church in many other places in the world. Even within Western Christianity the rise of liberation movements, for example, among women and black African-Americans, also brought the traditional representation of Christianity as singular and universal into question. A monolithic Christianity was coming under scrutiny from so many different areas and not all of them far away from Western Christian bases. Theological activity reflecting and also responding to a level of discontent began to develop. Schreiter characterizes this disquiet and concerns as the development of theologies which were reflecting '*a new kind of Christian identity*' (Schreiter, 2007:3). Schreiter sees radical and deep-seated change occurring in such theologies and this change, he argues, was characterized by a 'sensitivity' to three particular concerns: those of 'context, procedure and history' (Schreiter, 2007:3). As such, for Schreiter the first of these concerns, context, becomes an important theological component and not just an incidental of Christianity. Context, he argues, emerges as key to the theological enterprise rather than peripheral. This new theological approach moved away from the application of a universal theology to any context, regardless of the context, to a focus on the context first before then considering what Christian theology might look like in such a context (Schreiter, 2007:4). According to Schreiter without such analysis of context as part of the theological process a theology can 'become either irrelevant or a subtle tool of ideological manipulation' (Schreiter, 2007:4). As such, theology in Schreiter's understanding might be said never to be neutral.

For Schreiter from an awareness of the importance of context the second characteristic concern of this new theology emerges: a concern with procedure. By this he seems to mean that once an awareness about the role of context in theology developed there then followed a concern with how theology develops within and from the community. Here the community is not only the locus or shaping influence for theology but the community takes more responsibility than has traditionally been the case in 'shaping theological response' (Schreiter, 2007:4). This then means that theology begins and remains with the community. He does concede that the theologian has a role within this process but this role involves making connections between the experiences of a local community and other Christian communities. This characterizes for Schreiter a shift away from what he argues is a model of theology that has determined Western Christianity since the thirteenth century. From a concern with 'clarity' and 'precision' (Schreiter, 2007:4) to different ways of doing theology which are challenging the domination of this model.

For Schreiter the third sensitivity of this new way of approaching theology is to history and specifically it is a concern with the ambiguous nature of history. In particular, attention is being paid to histories of suffering, which has a direct impact on the present and also involves a reclamation or reconstruction of the past. These three sensitivities, to context, to procedure and to history, are reflected in the use of different terminology in theology. Schreiter argues that new terms or new ways of using different terms have emerged in an attempt to describe and capture the spirit of this new way of doing theology. For him 'indigenous theology' although stressing the local nature of theological enterprise was a term compromised by its distinctive imperialist connotations (Schreiter, 2007:5). Similarly, 'ethnotheology', a term which he argues became popular among Protestant theologians for a while, suggested a hierarchy biased strongly towards a Western centralized theology written by people 'somehow inferior to the chosen people' (Schreiter, 2007:5). Schreiter rightly notes that 'inculturation' became another term to describe this new approach to theology, especially among Roman Catholic theologians. For him it refers to the adaptation of 'the theological principle of incarnation' (Schreiter, 2007:5) to cultural contexts. This was, and in some cases remains, a popular choice of words to describe the shift perceived in theological activity. However, Schreiter argues that it is the term 'contextual theology' (Schreiter, 2007:5) that has actually become to be extensively used in description of this theological shift and clearly reflects the significance of the role that context actually plays in this theology. ⁀ite this, Schreiter himself chooses to use the term 'local theology' in *Con-*
    Local Theologies because for him the term captures the essence of the
          ⁀oing theology that he is concerned to write about. For him the
                ⁀ts obvious and easily understood relationship to the local
                      ⁀lst recognizing that a significant shift is taking place he

argues that not all should be described as contextual theologies which for him means that 'This allows keeping the term "contextual" for those theologies that show greater sensitivity to context' (Schreiter, 2007:6).

What is apparent and important here is that although Schreiter recognizes that a key shift has taken place in theology which involves the incorporation of an awareness of the significance of context, he is not willing or prepared, it appears, to describe this shift as a generically new way of doing or new awareness of ways of doing theology. Whilst on one level he recognizes and heralds the new theological awareness of the significance of context, at the same time he wishes to differentiate between those advocating a consciously contextual approach to theology from those who are not. The term 'contextual theology' is reserved in his theology for the former. He notes that different theologies have incorporated different relationships to context and use context in different ways and this leads him to reserve the term for theologies which demonstrate a high level of awareness of the role of context in their theological enterprise. Writing originally in 1985 this approach in many ways precedes the fuller recognition of the validity and appropriateness of the term 'contextual theology' which develops a few years later.

Before moving on and considering the ways in which understandings of contextual theology developed after Schreiter's important insights and arguments in *Constructing Local Theologies*, it is important first to understand what he actually means by local theology so that understandings of contextual theology can be compared to it and differentiated where necessary. Influenced as many other writers in this field are by missiology and theologies of how Christianity has been taken in its very Western forms to many different contexts around the world, Schreiter identifies three basic types of local theologies. Each of these is determined or characterized by the relationship it incorporates between 'theology and community in which it takes place' (Schreiter, 2007:6). These three ways of doing local theology he refers to as 'translation', 'adaptation' and 'contextual'.

The translation model as understood by Schreiter, and indeed many others, is one in which the Christian message is in some ways removed from its own contextual roots and trappings and then translated according to the local situation or context. Here there is an understanding of a fundamental core of Christianity which needs to be freed from the restraints of its original expression and then translated accordingly. Schreiter notes the significance of this model historically to missionary Christian activity but acknowledges that the theologian has the task of understanding the culture into which the gospel or Christianity is to be translated, usually asking the untrained missionary or theologian to engage in cultural analysis for which they are not usually equipped. This model also presumes parallel situations where Western Christianity can be taken from one context and translated into another context, which underestimates the complexity of cultural diversity. It also presumes some core universal unchanging Christian truth that can be taken and translated into whatever situation the missionary is faced with in her or his Christian work. Whilst this is a straightforward and in some ways reassuringly conservative approach to understanding

Christianity in its many settings, it is, at the same time, also hugely problematic. It is conservatively restrictive of what is perceived as the core of Christianity and goes against the essence of contextual theology itself with the notion of an unchanging essential Christianity which is context free and universally applicable. Schreiter acknowledges this weakness to some extent, with the words that 'Rather than the kernel-and-husk image of an incarnate Christianity, which allows for a ready hulling to reveal the kernel of divine revelation. Perhaps the image of an onion would be more appropriate: the kernel and husk are intimately bound together' (Schreiter, 2007:8).

For Schreiter the validity of the translation approach is limited in relevance and time and so a more thoroughly contextual approach is needed in the long run. This brings us to the second type of 'local theology' described by Schreiter, the adaptation approach. He sees this almost as a development of the translation model but incorporating a more sensitive and inclusive approach to both Christianity and local culture. This model in his understanding is characterized by the use of Western theological tools and methods but with genuine dialogue between these tools and local culture and contextual needs. But again limitations of the essentially prioritizing of the Western theological perspective and method are problematic, even if it does give more credence to local culture. This brings Schreiter to the third type of local theologies, contextual theologies. For Schreiter, writing in 1985, contextual approaches are concerned with and take seriously the local context. He differentiates between two basic types of contextual theology – 'ethnographic approaches' and 'liberation approaches' (Schreiter, 2007:13). He argues that those theologies which are primarily concerned with focusing on cultural identity are ethnographic approaches and engage in developing a dialogue with the traditions of Christianity. Different to this are liberation approaches which are fundamentally concerned with challenging oppression and bringing about social change. He notes the strength of the presence of liberation theology in the 1980s and describes them as 'a major force, if not the major force, in contextual theologies today' (Schreiter, 2007:15). He argues that of all the local theologies he identifies contextual theologies as being the most important and likely to be the most effective in the long term.

Schreiter stresses the significance of the local community in local theologies. The notion of professional, academic theologians being wholly or even primarily responsible for the development of Christian theology is being challenged by the very methodologies of local theologies. The power and authority of institutional Christianity is shifting away from central authorities and towards the local community, as the local community responds to its own contexts and needs in a culturally appropriate way. Drawing on scripture and tradition in a way that is best suited to the cultural framework within which it is being utilized and developed is the task which is being taken on by the local, contextual theologian. Within the local community those with particular talents and gifts will contribute to the theological enterprise facing the community. Such individuals come to articulate both collectively and individually the concerns and hopes of the community in a theological way. This introduces a significant shift to the concept of the theologian, according to Schreiter, and is characteristic of contextual theology as a whole. The theologian is no longer the specialist academic or ordained individual who is in some way privileged and set apart from the rest of the community by virtue of his or her theological ability or centrally invested authoritative status. The theologian is potentially anyone within the community who has a valid and appropriate contribution to make in the development of a local theology. Such an understanding of theological activity and of the theologian invests the community with theological authority and power.

Schreiter recognizes that doing theology on a local level in a contextual way raises questions about the rise of different local theologies and the relationship of these theologies to each other and to tradition. In recognizing culture, local experience and context as significant to theology the role and place of scripture and tradition need to be reconsidered and Schreiter relates this to the question of identity, of Christian identity. An interesting statement by Schreiter relates to how contextual theology or local theologies are to be perceived given the strong relationship they have to the local context and community and given the fact that such contexts and such local theological needs change often and quite significantly: 'More and more, local theology is pointing the way to a return to theology as an occasional enterprise, that is, one dictated by circumstances and immediate needs rather than the need for system-building' (Schreiter, 2007:23).

As such, local or contextual theologies are not systematic in the sense of methodologically contributing to building up a theological picture of Christianity with all of the various interrelated layers and components gradually slotting into or claiming its own place. If one accepts an understanding of the shifting nature of human experience and context then the need or possibility for the development of a systematic and universal theology simply is not feasible or even possible. Hence the emerging issue then of how local or contextual theologies relate to other contextual theologies, to tradition and to traditional theologies. For Schreiter the nature of local theologies, because they speak both to and of the experiences of the community and reflect the cultural traditions of these communities, are tools in spiritual growth and themselves engage fully with the gospel (Schreiter, 2007:24). He expresses this in very direct and uncompromising terms; for him the development of local or contextual theologies is the way to developing Christian spirituality:

> Another way of speaking about this context created by the movement of the Spirit and by the power of the gospel in a community is that it creates a certain spirituality among the believers. A way to God is charted out, a pathway to deeper faith and commitment opens out before the community. This pathway provides the essential context within which the local theology is then developed. Theology has to be more than an acute analysis of culture and tradition. It is always done for the sake of the community.
>
> (Schreiter, 2007:24)

Given the way in which Schreiter sees the theological process of development taking place local theologies, as he understands them, are less academically orientated than traditional theologies and more concerned with 'wisdom style of theology *(sapientia)* over the sure-knowledge style *(scientia)* preferred in academic settings' (Schreiter, 2007:24–25). Schreiter argues that as situations change so new local theologies will need to develop to respond to the needs of the local communities. What then becomes of existing local theologies? He notes that they may be seen as 'obstacles' (Schreiter, 2007:27) but is concerned to stress their role as reminders of what the community has experienced and indeed the oppressions it may have faced in its journeying. As such, these theologies, according to Schreiter, have a continuing role to play within the tradition of the local community, if only as a theology of memory. This then allows Schreiter to stand short of a full commitment to the most radical implications of a contextual reading of Christian theology, by emphasizing the presence of what for him is a genuine and crucial relationship between new and past theologies. This creates a tradition, perhaps a new kind of tradition it might be argued, but a tradition nevertheless. Once tradition is in place Christian theology has a sense of identity and a sense of continuity, both so important to traditional understandings of the nature of Christianity as a religion.

To begin the development of a local, contextual theology Schreiter argues that an associated methodology and an appropriate theory of culture must be in place. To acknowledge culture as a key component of human existence is not in itself enough, however. Culture needs to be investigated in order that we may appreciate its depths and the many facets that constitute any particular culture. Clifford Geertz, as Schreiter points out, has developed what he terms a 'thick description' of culture (Schreiter, 2007:28) which is an attempt to recognize the many aspects of a culture and necessary to be able to develop a culturally appropriate local theology. As a cultural anthropologist, however, Geertz was more concerned with description and observation, but fundamental to local and contextual theologies, in so many ways, is change. So whilst the thick description to culture approach of Geertz may be helpful and illuminating in itself it is not adequate for the task of developing local theologies. Schreiter argues that Christ stands at the centre of the theological enterprise of local theology. Christ needs to be located within culture and if necessary needs to be brought to the culture itself (Schreiter, 2007:29). Schreiter is concerned here not to lose sight of the purpose and fundamentals of Christian theology within the context about meeting the needs of local communities which are in search of social change. He is pointing us back to the central Christian concern of God's revelation in Christ and its place within developing local theology. He argues that the local community 'must be able to recognize the signs of Christ's presence in its midst' (Schreiter, 2007:29).

Schreiter develops this further by arguing that in studying and understanding a culture attention should be paid to locating Christ within the existing culture rather than importing or bringing Christ into that culture. Introducing Christ into a culture bears elements of imperialism and colonialism. Whilst the task of listening and finding Christ is by no means a straightforward or simple one, it is a crucial one, according to Schreiter. He challenges structuralist theorists such as Claude Lévi-Strauss and argues that 'native exegesis is important to listening to a culture and plays a leading role in the analysis of a culture' (Schreiter, 2007:41). Schreiter goes into some depth exploring different approaches to studying culture from the functionalist approaches influenced by Durkheim and Weber, to ecological and materialist approaches such as those employed by Roy Rappaport and Marvin Harris, to the structuralist approaches most closely associated with Claude Lévi-Strauss, to the semiotic study of culture influenced by the work of Ferdinand de Saussure and Roman Jakobson and also associated with Lévi-Strauss, Geertz, Victor Turner and Mary Douglas.

Schreiter challenges traditional modes of transmission of the gospel or the modes by which Christianity has been spread: 'we now know that what had often been called the Christianization of a people was in fact their westernization, depriving them of their own past' (Schreiter, 2007:75–76). Different local theologies develop different approaches to dealing with tradition and with the authority of the Church, but this often remains a problematic of contextual theology. Another area that is somewhat contentious but highly significant in local and contextual theologies is the inherent challenge it incorporates to the universal acceptance of theology as 'true' and universally applicable. Schreiter traces this tradition back to the Greek apologists and its reiteration in the Middle Ages in Thomas Aquinas's *Summa Theologiae* (Schreiter, 2007:88). He also traces its roots culturally to a number of factors including the development of the Western university with its faith-based task of systematizing and professionalizing theology. This has then led through the years to the imposition of a 'true' theology or theological knowledge in situations to which that knowledge does not speak and has no real meaning. Schreiter identifies the hugely problematic issue facing local theologies – that of their relationship to tradition, to the scriptures, the Church and creedal and conciliar statements. He attempts to engage in some analysis of it but fails to give any kind of satisfactory response to the issue as a whole. In places Schreiter's arguments about the resolution of potential clashes between local and universal theologies are limited and unconvincing. But what is important is that in 1985 he was raising these questions in a coherent and meaningful way and recognizing their significance to understanding contextual theology and Christian theology as a whole.

A key thing that Schreiter draws attention to in *Constructing Local Theologies* is the importance of tradition to humanity. He argues that tradition is very important for human community in that it provides 'identity, a communication system with cohesion and continuity, and resources for dealing with innovation' (Schreiter, 2007:113). He talks of 'a matrix within which a theory of tradition can be developed' (Schreiter, 2007:113), and proposes a model of tradition based on communication and on Noam Chomsky's theory of language acquisition. Now widely popular, the linguistic theories of Chomsky have come to influence theorists in many different areas. For Schreiter the significance of

Chomsky's work is that the model of language acquisition he proposes can be applied to Christian tradition. It allows the coexistence of different traditions or theologies and allows room for the development of new ones. For Schreiter when asking about normativity:

> The loci of grammar in Christian tradition would be the loci of orthodoxy. These loci have grown up in the course of Christian history, beginning with the Scriptures ...
>
> To continue the analogy, the loci of orthodoxy do not, therefore, create theology for a community. Theology will not flow from these loci any more than performances flow from grammar. Thus while a kind of magisterial theology can be articulated, and it is certainly correct, it of itself cannot be the theology of a community. To derive the community's theology solely from a magisterial (or biblical) theology is like trying to derive idioms from grammatical rules.
>
> (Schreiter, 2007:116)

Schreiter can be seen to have made a significant contribution with *Constructing Local Theologies* to the understanding and development of contextual theology. His work will be returned to later when the question of Christian identity in the face of multiple contextual theologies will be explored. What does need to be said here though is that Schreiter places the loci of orthodoxy with the local community and is not based on or tied to a magisterial, central theology. Rather, whilst rejecting the notion of a magisterial theology Schreiter is insistent that local theology is bound to Christian tradition by its use of and relationship to Christian scripture.

Stephen Bevans: *Models of Contextual Theology*

There are few texts that give specific sustained and critical attention to the description of Christian theology as innately contextual. Without doubt Stephen Bevans' *Models of Contextual Theology* originally published in 1992 still leads the field in this respect nearly twenty years later. Bevans is Louis J. Luzbetak, SVD, Professor of Gospel and Culture at Catholic Theological Union in Chicago. Bevans' now classic study proposed to the theological audience a systematic reflection on the nature of Christian theology into different models of contextual theology. His original schema of five models was expanded into six in the revised and expanded 2002 edition. The amount of space given to Bevans' text in this book does not rest solely on its academic significance but rather on its impact and continuing significance to the field that is still emerging in its infancy into contextual theology. His study and proposal of six models of contextual theology is heavily inspired and shaped by Bevans' own missionary theological background and interests and so he is interested in the role of context and culture within this particular framework. This then significantly shapes the way in which Bevans writes about contextual theology or the contextualization of

Christian theology and also the way in which he describes and even constructs his models of ways of doing theology contextually.

Robert Schreiter contributes a foreword to the revised and expanded edition of Bevans' *Models of Contextual Theology* in which he talks of the author's use of models as ' ... a map through the sometimes bewildering array of contextual theologies today' (Schreiter in Bevans, 2002:x). Bevans' approach of schematizing Christian theology into types or models is interesting and can at times be helpful to get a sense of just how different theological types or approaches might be termed 'contextual'. However, the description of Christian theologies as a map of contextual models needs to be used carefully and can be seen to be open to criticism. Models can be illustrative but also if used uncritically may well be confining and limiting. Bevans' classification focuses on the very nature of Christian theology and organises it into a schema which may at best be misleading and at worst misrepresentative and do a disservice to the plethora and spectrum that is Christian theology. So, Bevans' use of the schema of models must not be taken as fixed or beyond development or change.

Having said all of this, nevertheless, in the field of the study of theology as contextual his work clearly stands as groundbreaking. Not many theological texts survive the relevance of ten years and *Models of Contextual Theology* remains a key and groundbreaking text for any student of theology. Critical engagement is a mark of development so whilst acknowledging all that Bevans achieved in this book here we will focus on a critical exploration of his claims, models and underlying presuppositions, especially because he has reiterated his fundamental principles and insights ten years after the original text. If this text is as important to understanding theology as contextual as it appears and if it is shaping wide understanding of the nature of Christian theology as contextual then it must be open to critical interrogation.

What is it that Bevans actually proposes in his analysis of Christian theology as contextual? Inspired by the perception of the irrelevance of Western symbolism, liturgy and theological imagery for non-Western cultures (Bevans, 2002: xix) as a student in Rome and then as a missionary in the Philippines, Bevans became increasingly aware of the significance of culture to understanding and conveying the Christian message. He argues that 'There is no such thing as "theology"; there is only *contextual* theology, *feminist* theology, *black* theology, *liberation* theology, *Filipino* theology, *Asian-American* theology, *African* theology, and so forth. Doing theology contextually is not an option ...' (Bevans, 2002:3). This, then, sums up well the author's perspective and the underlying theological presuppositions of his work. He talks of contextual theology as a 'theological imperative' (2002:3), but at the same time stresses that this is not a new idea but one that is very much in line with the traditions of Christian theology (2002:3).

Approaches which stress the necessarily contextual nature of Christian theologies challenge the notion that Christian theology, and indeed all human knowledge, is objective, dispassionate and 'true' in a universal sense. As Bevans develops his argument here he points out that traditional or classical theology centred on two unchanging and culturally transcendent 'logi theologici' (theological sources) (Bevans, 2002:3) – those of scripture and tradition. Bevans proposes a widening of theological sources in a challenge to traditional understandings. He argues for the addition of a third locus theologicus – that of current human experience (Bevans, 2002:4). This then allows for the recognition and valuing of culture and situated human experience alongside the more traditional sources of Christian theology. Bevans recognizes that the inclusion of experience as a Christian theological source has radical and far-reaching implications. His claims and statements are bold and do not flinch from some of the inevitabilities of his proposals:

> The time is past when we can speak of one, right, unchanging theology, a *theologia perennis*. We can only speak about a theology that makes sense at a certain place and in a certain time.
>
> (Bevans, 2002:4–5)

Past theology is not redundant according to Bevans; we can learn from it whilst still recognizing its contextual nature. Bevans does not reject the past, tradition and scriptural interpretation but argues that it needs to be appropriated (2002:5). At times Bevans' interchange of the terms 'context' and 'culture' can be confusing. He sees a dynamic interchange between the past (including scripture and tradition) and present context and culture.

Individuals that Bevans names as examples of theologians influenced and shaped by their context include Clement of Alexandria, Origen, Augustine, Aquinas, Luther, Schleiermacher, Tillich and Barth (2002:8–9). Arguing then that theology shaped by context is by no means an exclusively new phenomenon he puts forward the argument that Christian theology 'today must take into more serious account the context in which a particular theological effort is articulated' (2002:9) and he also talks of dissatisfaction with 'classical approaches to theology' (2002:9). He argues that there is widespread realization and dissatisfaction with what he calls classical theology because of its irrelevance and inevitably Western cultural underpinning (2002:10).

Underlying this is a rejection of a classical notion of culture which holds to a universal view of culture, valid regardless of time or place. Bevans moves away from this restrictive and rigid view of culture to a more empirical understanding of culture (2002:11). Influenced by Bernard Lonergan here (and especially his views in *Method in Theology*) Bevans sees theology as the means of translation and the means of making sense of religion in particular cultural contexts. For Bevans the call to contextualization is imperative but at the same time Bevans believes that Christian theology is necessarily contextual.

Bevans places blame for colonialism and for the impact of the colonization process in particular with Christian theology. He argues that there is an increased awareness of the limitations of Western theology, the need for local theologies and the oppressive nature of classical theology. Colonialism imposed a homogenous, elitist interpretation of Christianity on Christians throughout the world. According to Bevans the historical processes of colonialism have come to face scrutiny so the realization of the importance of local and cultural relevance in theology has become clear. Bevans raises the issue of orthodoxy (2002:22) noting that cultural relevance and contextualization could compromise Christianity (2002:22). There is a real issue here which will be explored later and sits at the heart of this study. It is an issue that is itself hard to formulate but which focuses on the challenges and ensuing implications of a reading of Christian theology as radically contextual. If Christian theology is radically contextual and therefore very fluid and different in different contexts how then can it be determined what is Christian and what is not? If Christian theology is contextual then there will be many, many local, contextual theologies all having arisen out of particular situations and having relevance for specific situations. If this is the case then what are the limits or boundaries of orthodoxy? Or to put it another way, what is it that holds all of these theologies together under the umbrella of the identifier 'Christianity'. What in fact is the identifier 'Christianity'? These questions, whilst challenging and often uncomfortable, seem perhaps an inevitable by-product of such a reading of Christianity, and will be returned to later.

In writing against a backdrop of colonialism, westernization and its counterpart, the missionary movement, Bevans is driven by his experiences in what might be said to be a largely negative capacity and is looking for a more positive reading or solution of Christian theology. His justification or reason for writing *Models of Christian Theology* stems in part from this and his own related experiences. Underlying this critical examination of Bevans' own missiological task in this study is to outline the various processes of contextualization of the Christian message by which the Christian gospel can be communicated, translated and interpreted. Bevans proposes contextualization as a replacement for inculturation and indigenization (2002:26). He argues for this based on the need for contextual theology to respond to social and cultural change (2002:27). Bevans proposes the notion of contextual theology despite the popularity and currency of terms such as 'inculturation' and 'indigenization'. The reason that Bevans rejects these is that whilst they do represent the kind of theological concern and motivation which are indeed being called upon by contextual theology at the same time he sees them as somewhat limited.

Bevans' proposals of the use of models

Bevans argues that there is an increased use of the term 'model' in Christian theology (2002:28) and he points out its importance especially in relation to the work of theologians such as David Tracey, Sallie McFague and Avery Dulles. Bevans stresses that models are essentially constructions (2002:29); they are not to be read literally but are useful ways of knowing reality (2002:30). As such, Bevans stands within a theological tradition that attempts to organize and in some senses systematize complex theological ideas in a consistent and functional way. Models are helpful ways of organizing and representing different ways of theologizing but they are limited in their capacity to capture in a representative way diversity and depth, and they might even be said because of this to be potentially exclusivist. Bevans helpfully characterizes his own use of models as inclusive in the following way: 'It is a "case" that is useful in simplifying a complex reality' (Bevans, 2002:31). Models for Bevans are 'models of operation, models of theological method' (2002:31) and the ones that Bevans identifies differ in their theological approaches, emphases, concerns and stating points (Bevans, 2002:31). They are a tool of theological reflection and analysis.

Whilst acknowledging that models are limited in their ability to convey information and to represent diversity and depth, nevertheless, given the significance of the six models for understanding Bevans' argument, these six need to be outlined individually and then collectively to understand Bevans' argument about the nature of Christian theology. That is, in order to work out what it is exactly that Bevans is proposing with his analysis of Christian theology through models of contextual theology. Whilst different models demonstrate different emphases the underlying fundamental message according to Bevans is that Christian theology is contextually determined whatever type of theological position or message it incorporates. Close examination of the models also reveals how Bevans understood the relentlessly persistent impact of personal experience on Christian theology. This is something that has so far largely gone unacknowledged in a world calling out for a relevant Church and for relevant theologies.

Bevans maps out his models along a conservative to radical spectrum. This spectrum incorporates various positions of traditionalism and radicalism and this enables Bevans to account for all types of Christian theology whatever its implicit or explicit approach and whatever value it places on culture or context. As such, his theology or interpretation of Christian theology is not bound by or limited to one particular type of theology nor can only accommodate one particular theological type. The spectrum of six models is wide enough in its reference and the models themselves sufficiently overlap to incorporate most if not all theologies and also allows for a particular theology to fit more than one model of the six that Bevans has on offer.

Translation model

At the conservative end of Bevans' spectrum of models is the translation model of contextual theology. Bevans argues that this is the most frequently used model and also the model most often envisaged or used (often unconsciously) by those engaged in contextual theology (Bevans, 2002:37). This model involves the translation of the Christian message or gospel in specific or particular contexts. It is characterized by its unrelenting insistence on the 'message of the gospel as an unchanging message' (Bevans, 2002:37). Truth does not change, the message does not change. Bevans stresses that translation incorporates not only form but also meaning (2002:38), so the gospel or meaning of the gospel is translated into culturally appropriate terms (Bevans, 2002:39). This model sees a core, unchanging or in Bevans' words 'supracultural or supracontextual' (Bevans, 2002:40) Christian message. However, discerning or agreeing on the nature of this supracultural Christian message is another matter altogether. The most important thing, however, for this analysis of Bevans' models and the development of the understanding of Christianity as contextual is his proposal that there is a conservative contextual model in which the contextual form can be differentiated from core Christian truth or 'naked gospel' (Bevans, 2002:40). The role of culture here is subordinate to the naked gospel, clearly, but at the same time the role of culture is very important and is almost a necessary by-product of the processes of Christianity. This is an interesting attempt to incorporate a conservative reading of the gospel into a contextual model of understanding Christian theology.

In the translation model the gospel is clearly prioritized over culture. A simple uncomplicated Christian message or gospel is sought to be translated in different cultural contexts. The specificity and genuine differences of different cultures are not really accounted for or taken seriously. A basic and undiffer-entiated message is sought to be translated. The culture encountered within the theological process is not really valued for its difference and uniqueness; it is simply 'a culture'. Within this model the Christian message is also reduced to a minimal message. The message is short, largely unquestioned and value lies with the message and not with the form at all. This is a model that many theologians would question. It almost defies the definition of contextual theology. It is almost, but not quite, a step too far in Bevans' desire to be inclusive and to account for all theological positions. Bevans himself is both critical of this model but also envisages situations 'when a translation of one's own understanding of Chris-tianity is necessary' (Bevans, 2002:44). Examples of theologians who Bevans argues employ a translation model of contextual theology include David Hesselgrave, Pope John Paul II and Byung Kato (Bevans, 2002:45).

Anthropological model

For Bevans the anthropological model of contextualization of Christian theology is more radical in terms of its valuing of culture. He sums this up well by contrasting it with the translation model:

> If the primary meaning of the translation model is the preservation of Christian identity while attempting to take culture, social change, and his-tory seriously, the primary concern of the anthropological model is the establishment or preservation of cultural identity by a person of Christian faith.
>
> (Bevans, 2002:54)

The terminology used by Bevans in description of this model is helpful and the model can be described as being primarily person centred. The measure of meaning, values and even truth is not exclusively tradition and scripture but incorporates and stresses human experiences (Bevans, 2002:55). Human experiences become important sources for theological reflection and for doing theology generally. The Anthropological Model focuses on culture for discerning faith and identity. Scripture, tradition and human experience stand alongside each other 'as the place of divine revelation and as a source (*locus*) for theology' (Bevans, 2002:56). The model values and celebrates humanity because it suggests that humanity itself is the context of God's revelation (Bevans, 2002:56). Bevans suggests that those using this model will often see Christian doctrine as determined by the cultural conditions and contexts of Western Europe (Bevans, 2002:56). Those practising this model would not envisage exclusive change for the cultural context but 'mutual benefit for both the particular culture and wider Christianity' (Bevans, 2002:57).

Bevans seems to be arguing that in some ways the anthropological model is isolationist in that as it values and sees each culture as unique it does not really draw on or relate to other theologies, traditions and faiths in other cultures (Bevans, 2002:58). The Christian message or the word of God is embedded in the very cultures and it is for the practitioners to listen and hear (Bevans, 2002:58). It relies then not on a necessarily Western Christian theology but on the lives of individuals and is about these lives and their concerns. Bevans is critical of this model for its potential to romanticize culture and for what he sees as its potentially uncritical acceptance of the cultural context (Bevans, 2002:60). Practitioners of this model, claims Bevans, include Robert Hood and Vincent Donovan. Whilst this model again has clear limitations (as any model will inevitably have) and this model is not presented by Bevans uncritically, it does offer another configuration for understanding the relationship between Christian theology, culture and context or in Bevans' words for understanding the contextualization of Christianity.

Praxis model

Practitioners of the praxis model are concerned with a particular context, with Christianity in that context and with developing a way of expressing a Christian faith approach to that context. A marked feature of the praxis model is its concern with social change (Bevans, 2002:70). As such it is not only concerned with the expression of Christian faith within a particular context but also with the role of Christianity in bringing about social change. The context experienced is one in which social change is a concern and particular focus. As Bevans notes this praxis model can be variously described as practical theology or liberation theology. The use of the word 'praxis' in description of this model is intended to express God's presence in culture, among people, history and action (Bevans, 2002:70). Taking praxis and social change as its starting point or concern it claims biblical precedent in action as well as hearing the word (for example Isaiah and Amos) and James 1:22, 'Do not merely listen to the word, and so deceive yourselves. Do what it says.' Action or praxis is an identifying feature of this model of contextual theology.

Bevans acknowledges the roots of the word praxis in Marxist thinking and in the work of such thinkers as Habermas and Freire. He claims it marks a distinctive theological approach, calling on Sobrino's use of Marx's now famous critique of Feuerbach in explanation of his argument for a shift in theological understanding: 'the philosophers have only *interpreted* the world in various ways; the point is to change it' (Marx, 1967, *Theses on Feuerbach*, quoted in Bevans, 2002:72). Bevans tries to clarify what is meant by praxis when it is used in contextual theology. Contextual theology, argues Bevans, is not simply about the development of a socially, culturally relevant expression of Christianity. It is an extra, crucial dimension that makes it distinctively con-textual in its methodology – it is committed to action, Christian action. This brings many questions for change and action, specifically, what kind of action and what kind of change? Those committed to the praxis model would argue with the liberation theologians and theologians like Moltmann and Metz (Bevans, 2002:72) that the world in which we live has social, political and pragmatic dimensions for the Christian committed to his or her faith. This is because of the structural nature of sin. A world that supports sin must be challenged on a practical basis for change and for the development of alter-native structures. Bevans argues that justification for such a theological approach to sin and structure, given the inevitable accusations of politicizing the spiritual, can be found in biblical accounts of human oppression and lib-eration through human challenges to such oppression. Interestingly Bevans is insistent that this model is not simply to be aligned with liberation theology because the model does not have to be concerned with liberation; praxis is its concern primarily, not liberation.

Bevans argues that the commitment to praxis brings implications for traditional ways of doing theology but is concerned to point out that the result will be a more relevant, more socially vibrant theology. It is the starting and in many ways the ending point of theology:

> By first acting and then reflecting on that action in faith, practitioners of the praxis model believe that one can develop a theology that is truly rele-vant to a particular context. What becomes clear is that theology done in this way cannot be conceived in terms of books, essays, or articles. Rather than something concrete, permanent, and printed, theology is conceived more in terms of an activity, a process, a way of living.
>
> (Bevans, 2002:74)

The pool of resources which has traditionally informed the practice of Christian theology needs widening and other resources such as human experience, culture and local values need to inform an expanded approach to Christian theology. Culture and human experience are essential to understanding Christianity and to understanding God's revelation in history. God's presence is understood by the praxis model as in everyday life and, very importantly, as committed to revealing and challenging oppression and injustice. More than this, the praxis calls on women and men to work with God in history, 'in partnership God' (Bevans, 2002:75). Bevans clearly values the praxis model, arguing ... the praxis model is as such basically sound. It is based on an excellent epistemology, its understanding of revelation is very fresh and exciting, and it has deep roots in theological tradition' (Bevans, 2002:78).

Synthetic model

The fourth model that Bevans outlines in his scheme of models of contextual theology is what he terms 'the synthetic model'. Bevans sees this model as one that includes features of the other models, and he describes it as ' ... a middle-of-the-road model' (Bevans, 2002:88). It has traits of what Bevans considers the more traditional approaches of contextual theology but at the same time it values and acknowledges the significance of culture within which the Christian message is delivered or translated. Bevans' use of the word 'synthetic' here relates to the concept of synthesis, a synthesis of the other models of contextual theology that he presents. It attempts a careful balance, as Bevans presents it, between commitment to tradition, scripture and doctrine and to the con-temporary local context. Bevans describes the methodology of this model as Hegelian, as dialectical in its attempt to work with the traditional and the more contemporary. Within this Bevans clearly sees a significant dichotomy between the resources and aspects of the Christian faith along the traditional and con-temporary lines. Perhaps the dichotomy might be said to be between tradition (including doctrine and scripture) and human experience and culture. He com-pares this model to David Tracey's approach of analogical imagination (2002:90) or dialogical imagination as it is sometimes called but which Bevans referred to as 'inculturation' or 'interculturation' (2002:90). Interestingly, Bevans agues that this model does not understand culture as monolithic but rather as constituting different layers with the consequence that value can be placed on some aspects of a particular culture whilst others must be open to and undergo critical scrutiny. Also, contextual theology when understood in terms of the synthetic model is an ongoing theological movement. It has to be ongoing given its dialogical nature and the changing nature of experience and culture.

Transcendental model

The fifth model that Bevans outlines in his scheme of contextual ways of doing Christian theology is what he terms 'The Transcendental Model'. At the heart of this model is a shift in perception without which understanding simply cannot be reached (Bevans, 2002:103). This model focuses on the person engaged in theology, the person at the centre of theology:

> What is important is not so much that a particular theology is produced but that the theologian who is producing it operates as an authentic,

converted subject. In the same way that Bernard Lonergan ⸌
metaphysics, a contextual theology will not appear primarily in booĸ
in men's and women's minds.

(Bevans, 2002:103)

In using the term 'transcendental' Bevans refers back to Kant's method, subsequently developed by such thinkers as Rousselot, Rahner and Lonergan (2002:103). It rejects the notion that to know is to comprehend a reality divorced from or distinct from the human subject but instead sees it as intrinsically dependent on humanity and on human knowledge. It begins by trying to understand the human before going on to ask the 'bigger' questions. This 'transcendental subjectivity' begins with the human in the process of coming to know or discern truth.

As such, the transcendental model begins with human experience, whatever the nature of that experience, but in particular with religious experience. In recognizing the nature of humanity we inevitably recognize the nature of humanity as communal and so the transcendental model is in many ways contextual through communality (Bevans, 2002:104). Within the context of explaining the transcendental model Bevans considers the implications of radically different contextual experiences. He argues that rather than asking questions such as how can the Christian faith be authentically expressed in a particular context in order to demonstrate both the 'Christian' and cultural or contextual nature of that theology, the question should be such as, 'How genuine is the religious experience I am trying to interpret, how well does my language express this experience? ... Do I really understand what I am trying to articulate?' (Bevans, 2002:104–105). Revelation, then, is not seen as something outside of the human self, as of a different realm, but rather it is 'The only place where God can reveal Godself truly and effectively is within human experience, as a human person is open to the words of scripture as read or proclaimed. Open to events in daily life, and open to the values embodied in a cultural tradition' (Bevans, 2002:105). Revelation only actually occurs when a person is open to it.

One problematic feature of Bevans' transcendental model is the claim that despite cultural and historical diversity 'the human mind nevertheless operates in identical ways in all cultures and at all periods of history' (Bevans, 2002:105). This then allows Bevans whilst recognizing and claiming radical contextual diversity at the same time to claim a shared fundamental human experience or 'basic cognitive operations' (Bevans, 2002:105). So from this he is then able to conclude that contextual diversity is important but that 'As real as historical and cultural differences are, in other words, a historical or cultural subject's way of knowing transcends those particular differences' (Bevans, 2002:105). This, then, in a sense wipes away all of Bevans' claims about radical contextuality. Reality is within but that reality is in a sense shared and determined, despite radical differences. Important in this model is the person attempting to express or live out their faith and their authenticity in doing this (Bevans, 2002:106). The individual moves towards authenticity in their theology through their existence in a community or communal setting of faith. This forum for dialogue is almost a safety net to make sure that the emphasis on the individual's experience does not leave the individual without any form of external authority or checking point. Experiences between different people may be both positive and negative but they are a constant reminder or challenge to an individual's authenticity.

In Bevans' models theology as an activity becomes an ever widening and diverse activity. It is not confined to the trained and qualified theologian and this is one reason that he has come to refer to it as an activity (Bevans, 2002:8). It is concerned with doing, with activity, rather than with content or with discovering the answers to complex theological questions through content. Bevans argues that this reflects Anselm's understanding of theology as 'faith *seeking understanding*' (quoted in Bevans, 2002:108). Bevans acknowledges that many readers have found the transcendental model too abstract and difficult to work effectively with. He puts this down to the shift necessary from content to activity. He also acknowledges that

> ... the very universality that is one of the model's advantages is not really universal at all, but is the product of western, male-dominated cultural thought forms. Do people really come to understand in the same way, or are there really different ways of knowing? Is the transcendental model of contextual theology just another subtle way that western (and perhaps patriarchal) thought attempts to domesticate attempts to think in alternative ways?
>
> (Bevans, 2002:108)

Bevans interestingly suggests in relation to the transcendental model that the authentic believer and authentic human being are so utterly unattainable that perhaps these should be seen instead as a 'metamodel' (Bevans, 2002:108).

Countercultural model

The final model in Bevans' scheme is 'The Countercultural Model' which can be seen as a radically contextual model based firmly in history and human experience, and committed to social change, whilst at the same time adapting a hermeneutic of suspicion towards the role of context and towards context itself. As such, it is an analytical and deeply challenging model of contextual theology. It is embedded in scripture and in the importance of scripture and tradition, and should not be confused with 'anticultural' (Bevans, 2002:1180). Within this model the gospel, not human experience, culture or context, is the driving force. Indeed, Bevans points out that an appropriate alternative title for this model might be '*the prophetic model*' (Bevans, 2002:119). Bevans' explanation of his use of the term 'countercultural model' is helpful and insightful. He argues that there can be no such thing as a gospel that is culture free (2002:120) because context is crucial to understanding the gospel. However, at the same time he is careful to insist within this model that the gospel stands at the very centre experienced on a personal level and leading to conversion. Newbigin who Bevans cites as perhaps the strongest proponent of this model himself argued that the gospel cannot simply be taken to a context but has to be genuinely heard and received within that context. Given the significance of the gospel and so of revelation it is not surprising that Bevans argues that those advocating this model see Christ as the ultimate revelation and this is a revelation that can establish itself in any context or culture. Most importantly, however, the revelation is Christ, Christian revelation and Christ cannot be separated. Christ as God incarnate is accessed through the gospels and ensuing practices. Bevans points out that this model is being used by Newbigin, Hauerwas and Milbank. Bevans is critical of this model, arguing for the need to ensure that it is countercultural rather than anticultural (Bevans, 2002:125). Also, no particular culture should be idealized or be seen to be without its own problems, and possible corruptions.

In terms of valuing the different models, in comparing their strengths and weaknesses, Bevans in the conclusion of *Models of Contextual Theology* asks 'Is One Model Better Than Another?' He points out that each has different strengths but he argues that it is not necessary to be confined to working with one model. Bevans talks of 'healthy pluralism' (Bevans, 2002:139), the relevance of a model is itself contextual. A model that might be appropriate in one setting is not necessarily appropriate for another. This Bevans refers to as the inclusivity of contextual models of theology. In conclusion, Bevans argues that

> The move to understand all theology as contextual is also a move to recognize the complex reality of theological pluralism. In times past we could confidently speak of the unity of theology, and theological students from Manila, Chicago, São Paolo, and Accra all studied the same theology out of pretty much the same books – Ott or Tanquerey or van Noort were all cut from the same theological cloth. The question of the best model of contextual theology is an appropriate one, but within today's world of radical plurality and ambiguity the best answer to the question can only be: 'it depends on the context.'
>
> (Bevans, 2002:xxx)

The Blackwell Reader in Pastoral and Practical Theology – differentiating between and comparing contextual theology and practical theology

The Blackwell Reader in Pastoral and Practical Theology does not wholly and explicitly address the issue of contextual theology. However, it does touch on and deal with many of the key issues that are of concern for contextual theology. It is also a helpful way for us to differentiate or at least to explore whether it is possible to differentiate between contextual and practical theology. There are parts of this book that are extremely important to contextual theology and are helpful in understanding the nature of contextual theology, and not least it helps us to consider whether what various theologians refer to as practical theology might also rightly be called contextual theology. Is the difference one of semantics or theological method and content? There is, as will become clear, some confusion between the two terms especially in terms of the way in which they are used in description of particular theologies. It will be argued here, however, there are distinctions between practical and contextual theology but at the same time there are many, many points of similarity in terms of method, commitment and theological integrity. It will also be argued that some theologies can be described as both contextual and practical, bearing in mind that 'contextual theology' within this book is used as a term to refer to those theologies which explicitly and often politically place the context of the community or the theologian at the centre of theology, as a key guiding, informing, even revelatory aspect of theology.

The Blackwell Reader in Pastoral and Practical Theology is a collection of papers edited by and contributed to by James Woodward and Stephen Pattison. The collection explores some of the different ways in which pastoral and practical theologies are carried out. Within this collection there are a number of papers that have immense theological significance for understanding contemporary theology and specifically for understanding the nature and activities of contextual theology. First published in 2000 the book has proved to be a very important text for many people but especially for students of theology as an academic discipline. Contributors to the book include Paul Ballard, Elaine Graham, Don Browning, Gordon Lynch and Alistair Campbell. However, the particular papers which are going to be explored here are:

(1) Stephen Pattison – 'Some straw for the bricks: A basic introduction to theological reflection'.
(2) Emmanuel Lartey – 'Practical theology as a theological form'.
(3) Edward Farley – 'Interpreting situations: An inquiry into the nature of practical theology'.

In the preface and introduction to *The Blackwell Reader in Pastoral and Practical Theology* Woodward and Pattison argue that pastoral or practical theology is becoming an increasingly important aspect of Christian theology and of the study of theology and they offer as a start to the book the following definition which they formulated for an earlier joint project in 1994 *A Vision of Pastoral Theology*:

> For preliminary purposes, pastoral or practical theology can be defined as a prime place where contemporary experience and the resources of the religious tradition meet in a critical dialogue that is mutually and practically transforming.
>
> (Woodward and Pattison, 2000:xiii)

For Woodward and Pattison it is possible to identify quite precisely a method that is common to the papers that make up the reader in pastoral and practical theology. For them it is a method in which experience and tradition, in which theory and practice work together and interact interdependently (Woodward and Pattison, 2000: xiv). In effect it would seem they envisage a common method that supports and is dependent on this interdependent relationship, one that gives appropriate and balanced credence and significance to tradition and experience and theory and practice. Woodward and Pattison are very eager to stress the uncontested place and significance of tradition within practical and pastoral theology.

In arguing for the interdependence of tradition and experience, practice and theory, they argue for a holistic approach to theologizing which brings together the different elements which they and others have identified as key components of theology. It seems that the interdependence of these different elements is essential for the Christian faith to be genuinely represented and present in any given situation. In differentiating between pastoral and practical theology Woodward and Pattison argue that the roots of pastoral theology lay with the basic theological notion of care to ensure 'the individual and corporate well-being and flourishing of the Christian "flock"' (Woodward and Pattison, 2000:2). They argue that practical theology as a theological term can be traced in its roots to eighteenth-century Protestant theology in Germany and grew out of pastoral theology with a concern for the application of certain theological principles to theology in all of its many aspects such as preaching and education. They note the shared concerns and practices of pastoral and practical theology and in effect tie the two together in the way in which they describe both the origins and operations of these theologies. On one level the difference between the two is a matter of preference and tradition, tradition in terms of usage. Similarly, they also discuss the use of the increasingly outdated term 'applied theology', arguing that 'Practical theology might be taken to imply a more mutual, dialogical process than the simple application of theological truths and conclusions in practice' (Woodward and Pattison, 2000:3). Whilst their argument is a valid one their understanding and description of applied theology might be open to challenge from those preferring the term to 'practical theology' in description of their theology. What is clear is that terminology in this area, be it 'pastoral theology', 'practical theology', 'applied theology' or 'contextual theology', is potentially confusing and usage of any of the terms needs clarity and consideration. Woodward and Pattison argue that both pastoral and practical theology are not single contained methods as such but rather can be seen themselves to use a variety of methods in order to remain sensitive to and responsive to different situations, they need to remain flexible (2000:9). They place practical theology largely within 'the academic setting of universities, seminaries, and colleges' (2000:11) but resist any narrow attempts to confine it to these settings.

In attempting to offer some kind of general way of identifying practical theology Woodward and Pattison name a number of characteristics that might be present in a practical theology. This is not meant as a definitive definition but rather as an attempt to offer a way of identifying or characterizing a theological approach whose boundaries are often unclear or overlap to include other kinds of theological approaches. As such, it is possible to argue that in many cases contextual theology might also be described as practical theology, according to Woodward and Pattison's characterization. They offer fourteen characteristics of practical theology, arguing that it:

(1)   Is 'a transformational activity'.
(2)   Goes beyond the rational and logical to incorporate the full range of human experience and ways of communicating.
(3)   Is 'confessional and honest' by which they seem to mean that it arises out of faith and commitment to Christian truth.
(4)   Is 'unsystematic'.
(5)   Is 'truthful and committed' and this seems to mean that it will face difficult situations with faith to seek change.
(6)   Is 'contextual and situationally related'. Here Woodward and Pattison refer to Schreiter's work on local theologies claiming that practical theology is local theology in so far as the local context is a significant theological factor. They also argue that 'Whilst historical data, classic texts, such as the Bible and experiences from elsewhere may help practical theology in its main task, its main concern is to explore and contribute to immediate contexts, situations, and practices'. This makes a strong and interesting link between what is understood in this book to be contextual theology and what Woodward and Pattison refer to as practical theology.
(7)   Is 'sociopolitically aware and committed', and they place a liberationist agenda with practical theology.
(8)   Is 'experiential'. It begins with people's experiences, placing authority with experience in a way that has traditionally been accorded to texts like the Bible.
(9)   Is 'often reflectively based' and by this the authors seem to mean that practical theology involves reflection on experiences and situations.
(10) Is 'interrogative' and here Woodward and Pattison are making an important distinction between the ways in which theology has often been perceived and in reality involved as 'monolithic and instructional' and instead practical theology is less restrained by the limitations of an imposed orthodoxy which prevents key questions and issues being pursued.
(11) Is 'interdisciplinary', which is again a significant break away from understandings of the nature of theological reflection and engagement. There is an increasing use of disciplines other than theology to inform and develop theology on the basis of the usefulness of such disciplines to theology.
(12) Is 'analytical and constructive', it aims to both be a tool of understanding but also of change or development.
(13) Is 'dialectical and disciplined'. By this Woodward and Pattison mean that practical theology often holds different polarities in tension, such as experience and tradition or theory and practice.
(14) Finally, the authors characterize practical theology as 'skillful and demanding'.

(Woodward and Pattison, 2000:13–16)

Whilst acknowledging that in theory anyone could engage in practical theology 'there is much to learn about how to work with different methods, types of material, situations etc'. So whilst on one level Woodward and Pattison are prepared to concede that practical theology need not remain wholly in the domain of the trained and skilled academic theologian, they still express some reservations about the actual practice of theology in terms of experience and expertise. In conclusion to their initial analysis of practical theology Woodward and Pattison argue that whilst on the one hand this is a rapidly expanding and vibrant area of theological activity at the same time it is an area wrought with confusion (2000:16).

Stephen Pattison is Professor of Religion, Ethics and Practice at the University of Birmingham. In his contribution to the reader 'Some straw for the bricks: A basic introduction to theological reflection' Pattison explores the nature of theological reflection. He proposes the model of the three-way conversation as the basic function of critical theological reflection. His model is heavily dialogical and is an attempt to offer a fairly basic and simple model for understanding the complex interactions and methodologies that he claims are taking place in critical theological reflection. The three-way conversation concept proposed by Pattison understands that those engaged in critical theological refection are being involved in

> a three-way 'conversation' or dialogue between their own ideas, beliefs, feelings, and perceptions; the beliefs, assumptions, and perceptions provided by the Christian tradition; and the contemporary situation which is being considered.
> (Pattison in Woodward and Pattison, 2000:135)

Pattison in his paper is drawing on Exodus 5:16 'No straw is provided for your servants and still the cry is "Make bricks!"'. He claims that the need to engage in critical theological reflection is at the heart of many theological programmes of study and yet notes, quite correctly, that 'theological reflection' is a vague and variedly understood term. In fact he argues that theological educators themselves, although encouraging the need to engage in theological reflection, often have difficulty actually clearly stating what they mean by this (Pattison in Woodward and Pattison, 2000:136). Pattison makes an excellent point here. There is much emphasis in contemporary theological education and training on theological reflection but that said, what this means has largely been a very subjective and even then vague understanding by the educator giving the instruction. In 2005 Elaine Graham, Heather Walton and Frankie Ward published *Theological Reflection: Methods* addressing and exploring this very issue with a strongly pragmatic slant. The very fact of the existence of such a book demonstrates both just how significant theological reflection is and also how elusive and confusing the term has become.

Pattison argues that there is an almost 'mystic' quality attached to the notion of theological reflection, such is the elusiveness and lack of shared understanding about what is actually meant by it (Pattison in Woodward and Pattison, 2000:136). The model that Pattison proposes of the three-way conversation, as he acknowledges, is neither original nor is it without problems, but it is the simplicity and proved effectiveness of the model among his students that brings Pattison to propose it as a workable model for critical theological reflection. Pattison in this paper proposes the dismantling of traditional understandings of what 'theology' actually is, and this is part of the reason for the inclusion of this paper from the edited collection here. Pattison's model incorporates a fundamental characteristic of contextual theologies, the conviction that theology is not solely the activity of an elite and highly educated group of people but is potentially an activity which anyone can engage in. This challenge to the notion of theology as the queen of the sciences, as something removed from everyday activity and guarded by the privileged and authoritative, is absolutely fundamental to the understanding and approach of contextual theologies.

> The word 'theology' seems to frighten people. One suspects that the images that it brings to their minds are those of serried ranks of learned tomes written by elderly and authoritative men of incomprehensible profundity which bear no relation to present day reality or to their own situation.
> The word 'theology' must be set free from dusty academic bondage.
> (Pattison in Woodward and Pattison, 2000:137)

Pattison stresses that theology is not an out of date activity but rather that it is a contemporary and an appropriate method of enquiry. He also rejects ideas of theology as static and ancient; for him it should be 'dynamic, searching and open-ended' (Pattison in Woodward and Pattison, 2000:137). Given the place of experience in theology and its dynamic nature Pattison argues that theology should really be spoken of in the plural as 'theologies' rather than 'theology'. He challenges the idea that there is a right and proper way of doing theology that is in line with the norm, with the words 'The fact is that there is no formal norm' (Pattison in Woodward and Pattison, 2000:137). He also raises the inevitable question that lies at the heart of this book, that of Christian identity and the inescapable question of: what do all of the different theologies that exist have in common if we accept the notion of radical contextual theology?

> There are all sorts of ways of doing theology which are so different that it sometimes seems that the only thing that unites them is a common claim to be talking about God and religious experience.
> ... if theologians are so different in their approaches and cannot agree on what theology is, there can be no one right way of doing theology and perhaps one's own way is as good as anyone else's. It has its own validity and usefulness within one's own situation.
> (Pattison in Woodward and Pattison, 2000:138)

For Pattison theological reflection has a crucial place in contemporary life. It is not something that is limited or restricted to the academy or the institutional Church, rather, given the way he understands and models it, theological reflection by its nature ensures an ever evolving and relevant relationship with the contemporary. It is theological reflection, argues Pattison, which is effective in ensuring the relevance of Christian faith in any given age. It is dynamic and constantly renewing. Pattison brings this together with his proposal of understanding theological reflection as critical conversation (Pattison in Woodward and Pattison, 2000:139). Conversation by its very nature is dynamic, dialogical and unpredictable. Pattison proposes that his model of theological reflection as a critical conversation involves envisaging a conversation that is in effect held between

(a) her own beliefs, feelings, perceptions and assumptions, (b) the beliefs, assumptions and perceptions provided by the Christian tradition (including the Bible) and (c) the contemporary situation which is being examined.
(Pattison in Woodward and Pattison, 2000:139)

As a tool to aid this process, using this model Pattison suggests that each of these three be personified so that what is being envisaged is a conversation between three people. His stress on theological reflection as critical means that each of the participants in the conversation should ask questions which may be probing and in fact Pattison argues that it should not be presumed that all three participants will agree by the end of the conversation. One of the strengths of Pattison's proposal is that conversations can be notoriously difficult 'because participants start from very different assumptions and understandings' (Pattison in Woodward and Pattison, 2000:140). This is an important point and relates to the diversity of human experience, the diversity of context and the diversity of the presence of institutional Christianity. Also, he argues that lack of agreement may be the result of the conversation or even just silence. This is okay in Pattison's model and in fact more faithfully mirrors the reality of theological reflection in that it does not encourage the development of key systematic principles which can then be universally applied regardless of context. Rather, it allows for the fact that there are, at times, real gaps between the tradition and contemporary experience. Theological reflection does not have as its endless task the closing of these gaps and resolving any kind of unanswered or conflictual issues. Rather, the model of theological reflection as a conversation with all of the characteristics of a conversation allows for the existence of gaps and living with these gaps (Pattison in Woodward and Pattison, 2000:140).

Pattison gives an example of how this model of three-way conversation might work as a model for theological reflection. He describes a situation in which a trainee minister is on placement to the Marriage Guidance Council (Pattison in Woodward and Pattison, 2000:141). The student approaches this placement with certain presuppositions and beliefs about marriage with the central one being that the role of the minister should always be to encourage a couple to stay together regardless of the situation. Pattison argues that during her time at the placement the student may encounter some situations and experiences that support and affirm her commitment to and faith-based belief about the sanctity of marriage and the role of the minister. However, she may also experience situations that may challenge or lead her to question her approach in under-standing the role of the minister. There may be a clash, for example, between traditional Christian approaches to marriage councelling and the practice of the Marriage Guidance Council with its appraoch of not telling or advising people what to do. The student, then, argues Pattison, is potentially faced with a pro-blem: that there is a clash between what her faith-based understanding of the role of the minister is in such situations and the practice of the Council. The student is now faced with some important questions if not actual decisions to make because of the clash in practice and beliefs. She may contemplate leaving the Council because its values and practice do not line up with those of her Christian faith and the tradition that underpins this faith. Alternatively she could adapt her own approach to counselling to bring it into line with that of the Marriage Guidance Council. In the process of considering whether to change her practice or leave the Council the student has in effect been engaging in a three-way conversation. This conversation has been between her own beliefs and assumptions, those given to her by the Christian tradition and the actual contemporary situation in which she finds herself. For Pattison this is real critical theological reflection at work. It is vibrant, probing and real. The student's own process of question might well at times be painful and testing to her faith but it is grappling with the realities of Christian faith in contemporary situations which for Pattison is the mark of critical theological reflection.

Pattison himself notes that his model has limitations. First that it is not a model designed to produce lasting and transferable faith-based responses to issues. Rather, as he notes (Pattison in Woodward and Pattison, 2000:142), his model in reality actually leads to more questioning rather than any universally applicable answers or transferable truths. As such it cannot in any real way be said to encourage a systematic theological way of approaching questions and issues. Another criticism Pattison envisages might be made of his model, is in terms of the depth of conversation that is actually being entered into. He notes that anything beyond a superficial dialogue would require academic research by the student. He also notes that the theological reflection that might emerge from all of this will only really be valid for the context with which the student is concerned. Here Pattison challenges high understandings of what rightly constitutes theological reflection:

> We need to get used to the idea that theologies can be disposable and contextual; the conclusions of any particular theological reflection do not need to be seen as relevant for all people in all places and they may, indeed, be thoroughly idiosyncratic.
>
> (Pattison in Woodward and Pattison, 2000:143)

Emmanuel Lartey 'Practical Theology as a Theological Form'

The second paper to be examined from Woodward and Pattison's reader is a contribution by Emmanuel Lartey, who is a Ghanaian theologian who is now

Professor of Pastoral Theology, Care and Counseling at Candler School of Theology, Emory University. He is known widely for his work on black theology and pastoral theology. Lartey in his paper 'Practical Theology as a Theological Form' maps out his understanding of the place of practical theology in contemporary theology as well as the general characteristics of this theological 'form' as he refers to it (Lartey in Woodward and Pattison, 2000:129).

He begins his critical exploration of practical theology with the following words: 'The pluriformity and ambiguity of practical theology are at once its highest promise and its greatest pitfall' (Lartey in Woodward and Pattison, 2000:129). He argues that practical theology has been used by specific groups, these being '(1) ministry (specifically Liturgy and Homiletics); (2) pastoral care and counseling; (3) religious education; and (4) ethics' (Lartey in Woodward and Pattison, 2000:129). Turning to the task of characterizing practical theology Lartey offers the following definition:

> There are a number of ways in which practical theology has been characterized, engaged in, or understood (sometimes by people other than those actually seeking to practice it). In my view these can be categorized into *three* distinctively different streams, although at times they flow into each other and exert relative influence upon each other. What is common to all three is a concern to relate faith (or doctrine) with practice (or life) and to do so in ways that are relevant and useful.
>
> (Lartey in Woodward and Pattison, 2000:129)

The three streams that Lartey argues practical theology can be categorized into are as follows. First, 'the branch approach' sees practical theology as a branch of theology (Lartey in Woodward and Pattison, 2000:129) and Lartey talks of this approach as one in which practical theology serves as a kind of 'church government', or else the 'church's action' (Lartey in Woodward and Pattison, 2000:130) through the application of doctrine, for example, to the job of managing the Church. Second, practical theology can be seen as a 'process' (Lartey in Woodward and Pattison, 2000:130). Here, concern is with developing effective methods which will then help the practical theologian in their theological task. Lartey points to Tillich's correlation method as an example of this and to Tracey's revision and development of Tillich's approach. Finally, the third approach identified by Lartey is that which sees practical theology as a '*form*' of theology. Here focus is on ways of doing theology. It is concerned with the pragmatic, with ways of doing theology. For Lartey liberation theologies are examples of this understanding of practical theology.

Having described these three ways in which practical theology might be and has been understood Lartey goes on to offer his own account of how practical theology might be understood, and understood specifically for use in the academic setting, his own context. He develops his understanding of the pastoral cycle (Lartey in Woodward and Pattison, 2000:132) which incorporates the following five phases:

(1)   The pastoral cycle begins with an actual or 'concrete' situation, a situation which involves some sort of encounter with people, which for Lartey lies at the centre of incarnational theology. In other people we have the opportunity to encounter God and Jesus.

(2)   Moving on from the concrete situation the next phase in the cycle is what Lartey calls '*situational analysis*'. Here the situation encountered is analysed using different analytic tools and disciplines to try and discern the dynamics of the situation that demands some sort of response or in which an individual may find themselves. Lartey argues that God's truth is to be found not only in theology but can be encountered in other disciplines. Appropriate disciplines, then are used to get as full a picture as possible of the situation through situational analysis.

(3)   In the third phase Lartey argues that the situation is analysed from a committed or faith perspective. In this sense it complements situational analysis in that it is personal and faith based.

(4)   In the fourth phase it is the faith perspective that is itself questioned by situational analysis.

(5)   In the fifth and final phase exploration is then made of the options that are actually available to the individual who then, as a result acts accordingly.

For Lartey, then, like Pattison, theology and in particular practical theology is not static or fixed but rather is changing with human experience.

Edward Farley 'Interpreting Situations: An Inquiry into the Nature of Practical Theology'

Edward Farley in his paper stresses the contextual nature of human existence, stressing that human beings 'exist and act in situation and engage in interpretations of situations' (Farley in Woodward and Pattison, 2000:119). Farley who is Drucilla Moore Buffington Professor Emeritus of the Divinity School at Vanderbilt argues that faith has a special role to play in understanding and interpreting the situations in which human beings find themselves. He refers to this as 'a special hermeneutic task, differentiable from other hermeneutic or interpretive dimensions of theology' (Farley in Woodward and Pattison, 2000:119). Recognizing that the full description of this hermeneutic task would be a significant and lengthy task Farley offers instead a description of some of its features. These are features which he believes to be almost definitely present when a situation is being analysed from a faith or faith-informed perspective. Farley stresses the fluidity of life, or situations that human beings find themselves in. Responding to change, then, is part of situational living, where situations can be short or prolonged, local or global, experienced by an individual or by groups (Farley in Woodward and Pattison, 2000:120).

Farley argues that the task of interpreting a situation must begin with the identification and description of the situation. This he argues is a difficult task, given the often complex nature of a situation and also given the fact that as human beings we are biased and hold strong preconceptions which will influence and determine the way in which we see and describe a situation. The second feature or task that Farley identifies in the task of interpreting situations relates to the past. This is because present situations incorporate on some level past experiences and situations:

> ... the present is comprised of and structured by these disguised repressions of the past. And only a certain way of studying the past will uncover these repressions and in so doing will thus uncover something at work in the present.
>
> (Farley in Woodward and Pattison, 2000:121)

Farley describes the third task as relating the local situation at hand to the bigger picture. It may be globally related pictures or a wider series of situations that are related in some way to the situation being analysed. This prevents a limited and wholly inward looking analysis and recognizes the significance of the possible relationship it may bear to other situations. Farley describes a fourth task in which theology is central. All situations which face human beings demand responses and one aspect of this is the faith response.

The Woodward and Pattison reader whilst not being directly concerned with contextual theology as such *is* concerned with practical and pastoral theology. The three papers examined here demonstrate that there is theological concern with the same issues that are central to contextual theology even if they are not being raised or addressed under the umbrella of contextual theology. This chapter will now move on to examine the final text that has been identified as significant to the emergence of contextual theology as a distinct and important theological approach. The text, *God in Context: A Survey of Contextual Theology*, is the most recently published of the texts being examined here and was published in 2003 and written by Sigurd Bergmann.

Sigurd Bergmann *God in Context: A Survey of Contextual Theology*

Sigurd Bergmann is Professor of Religious Studies at the Department of Archaeology and Religious Studies at the Norwegian University of Science and Technology in Trondheim, Norway. He is very committed to the study of contextual theology and to uncovering the meaning of Christian theology as contextual. In 2003 he published with Ashgate *God in Context: A Survey of Contextual Theology*, which, as Mary Grey says in the Introduction to the book:

> *God in Context* pays full attention to the revelatory situation and to reve-lation in action. *God In Context* captures the dynamic, communicative aspect of revelation as appealing in an integrated way to persons-in-community, to heart, mind and body. The author rightly recovers the power of symbol and image often overlooked by 'tradition'. Symbol, he writes, both refers and manifests. But the arguments only work because Bergmann offers an

interpretation of tradition that is no mere handing on of knowledge, but is respectful of local traditions, encourages the integration of suppressed and invisible groups, gives priority to this underside and encourages ecological expressions.

(Grey in Bergmann, 2003:x)

So, for Bergmann, as will be demonstrated, what is important is the combination of tradition and revelation in tradition and in human experience in context, but always guided or validated in some way by tradition.

Bergmann begins his study by acknowledging the increasing awareness of the significance of context for Christian theology and notes specifically how context is impacting on and determined the shape of Christian theology to the point of relevance (Bergmann, 2003:xiii). As Bergmann notes, the development of this awareness was against a backdrop of religious pluralism and the Christian theological attempts to understand the implications of pluralism for Christianity. Also, other factors contributing towards a general shift in understanding about how and by whom Christian theology could be done included 'discontent with conventional generalizing ways of approaching theology' (Bergmann, 2003:xiii) and also the increasing recognition that in general an awareness of cultural diversity and changing cultural situations demanded some kind of appropriate theological response. This setting, argues Bergmann, provided a theological ground ripe for a new way or ways of doing theology. It is from this, according to Bergmann, that explicitly contextual theologies began to develop and he names some as Latin American liberation theology, feminist theology, North American black theology, Minjung theology, Palestinian theology, African black theology and eco-theology (Bergmann, 2003:xiii).

Bergmann's driving thesis in *God in Context* is the contextual expressions of the ongoing revelation of God. For him this is the point and function of contextual theology, to be open to God's revelatory presence in the very places that people find themselves. Bergmann's intention in this book is to examine how different contexts reveal God's ongoing revelation; this is his fundamental aim. He is not attempting to present a new systematic theology as such but is arguing for a paradigm shift (Bergmann, 2003: xv), a theological paradigm shift to a different way of doing theology than has traditionally been done. We see here very clearly a common concern, then, with Schreiter, Bevans, Pattison, Lartey and Farley.

Bergmann begins his study with a strong assertion that 'Theology today ought to be contextual theology' (Bergmann, 2003:1). He argues that the claimed postmodern age in which we find ourselves at the time of writing *God in Context* demands a theological response to the multiplicity and spectrum of competing and diverse claims about truth and the range of worldviews that we are not only aware of but that we often live among. In relation to this he asks questions about the location and function of theology today, whether it should be a confessional activity which takes place so to speak behind closed doors among believers or whether there is a place for theology in contemporary discourses. He begins with attempting to differentiate between contextual and non-contextual theology and then puts forward a strong argument for the so-called contextualization of Christian theology. Bergmann in his analysis deconstructs the word 'context' in an attempt to locate meaning through analysis of the roots of the word:

> 'Context' is an immigrant from philology. It refers to that which surrounds (Latin con-) a text. Context means the parts of a text that precede and follow the text in question and which are of importance for its understanding.
>
> The linguistic meaning of context can be transferred to other fields. Today the word also denotes the particular social, cultural and ecological situation within which a course of events takes place. A theological text, for instance, comes into being within a wider context, that is, it is determined by the traditions and circumstances that have an effect on the complex situation of the author and the reader.
>
> (Bergmann, 2003:2)

Bergmann argues that in the 1970s and 1980s more theologies began to place human experience at the centre of theology, or put in a different way, more theologies grew out of the significance of human experience. He rightly notes that at this time there was no conscious move to categorize or develop this theological development as a clear and distinct theological type of method. A particular feature of this concern with theology, which valued and saw human experience as fundamental to the theological process, was a focus on human experiences of oppression and of 'suffering and structurally conditioned repression' (Bergmann, 2003:3). This, in turn, inevitably reflected the kind of theologies that were developing, as concerned not just with the context of human experiences but the contexts of human experiences of suffering and oppression.

As we will see in the next chapter by the 1970s the emergence of theologies of liberation, in the first instance in Latin America, reflected this valuing of human experience and particular focus on situations of human oppression. The roots of liberation theologies can be traced most definitely to Latin America but the core theological concepts and concerns of liberation theologies soon spread and we see a plethora of theologies of liberation develop, some very different to each other. These include black theologies, feminist theologies, Minjung theologies, sexual theologies, ecological theologies and queer theologies.

Bergmann offers a number of characteristics of contextual theologies that he argues aid in the identification and description of contextual theology. First, Bergmann argues that contextual theology is concerned with developing a method, one in which theology 'is an interpretation of Christian faith, which arises in the consciousness of its context' (Bergmann, 2003:4) and is specifically concerned with experiencing God. What Bergmann is arguing here is that when we talk about contextual theology as a distinct theological type or approach then we are talking about a theology which not only values and promotes as central to its theology the human context, but does this in a conscious and reflective way. It is fully aware of the significance it is placing with experience and context, and indeed, aims to do this. The significance of experience and context is not incidental to contextual theology but deliberate and at the heart of any attempted classification of contextual theology. Very importantly, for Bergmann, context is not only recognized and valued in this theological approach but there is a fundamental concern with change. Concern is with change to the context that is oppressive and limiting to the fullness of human living, experience and faith.

Bergmann goes on to argue that contextual theologies can be seen to be attempting to apply the above described method of identifying, valuing and changing context in a number of ways. Here, value is given undoubtedly to human experience and specifically to human experience of 'suffering and deliverance' (Bergmann, 2003:4). As noted earlier, it is part of the growing tradition that challenges and rejects the traditional view of theology as offering universal truths that can be imported and are valid in any given situation. Such universalist tendencies are resisted and theology becomes informed and transformed by local culture.

What is clear is that Bergmann understands contextual theology as referring to a theological approach that is conscious of the context in which it is situated and to which it is responding, that it values this context as a theological resource and is an approach that is found particularly among those whose contexts are ones characterized by oppression and human suffering. Bergmann is aware of the difficulty that a radical reading of Christian theology as contextual actually brings, that all theology is determined and influenced and so inevitably, in some sense, bound by its context. Bergmann in arguing that all theology should be contextual is actually arguing that all theology should be aware of and place in a centrally determining position context and human experience.

He claims that there is a general dissatisfaction with traditional ways of doing theology, amidst questions of relevance. Also, that there is a growing interest with sociological theories of the construction of reality and with other disciplines that offer different ways of looking at the world and understanding its complexity and the place of human beings and Christian faith within it. Bergmann argues that this actually brings a central challenge to traditional theological claims, for example:

> Given our insight into the social prerequisite of religion, the theology of eternity seems to be an illusion. The reflection over God as an expression of the experience of meeting this God is and will remain bound to the sociocultural context in which these experiences occur.
>
> (Bergmann, 2003:9)

Bergmann is not willing to concede, however, that this limits all theology, and especially all explicitly contextual theology, in terms of its relevance and

insights to the context from which it arose and which is so central to its formation. Bergmann gets around the nagging question of theological relativism by
differentiating within contextual theology between that which remains tied to
context and that which in some way goes beyond the context and links with
Christian tradition. In this way he avoids the criticism often levelled at contextual theology that if all Christian theology is contextual then what is it
exactly that different theologies have in common?

> From the perspective of the science of culture, we can partly differentiate
> between concrete prerequisites for the determination of place in context
> and the prerequisites of persistence and over-dimensionality. The factors
> that are defined in time and place could be called 'culture' and the coded
> time-constant factors 'tradition'. A vital social cultural context always
> consists of these two elements functioning in the inter-subjective process of
> communication and action.
>
> (Bergmann, 2003:9–10)

Bergmann sees no clash here between tradition and the local. He argues that
rather than having a restrictive impact on Christianity in the sense of challenging
notions of universal claims to truth, contextual theology has the opposite effect,
in that it

> … creates new conditions for transcultural interpretation of the Christian
> faith, which could win extensive validity in a global society of many cultures.
> Only that which appears to be credible in a local context could be the
> foundation of claims of universal validity.
>
> (Bergmann, 2003:12)

Bergmann notes that Christianity, although clearly not *born* in Europe, was
shaped at significant developmental points in the dominant European Church,
especially in the medieval period. He argues that the theology that has so
dominated and many would argue has been so destructive and brought so much
oppression is in fact a local European theology that has then been represented,
transported and imposed as a universal theology throughout many different
parts of the world as part of the process of colonialism (Bergmann, 2003:13).
Bergmann formulates from this analysis of European-shaped theology a challenge which speaks to the heart of contextual theology, 'Can the Eurocentric
interpretation of Christianity, which so far has successfully defended its universal validity, remain normative for Christianity outside Europe?' (Bergmann,
2003:12) and most importantly, asks the question about Christian identity so
important to this study of contextual theology, 'Is there something which
remains unchanged through all places and times, or does perhaps the Christian
belief in God distinguish itself through the belief in the variability of God?'
(Bergmann, 2003:12). Given the focus on these questions Bergmann is concerned
to stress that the challenges of contextual theology should not mean that it is

dealt with and placed within the field of mission studies. Its concerns and relevance are much wider and the implications of raising the questions tied so closely to contextual theology, about Christian identity and the relevance of 'local theologies' and their relationship to traditional understandings of Christianity as comprising universal truths, are important theological questions.

As well as arguing that social and cultural studies call on and indeed demand critical reflection on theological concepts of universality, and in particular, universal theological truths, Bergmann also puts forward an interesting argument about the need for the contextualization of theology based on a fundamental understanding of Christianity as a religion of revelation through incarnation. Bergmann argues that the incarnation at the centre of the Christian faith is the incarnation of God in Christ, ' ... he is a male Jew, ideologically diffuse wandering freely around Palestine' (Bergmann, 2003:15). Bergmann argues that this specificity or particularity of the incarnation needs to be preserved as part of the Christian heritage and ongoing tradition. Also, Bergmann adds to this argument his conviction that the Christian belief in the revelation of God through creation gives authority to the worldly, human experience. Different communities now have the task of reflecting theologically on the meaning of the creation within their own context.

Persistent in Bergmann's theology is the belief that contextual theology is creation theology (Bergmann, 2003:17). He places creation at the very centre of all Christian theology and sees contextual theology as particularly reflective and receptive to this understanding of the place of creation in Christian theology. For Bergmann, the significance of creation in theology is that it 'aims at a reflection on experiences and encounters with the living God, who dwells in the Creation for the sake of its survival and renewal' (Bergmann, 2003:17). Contextual theology constantly revisits and renews the theological task of interpreting revelation through creation in particular contexts. Bergmann supports the claims which will be explored in the following chapters that the Christian God is essentially and inherently a God concerned with liberation, who condemns and opposes injustice and oppression wherever it occurs, 'God is not only everyone's God generally or the believer's Jesus especially. Contextual theology interprets God's actions as creative and liberating' (Bergmann, 2003:22). As such, there is a strongly liberative feature of Christianity most coherently expressed by contextual theology. Bergmann also argues that despite the common theme of liberation found in Christian theology and expressed most clearly in contextual theology, where contextual theology aims to meet the needs and respond theologically to different communities and contexts in different ways, 'The differences and similarities are, on the contrary, a sign that the same God acts in a liberative way in different places' (Bergmann, 2003:24). Any place could be the site of revelation.

Bergmann sees theology as something in which the practitioner of contextual theology is actively and actually involved with; it is not a distant or removed activity for the academic or the cleric, for example, but is the responsibility of every believer:

The road from the act of God to the experience of God and from there to a communicative expression or rite, and further to a verbal or figurative description of experiences may be long and tricky. The theologian who only devotes himself/herself to the studying of texts easily ignores the complexity, which distinguishes the flow of experience, expression and reflection in a Christian interpretation.

(Bergmann, 2003:31)

Bergmann argues that contextual theology demands methodologies which go beyond textual analysis. He also argues that systematic theology, as it has traditionally been understood, needs to be reassessed, or in his words, 'needs to widen the horizons of its interpreted objects from the texts to pictures, rites and the everyday course of events' (Bergmann, 2003:31).

Bergmann acknowledges that the contextual theology found in Latin America is often referred to by the participants as liberation rather than contextual theology. Bergmann offers an interesting overview of contextual theology in the five continents. For him, as noted above in Latin America, South Africa and Asia the term 'liberation theology' was often preferred, although there is now a very strong movement concerned with contextual theology in South Africa. Many papers are published in journals both within South Africa and internationally which reflect upon the place and vision of contextual theology in South Africa, and Bergmann notes that Minjung theology is a significant development in Asia. In the independent churches in Africa local contextual concerns are often offered combined with a concern with tradition, whilst in the Middle East the picture is very complex and 'contextual theology is still in a weak position' (Bergmann, 2003:33). In the Eastern Orthodox Church communities Bergmann argues there is 'an ambiguous interest in contextual theology' (Bergmann, 2003:33). Moving on to Australia, contextual theology has the same sort of place and significance as in North America and Europe. He notes that the political theology which emerged in Europe in the 1960s as it developed and was concerned with some of the issues now addressed by contextual theology. In the 1970s the emergence of liberation theologies attracted to various degrees and in different places enormous attention and in the early 1990s contextual theology became an explicit concern in the Nordic countries. Although Bergmann cannot give a fully extensive view of the history of contextual theology, the title of the book, *God in Context: A Survey of Contextual Theology*, leaves the reader a little disappointed with the lack of depth of analysis of the history and key developments of contextual theology.

Bergmann moves to consider the significance of the kairos movement in Europe and North America, and eventually South Africa, for the emergence and future development of contextual theology. For him it is an important part of the future of contextual theology. Eschatological in nature, kairos theology is concerned with responding to the needs and challenges of the local and global church. It stresses the need to respond in a particular age to the crises that face the world. For him the movement points towards solidarity among people who are oppressed or face injustice. It is a resource and action theology in the sense that it encourages people to identify, challenge and overcome through alternative ways of being.

When briefly considering feminist theologies Bergmann notes the divisive challenges that this group of theologies have faced, as will be seen in Chapter 3. Not only does he acknowledge the universalizing tendencies in feminist theologies to project the experiences of white, Western, middles-class women onto all women, but he also notes at an even more local level the problems facing feminist theologies of the diversity of contexts that impact on this theological movement. In reflecting on the work of the Asian theologian Chung Hyun Kyung and in particular her highly influential book published in 1990, *Struggle to be Sun Again*, Bergmann questions the basis of her claims to represent Asian women.

> Chung wants to be the voice of the poor and she pleads for an 'inductive, collective and inclusive method' for theology. The dialogue with the suffering women is the basic experience to which she wants to listen and on which she will build her theological reflection.
>
> Methodologically one may ask if the inclusiveness that she tries to attain is not rather a typically Western way of approaching human reason. The question is if an individual theologian really can include all of Creation in her personal and particularly shaped interpretation of life.
>
> Chung's theology leaves many questions unanswered. It is not distinguished by any special ability towards self-criticism.
>
> (Bergmann, 2003:39)

Bergmann's criticisms of Chung's theological approach (a criticism that can be applied to a range of contextual liberation theologies) are perhaps harsh, especially given the relative infancy of Asian women's theology and the many difficult tasks that they face to overcome not only traditional patriarchal Western biases and presuppositions but also those of white, Western feminist theologians.

Bergmann in fact identified ten 'social, cultural and ecological factors' (Bergmann, 2003:44), factors which he argues contribute towards understanding contextual theology, or rather as understanding the significance of context for theology. These are: (1) geography; (2) gender; (3) ethnic affiliations; (4) culturally constructed power; (5) class; (6) economy; (7) ecology; (8) generation; (9) education; (10) place (Bergmann, 2003:44). Bergmann picks up on the issue of tradition and contextual theology, arguing that contextual theology has yet to work out a 'new notion of tradition even if it has stressed the historical experience' (Bergmann, 2003:49). This, as Bergmann notes, has brought criticism to contextual (and especially liberation) theologies. But more than this it points to a central problem facing an increasingly significant and effective theology for local communities around the world. That is, how do contextual theologies draw on traditions that may directly contradict their own experiences, or at best, be unsympathetic to and unsupportive of the struggles and oppressions that they face? This will be one of the main concerns of Chapter 6, which attempts to work through some of the implications of a truly radical reading of Christian theology as contextual.

In conclusion Bergmann's 'survey' of contextual theology, whilst in some aspects is informative and important, in other ways is limited, given the great task that he has set himself. Nevertheless, the existence of such a text signifies the importance of contextual theology as an increasingly important theological approach, and one that is demanding a response from 'traditional' theologians because of the benefits it offers in terms of relevance and practical engagement with immediate social and community issues.

Conclusion

Whilst it cannot be said that studies of contextual theology and studies of the contextual nature of theology are extensive and well established within the field, clearly, however, there are a number of important texts that either directly address the relationship between context and theology or share the same concerns as those of contextual theology. The texts that have been identified and examined here all contribute to the developing understanding of contextual theology in some way. Schreiter's study of local theologies proposes a number of challenges to the perception of Christian theology and to the methods and functioning of Christian theology. He binds local theology very firmly to local culture and moves it away from a magisterial theology. Bevans' reading of Christian theology into six models of contextual theology makes an enormous contribution to the development of an understanding of contextual theology. Whilst the models he proposes may well be open to some criticism his achievement is to have formulated a strong and detailed argument about the inherently contextual nature of Christian theology. The three papers from *The Blackwell Reader in Pastoral and Practical Theology* whilst not directly or explicitly concerned with contextual theology demonstrate that in theology the concerns of contextual theology are shared and are being addressed elsewhere, in this case, under the umbrella of practical theology. Finally, Bergmann's study of the contextual nature of theology places the incarnation and the revelation of God firmly with contextual theology, as it is in different contexts that God's ongoing revelation takes place.

2 Starting from base

The roots of contemporary liberation theology in Latin America

Searching for the roots of explicitly contextual Christian theology is the search for the roots of liberation theology in the first instance. This is because liberation theologies, unlike many other types of Christian theologies, are open and explicit about their agendas and influences. The journey here begins in Latin America in the 1950s and specifically among the disillusioned Roman Catholics in Latin America living in poverty and often under oppressive rule. These were Roman Catholics disillusioned with a Church and theology which at best did not seem to reflect their own experiences and which at worst simply ignored their circumstances. The Roman Catholic Church was seen by many involved in the theological movements for liberation in Latin America as imposing an authority that did not recognize or seem to value contextual struggles. More than this it was a Church which through its actions had come to be identified with oppressive and often brutal political regimes and was seen to be both powerful and wealthy whilst many members of the Church suffered great poverty and injustice.

Pedagogy of the oppressed

In the late 1960s and 1970s Paulo Freire, a Brazilian-born educator, had an enormous impact on the development of thinking about injustice, oppression and the role of the poor in challenging these. So it is with the work of Freire that the search for the roots of contemporary liberation theology in Latin America really begins. Freire was a Christian from a middle-class family who studied law and philosophy at the University of Recife in Brazil. He then went on to work in the educational field where he remained in effect for the rest of his working life. He worked as an educator among the poor of Brazil and through this became aware of the kind of injustices and oppositions such people faced. His approach to education was pragmatic and he began to teach the poor, who were largely illiterate, to read and write. Reading and writing were important assets, not least because literacy was essential for voting rights in Brazil at the time. In 1946 Freire was appointed to the role of the Director of Education and Culture in Pernambuco and it was here that he began to bring together his educational and theological ideas into a framework encompassing both theory and practice. Freire's ideas and work did not go without notice from those that he criticized. In 1960 he was imprisoned following a military coup and classed as a traitor. After spending seventy days in prison Freire left Brazil for exile in Bolivia and then holding a variety of posts lived in many countries developing his theories and practice informed by both local and global knowledge of injustice and oppression. Freire died in 1997 but his legacy is strong and multidisciplinary and was effective in reaching and influencing many different areas of life and many academic subject areas.

His legacy is bound up closely with the publication in 1968 in Portuguese, and in 1970 in Spanish and English, of what is now to be considered to be a classic text in the development of understanding and challenging oppressive structures and hierarchies, *Pedagogy of the Oppressed*. For this study of contextual theology, the significance of the book lies with both its theological component and also with its influence over the liberation theologies which were to emerge in the 1970s in Latin America. It is a book that was very much written in context, as Freire himself describes:

> Thought and study alone did not produce *Pedagogy of the Oppressed*; it is rooted in concrete situations and describes the reactions of laborers (peasant or urban) and of middle-class persons whom I have observed directly or indirectly during the course of my educative work.
>
> (Freire, 1996:19)

For many, the core contribution of *Pedagogy of the Oppressed* lies with its emphasis on empowerment. Freire argued that the oppressed should challenge their oppression through literacy and awareness before moving on to engage in the actual transformation of the very situation and structures by which they were oppressed. Although Freire was clearly writing for Latin Americans in the first instance his words and ideas for many were also relevant in other contexts. Central to Freire's teachings was the concept of 'conscientização' which means to become aware of, to see political, social and economic situations and contradictions and in the light of this to engage in transformative action (Freire, 1996:17). According to Freire, by doing this the oppressed in effect become subjects as they begin to participate in and shape the historical process. He argued that the oppressed were in some senses afraid of freedom but that radicalism enables a person to enter into reality and genuinely know and see the world and so be in a position to transform it.

Freire argued that dehumanization needs to be recognized not simply as 'an ontological possibility but as an historical reality' (Freire, 1996:25). Within Freire's theorizing dehumanization is the distortion of the possibility to be human in the fullest sense. The task facing the radical or the revolutionary is to challenge unjust orders and to liberate themselves as well as those who oppress them. He claimed that such are the nature and processes of oppression that the oppressed may at first become oppressors themselves in the early stages of liberation as this is the dominant and perhaps only model of humanity that they know. He argues that there is a conflict between social forces that needs to be overcome for genuine liberation (Freire, 1996:28). His writing is wrought with contradictions about the nature of humanity and oppression, for example, arguing that although freedom is a central desire of the oppressed at the same time they fear it and may even resist it. What is clear, though, is that Freire presents a pedagogy in *Pedagogy of the Oppressed* that uncovers oppression and which he believes will genuinely enable the oppressed to see their situation as it is. From this he argues will come the realization of the necessity to challenge this oppression and to participate actively in opposing oppressive social and political structures. This can only be achieved, however, according to Freire, when the oppressed 'discover themselves to be "hosts" of the oppressor' (Freire, 1996:30). Once they have discovered this they will then strive for liberation as their pedagogy of the oppressed is owned and used by themselves, and not by those outside of the situation. In essence what Freire was arguing here is that there are two key stages in the process of liberation. First comes awareness and understanding and then from these comes action to begin transformation. In the second stage of the process of liberation the pedagogy of the oppressed becomes the pedagogy of all people as the way in which the world and humanity is perceived and ordered changes. It is for the oppressed, ultimately, to free the oppressors. He challenges a fatalistic view of oppressive hierarchies as the will of God with his claim that such a perspective incorporates 'a distorted view of God' (Freire, 1996:43). Rather, Freire argues that 'At all stages of their liberation, the oppressed must see themselves as women and men engaged in the ontological and historical vocation of becoming more fully human' (Freire, 1996:47–48). In recognizing their oppression, the oppressed, in Freire's thinking, then become responsible for overcoming this oppression through praxis and direct action in order to become more fully human. Freire also argues that it is crucial that as the oppressed participate in the processes of liberation and revolution that they do so with 'an increasingly critical awareness of their role as Subjects of the transformation' (Freire, 1996:108). Otherwise more oppression within a different order may be the result of the revolutionary action. Critical, reflective awareness, then, is very important within the process of liberation and transformation. Solidarity among all of those involved with liberating praxis is also essential according to Freire. Dialogue stands at the centre of the whole process and also at the centre of his pedagogy of the oppressed because 'once a situation of oppression has been initiated, antidialogue becomes indispensable to its preservation' (Freire, 1996:119). Freire talks about revolution as 'dialogical cultural action' (Freire, 1996:141), so it is through genuine dialogue, direct action and the reclamation and transformation of their disinherited culture (the result of cultural invasion) that people enable themselves to become 'historical *subjects*' rather than objects (Freire, 1996:141).

Freire's thinking and work as evident in *Pedagogy of the Oppressed* and in other publications started with the grounded experiences of oppressed people. He offered a framework through which such oppressed people might themselves challenge these circumstances and those who oppress them. This framework was concerned to enable and empower oppressed people to become subjects of transformation so that they might themselves recognize the reality of their own situation and then participate in the transformation of both their situation and of humanity as a whole.

Latin American liberation theologies

Did theology concerned with liberation begin in the Latin American countries in the 1960s? The answer to this question must surely be no. Did the theological approach and group of Christian theologies that we today term loosely as 'liberation theologies' have their roots in Latin America? The answer is a resounding 'yes'. As such, understanding the history, socioeconomic, political, cultural and religious contexts that nurtured and gave rise to the grass roots movement that in many ways has transformed Christianity since the 1960s is an important task in establishing how a specific, radical theology emerged from a particular context. Here a socioeconomic and political context provided the basis for a whole new Christian theology. A theology which is significant in so many ways and not least as marking the beginning of the emergence of explicitly contextual theologies.

The emergence of Latin American liberation theology in the 1960s marks the beginnings of the distinctive, but increasingly diverse, group of theologies that we today refer to as 'liberation theologies'. A number of texts, individuals, certain historical Church gatherings and conferences can all be identified as key indicators or formative events in the emergence of liberation theology in Latin America. Key texts here include Gustavo Gutiérrez's *A Theology of Liberation* (1971), Leonardo Boff's *Liberating Grace* (1979), José Miguez Bonino's *Doing Theology in a Revolutionary Situation* (1975) and Jon Sobrino's, *Christology at the Crossroads* (1978). Key figures in the development of liberation theology include as well as Gustavo Gutiérrez, Juan Luis Segundo, Leonardo Boff, José Miguez Bonino, Hélder Câmara, Oscar Romero and Camilo Torres. Finally, influential theological events include The Medellín Conference of 1968 and the Second Vatican Council. Some of these texts, the contribution of some of these people and certain theological events will be examined in greater depth later in this chapter.

Historical overview – setting the context for theological revolution

The history of Latin American liberation theology is a history of people who have been oppressed by religion but who have also come to use religion as a tool by which to challenge their oppression. The 'poor' is a term which will be used throughout this chapter to refer to the indigenous people of Latin America who suffered great economic, political, ethical and social exploitation at the hands of a much more powerful and prosperous elite. The history of Latin America is a history of colonization, oppression and violence which was supported by the Catholic Church with its missionary links to the colonial movement. Christianity in a sense rode on the back of the ruthless war of the colonizers and so became indelibly linked to it. Politics, state and religion (mainly Roman Catholicism) became inextricably tied together in a way that history has demonstrated has been difficult to resist. Ironically the Church came to Latin America with colonialism and was associated with the ensuing colonial oppression but religion became one of the key tools for challenging the oppressive colonial situation. The distinction between Church and religion or Church and Christianity is important. A brief history of the processes by which Latin America came to be colonized by foreign powers needs to be outlined, so that an understanding of the actual situation out of which liberation theology eventually arose can be reached, to understand how, from the oppression of Latin American people, we have the birth of liberation theologies. The term 'liberation theology' was a term that emerged in relation to Latin America in the late 1960s. Gustavo Gutiérrez in his introduction to the revised edition of *Teología de la Liberación* (*A Theology of Liberation*) 'Expanding the View' writes in relation to the term 'liberation theology':

> My lecture entitled 'A Theology of Liberation,' which had been delivered to a national meeting of lay persons, religious, and priests, was published first in Lima and then, a few months later, in Montevideo (MIEC, Pax Romana, 1969). It was expanded and delivered again at a meeting of Sodepax (Cartigny, Switzerland, 1969).
>
> (Gutiérrez, 1988:175)

Why did Christians turn to theology to challenge their situation, especially given its apparent role in being complicit in if not directly contributing to the wide-scale oppression being wrought by the state on the people? Why did Christians not simply turn to socio-political explanation and tools to firstly understand and then oppose their situation? What is evident from historical analysis is that from the ground upwards there arose a reaction to political and religious power in Latin America in the 1960s which subverted the religious basis upon which the colonial system was dependent. Religion challenged religion. Religion returns to its 'base' in liberation theology, to the basis of the Christian gospel, to challenge oppression and build a theology directly opposed to political and theological dominance and to the abuse of power.

In reviewing the history of Latin America to find the roots of liberation theology the period of Latin American history that is of specific interest begins in 1492 with the arrival in the Americas of Christopher Columbus and the many colonizers who came after him. The attraction of colonizing the Americas for Columbus was the lucrative silk trade, gold and many other wealths of materials that the lands he set out to conquer were thought to hold, along with the desire to challenge the Ottomans' claim over this following the fall in 1453 of Constantinople. After the fall of Constantinople the silk and spice trade became very costly and challenges were sought to depose the Ottomans' hold over this key economic asset and claim to power. Columbus' expeditions opened the flood gates to other European invaders seeking new lands and wealth. The Americas were besieged by foreign, usually European, attempts at rule and colonization. The arrival of Columbus and the ensuing actions of the Spanish and Portuguese conquerors changed the political and cultural landscape of Latin America. Indigenous civilizations were either destroyed or decimated. The Incas, the Aztecs and the Mayas were too often stripped of the identity, beliefs and practices that had defined them distinctively for so many years.

The conquistadors or conquerors who came to Latin America imposed their rules, beliefs and customs on the people of Latin America through subjugation and fear. These colonizers brought with them not only economic rule and systems but also religious ones. Roman Catholicism was the religion imposed on the people of Latin America. So that even to this day Roman Catholicism is the religion followed by most people in Latin America, with some adherence to Voodoo and indigenous religions. From Barbados to San Salvador to Haiti Columbus rampaged with the official backing of the Roman Catholic Church as his highest point of authority and legitimization. Pope Alexander VI in 1493 issued a papal bull in which, as Tombs argues, he gave his support for, 'further exploration to extend the Catholic faith to new people' (2002:6). Without doubt, Christianity came to Latin America as an integral part of colonization. As Smith puts it, 'Along with the musket and cannon came the Roman Catholic faith; behind the marching soldier walked the zealous missionary' (Smith, 1991:11). The two, in many respects, are bound together, the conquest of land with its associated acquisition of wealth along with the spiritual conquest of the 'heathens' and conversion to Christianity. Columbus himself was a Roman Catholic who frequently spoke of his conquests in terms of bringing Christianity to new lands, as well as speaking of the acquisition of these lands. As such, Church and state, from the earliest times of the Spanish and Portuguese conquest of Latin America, were tied closely together and interdependent in terms of power and authority. The colonial process was seen and interpreted within a Christian framework, and as Tombs and others point out, when Columbus 'started to claim the inhabitants of the Indies for the Spanish throne and the Christian faith, the Jews were expelled from Spain' (Tombs, 2002:15). Smith argues that not all Roman Catholics took such an aggressive approach to the conquests and subjugation of the Latin American people. He argues that some priests and bishops spoke out against the treatment of indigenous people (Smith, 1991:12–13). So that even in these early and dangerous times, some Christians can be seen to have challenged colonization and the Church's association with it.

History paints at times a romantic picture of the European colonizers and this is especially true in relation to the figure of the conquistador. This is a picture which will not go unchallenged in this account of Latin American history and in the account of the emergence of liberation theology in Latin America. Although the whole of the Americas were subject in some way or another to the invasion of the Europeans, from the Bahamas to Central and North

America, the American revolution in the eighteenth century leading to the United States Declaration of Independence in 1776 changed the political and social landscape in the North in a way that simply did not happen in Latin America. The very term 'Latin America' needs some explanation as it is often used interchangeably with 'South America'. 'Latin America' refers to those areas in the Americas in which the languages of Spanish, Portuguese or French are the dominant or significant languages. Understandings of what actually constitutes 'Latin America' are, however, disputed; this can only really be noted here, not debated.

Following the Spanish invasion and conquest, it was the Spanish conquistador who was so very influential in controlling and maintaining control of power in Latin America. The conquistadors were the soldiers, the conquerors who 'tamed' the lands of the Americas. Slavery was rife with the conquistadors holding great power and control over the indigenous peoples of Latin America. From the C16th to the early C19th the conquistadors continued their reign of exploitation and terror over the indigenous people of Latin America. Both Church and state reinforced the power of the other by political, social, spiritual and sometimes simply barbaric means and relied on the conquistadors to control and maintain control over the conquered lands. The Church remained tied to the state and depended on it for its dominance and control in Latin America. Tombs sums up well the complex and disturbing situation that the Church in the years spanning the C16th to C19th not only allowed it to exist but also proactively defended:

> Cross and sword arrived together, and the church offered divine sanction for colonial society. The colonial church was a highly conservative force, which stood firmly on the side of the powerful. Despite the celebrated prophetic exceptions, such as Montesinos and Las Casas, the church usually served as an uncritical chaplain to colonial power and encouraged its exploitative practices. It preached that life was a vale of tears, that God ordained social positions, and that obedience to God, to the church, and to the colonial order were inseparable. The ordinary people were left to find solace in their prayers for charity and their hopes for a better life in another world.
>
> (Tombs, 2002:25)

This collusion between the Roman Catholic Church and the colonial state powers left the Church firmly politically aligned to an oppressive regime that no amount of historical justification and explanation can undo. The Christian missionaries stood side by side with the conquistadors and the Church's power and authority were reinforced by the colonizers, a favour which was returned in kind. The two were interdependent; political and religious power lent enormous power to the regime that took many years to begin to unravel. To challenge one was to challenge the other. The inextricable marriage of Church and state ensured that the people of Latin America remained bound by oppressive rules which were backed by political and military power and sanctioned by theological authority. Some individual church members protested, even challenged the situation, but these were not surprisingly few and far between given the conditions faced.

The infrastructure set up by the colonizers enabled both Church and state to work hand in hand in an almost indomitable power alliance that enabled both to flourish in the ways that they desired. In 1508 the formal sanctioning of the Church and its ensuing structures came with Pope Julius II's *Patronato Real*, which was an agreement between the Roman Catholic Church and Spainish civil rule. This set out the guidelines and gave authority to the establishment of a Church structure in Latin America which would involve the appointment of bishops and other church workers.

There were of course exceptions to the barbaric and devastating collusion of the Church with the colonial powers with individuals and sometime small groups seeking to oppose the seemingly impenetrable might of Church and state. However, these were often short lived and ominous for those involved. Colonialism continued in Latin America under different guises and also under different foreign powers. Various moves towards independence in different countries and areas of Latin America in many cases brought no real substantive change in terms of the conditions and inequities facing the people of the region. The Church resisted the moves towards independence, perhaps fearing that its own powers and status would be substantially diminished if not eroded. However, by the C19th many Latin American countries were well on their way to establishing independence of a sort. The prosperity of some areas of Latin America increased, encouraged (perhaps inevitably) by foreign powers. What became known as 'the independence movements' were officially opposed by the Roman authorities but gained some support at a local level from priests. As a result, as various countries gained, and sometimes lost, newly found independence so the Church stood at odds with the newly established regimes. The Church continued to advocate a largely conservative approach to rule in Latin America and was in turn defended by conservative forces and criticized and even attacked by more progressive political forces. The Church had made and stood by its decision to align itself with the colonial powers and so with all of the suffering and exploitation that brought. It was during the reign of Pope Gregory XVI in the mid C19th that the Church at last conceded and recognized independent Latin America.

The fight against the European powers and against the rule established by the systems of power imposed marked the early nineteenth century in Latin America. Independence from European colonizers was achieved in most Latin American countries by the mid to late nineteenth century. One of the consequences of this was that the traditional ties between Church and state were no longer stable or sometimes even in place. The Roman Catholic Church could no longer rely on the interdependent relationship which was responsible, in part at least, for securing and maintaining its power base in Latin America.

In this context, however, democracy did not automatically claim a place in the newly 'liberated' countries and regions of Latin America such as Costa Rica, El Salvador, Nicaragua and Brazil (Gilbert, 1990:8). In some senses, only the names of the rulers changed. The exportation enterprise that stood at the heart of the Latin American economy drove on furiously and branched out into new areas. Some countries benefited more than others in this economic climate. However, poverty among so many of the people of Latin America remained unchanged. The role of the Catholic Church in all of this demands comment if not criticism and condemnation. The Church singularly failed to offer any kind of resistance to the stringent and inhumane practices of the colonizers to the extent that Tombs argues that 'Most of the church authorities colluded with the genocide of the native people' (2002:8). The Church was so closely aligned, materially, politically and indeed spiritually with the aims and vision of the colonizers, and then with the regimes that replaced the earlier colonizers, that it could not in any meaningful sense be seen as distinct from the regimes. In some areas the relationship between Church and state remained in place along traditional lines despite the changes to political governance, in Colombia, for example (Smith, 1991:13). Others saw independence as an opportunity for challenging traditional ties to the Church, especially as the Church openly opposed the apparently more liberal regimes that were coming into power. Either way, for many Latin America people, not all that much changed in terms of freedom, justice and basic human dignity. The Roman Catholic Church continued to have a significant role in the lives and contexts of the people of Latin America until early in the twentieth century when certain factors led to challenges to the Church's often oppressive, or at least controlling, influence over the lives of poor Latin American people. With the rise of challenges from often liberal or left-wing political groups, nationalistic groups and Protestantism the Roman Catholic Church was being increasingly pushed towards reassessing its role in Latin America.

By the 1930s the Church in Latin America can be seen to have attempted to in some ways reinvent or reconstitute itself in the light of the many changes that were taking place, recognizing that it was simply unable to halt or even effect these. However, to what extent one can really talk of this as a discernible and coherent movement that pre-empts the liberation theology movement of the 1960s onwards is open to question. Clearly, some pockets of the Roman Catholic Church were attempting to respond to the desperate context of Latin America but prior to the 1960s this was sporadic and disjointed.

What we can say is that by the twentieth century the economic situation of Latin America was varied but almost universally dire. Debt, population growth and urbanization marked one point of Latin American life whilst the exportation industry in some areas of Latin America flourished (Gilbert, 1990:19–20). Hierarchical discrimination between and among blacks, Indians, mestizos (people of mixed indigenous and white European roots) and whites dominated the cultural scene. From this situation revolutionary stirrings were inevitable. The Cuban revolution in 1959 left Fidel Castro at the head of a newly socialist state and in Brazil a military coup in 1964 swept democracy away. As all of these things were happening voices of dissent, protest, but also of hope, began to emerge with consistency and increasing strength within the Roman Catholic Church on a number of levels.

Latin America in the 1950s and 1960s

To remain with the time period so crucial to us we need to focus on the 1950s and 1960s. It is difficult to sum up into one overall picture the economic, social, political and religious climate in Latin America in the late 1950s due in part to the different geographical contexts and experiences. There are, however, some things that can be identified as general factors that influenced or gave rise to liberation theologies in Latin America:

(1) Increasing disillusionment with the socioeconomic and political situations.
(2) Related discontent with the Catholic Church's role in these situations.

(1) Increasing disillusionment with the socioeconomic and political situations of Latin America

The first factor influencing the rise of liberation theology in Latin America to be examined here is the increasing and widespread disillusionment with the largely capitalist socioeconomic and political situations in many Latin American countries in the late 1950s and 1960s. In some cases capitalism gave rise to dictatorships as the countries of Latin America tried to compete with more developed economies, whilst at the same time trying to quell the initial stirrings of discontent from the poor and oppressed whose labour, and the exploitation of this labour, was so essential to the industrial development of the Latin American countries. Latin America, like so many regions, had been affected by the two world wars and the Wall Street stock market crash which led to the Great Depression. At this point different countries in Latin America responded differently to the situations that they faced. The different responses were often determined by each country's own natural resources and their response to sweeping modernization. Relations with the United States were increasingly difficult and often hostile and the United States increasingly imposed its control over the economies and exports of the countries of Latin America.

In the midst of all the changes in Latin America in the 1950s and 1960s the revolution in Cuba stands as a landmark on the political and social landscape of the region. Fidel Castro in 1956 had begun to express a deep-rooted Cuban nationalism (Bakewell, 2004:533) through which resentment of United States influence as the target market of Cuban goods and exports was expressed. The country was rife with corruption and military rule and instability resulted in civil unrest and even more poverty. Castro in this setting took hold of political and economic power in Cuba. The perceived Marxist threat of a revolutionized Cuba alarmed the United States. However, interestingly, this pattern of civil unrest and revolution was not played out right across Latin America. Rather, military-style dictator governments were established in many countries often accompanied by conservatism, poverty and oppression.

Countries like Argentina, Bolivia, Brazil, Chile and Uruguay (Bakewell, 2004:534–535) were controlled by conservative regimes which were supported by the Roman Catholic Church. Violence, poverty, death and the missing were problems that were rife in Latin American countries. Often change did not really begin to happen until the 1980s when many of the military dictatorships fell and other forms of government were established in their place.

(2) *Related discontent with the Catholic Church*

The Church in the 1950s and 1960s in Latin America was in turmoil. The previously impenetrable relationship between colonizers and Church began to show cracks, if not to actually crumble. Ironically, given Rome's previous support of the alliance between colonialism and Christianity, seeds of hope had already emerged from Rome itself with a series of papal documents which seemed to give permission, if not to actually sanction, some sort of change towards a more progressive society in which the Church was to have a formative role. Pius XI's *Quadragesimo*, which addressed conditions and rights for workers, was published earlier in 1931 and offered hope to Catholics for a more socially concerned Church. The encyclical seemed to advocate social justice through fair wages and property rights and called for cooperation between people. From this encyclical, coupled with other documents and events, a new kind of Roman Catholic response to social injustice and inequality began to develop. Groups under the umbrella name of Catholic Action were the leading force in this move for change and were effective and active in many different countries and areas by the 1930s.

Movements and organizations like Catholic Action made an important contribution to the shift in ecclesial and political power in Latin America beginning in the 1950s. The laity became more important and whilst the clergy still undoubtedly retained the clear balance of power a shift had begun and this in itself was very significant, especially with the power of hindsight. In different countries and regions of Latin America progress and the relationship between clergy, laity and state varied. There is no one uniform picture to describe the situation in Latin America in the 1950s but universally the situation for the ordinary person was neither prosperous nor promising.

In Cuba the Church responded to the revolution and spoke out and criticized the revolutionary regime. In response to this criticism the Church became the target of victimization. With revolution a reality in Cuba, and also potentially on the horizon in other places, the Roman Catholic Latin American Church strengthened itself with the arrival of European priests to replace those who fled the revolutionaries. At the hierarchical centre of the Roman Catholic Church the Vatican responded with key documents which attempted to address and offer theological justification for the actions it instructed the Church on a local level to take.

Communism, socialism, liberalism, revolutions in Brazil, Cuba and the threat from the Soviet Union were all party to shaping the landscape of Latin American politics and the United States response in the 1950s and 1960s. Christian Smith goes as far as to argue that it was the Cuban revolution, and the fears that this would have a knock-on effect in other countries, that was in effect a wake-up call for the Roman Catholic Church in terms of the situation in Latin America and the very real threat posed to its power base there and hold on the lives of the poor people of Latin America (Smith, 1991:91–91). The response of the Roman Catholic Church to this was to unite in defending itself and oppressing the perceived threat and also to commit itself to 'demonstrating that democratic capitalism was, indeed, workable in Latin America' (Smith, 1991). Pope John XXIII in recognition of the crisis called on the Church in Latin America to respond pastorally and through evangelization, and the priests of the Roman Catholic Church in Latin America were called upon to reach out to and engage with the poor, to go to the heart of the problem. Analysing the reasons for the call on the Church to engage directly with the poor is complex and difficult to justify at this stage as a genuine attempt by the Roman Catholic hierarchy to respond to the needs and recognize the injustices faced by the people. Rather, it seems more a recognition that the alternative philosophies and theories, which challenged the power base of the Church and indeed membership of the Church, were under genuine and direct threat. The Roman Catholic Church responded by drafting in priests and bishops and attempting to engage with some of the issues that were at the heart of the underlying problem.

In August 1955 an inaugural meeting of the Latin American Bishops took place in Rio de Janeiro. This was the Conference of the Latin American Episcopate (Consejo Episcopal Latinoamericano or CELAM 1), and followed a conference in 1952 of the National Conference of Brazilian Bishops. The force behind such gatherings and the subsequent organizations that emerged was the recognition on the part of some Latin American bishops that the situation in Latin America was not only dire, as it had been for so long, but that the Church was failing in its Christian mission in Latin America. Such recognition came from new voices and from those changing in their understanding of the role of the Church in the world.

Whilst in many ways the Conference of the Latin American Episcopate in 1955 was not radically socially visionary or even particularly liberal, it did mark the beginning of the coming together of the bishops of Latin America in recognition of their specific needs to discuss how the Roman Catholic Church might be able to operate within Latin America in such a way as to satisfy papal law and serve the needs of local communities. In particular, it recognized the context of Latin America as needing a specific kind of theological response. So, in this sense it was a historic event for the people of Latin America, the Roman Catholic Church of Latin America and for the emerging seeds of liberation theology.

The Second Vatican Council

In 1958, following the death of Pope Pius XII, Pope John XXIII initiated unexpected waves of revolutionary hope and promise through the liberal and socially conscious ranks of the Roman Catholic Church. John XXIII was expected to be an interim or caretaker pope, to hold the Church firm following the death of Pius XII. As it was, Pope John XXIII is seen by many as having changed the course of Christian, and especially Roman Catholic, history. Perhaps most significantly Pope John XXIII set in motion an ecumenical council which eventually began in 1962. This Second Vatican Council, as it became to be known, was remarkable in many respects. John XXIIII, who was Italian and born Angelo Giuseppe Roncalli, died in 1963 and did not live to see the end of the Second Vatican Council in 1965. If John XXIII had lived to the end of the council the religious and Christian landscape may have been even more radically altered than was eventually the case.

Preparations for the council were complex with advisors from many different areas and documents on many different issues produced. The two years' preparation for this council was a witness to the commitment of John XXIII to fully and adequately address the place of the Church in the world. During the papacy of John XXIII there were four council sessions planned and each produced important theological insights for the Roman Catholic Church and for the people of Latin America. Unfortunately John XXIII died after the first session and was succeeded by Pope Paul VI who declared his intention to carry on with the council. One of the key aspects of the Second Vatican Council that John XXIII is remembered for was his invitation to non-Roman Catholic people to attend and observe the council proceedings. This was seen by many as a huge step in the development of the Roman Catholic Church out of its self-imposed isolation. The first session of the council took place in 1962 and in his address *Gaudet Mater Ecclesia* (Mother Church Rejoices) John XXIII among other things was concerned to stress the mission of the Church to the contemporary world. His emphasis was on the pastoral role and concern of the Church and not its more formal doctrinal role.

The events of Vatican II brought theological sanctioning of a more progressive, liberative theology for Latin America. Vatican II in many ways changed the face of the Roman Catholic Church. Post-Vatican II, it was possible, drawing on council documents and papal encyclicals, to give authentic theological backing to a different vision of both Church and humanity in the world. Towards the end of the Council a statement emerged from a group of fifteen bishops who put their names to the important document 'A Message to the Peoples of the Third World'. These bishops were from Africa, Asia and Latin America and collectively recognized the opportunities gifted by the Council and the need to respond on a theological and organizational level to the realities of social, political and economic injustice as it occurred globally in a very real way. The majority of bishops were from Latin America, indicating how immediate the problem in Latin America was, especially in presenting itself to the Church. An influential figure in organizing both the meeting and the statement that emerged from the meeting was Dom Hélder Câmara. The statement is one of hope and commitment to social and political action (Hennelly, 1997:48). The statement built upon the encyclical *Populorum Progressio* (On the Development of Peoples) issued by Pope Paul VI and spoke of the need for revolution, understood in the widest sense of the term, to include the spiritual and the social. It stressed that the gospel has always been bound up with political and social issues (Hennelly, 1997:50) but it also differentiated between political and economic systems that were just and those that were unjust. It called upon the Church to respond to injustice. Whilst clearly challenging Marxist interpretations of religion at the same time it argued that religion 'is a force that exalts the lowly and casts down the proud, that feeds the hungry and sends the sated away empty' (Hennelly, 1997:55). Its vision is strong:

> The peoples of the Third World are the proletariat of humanity today. They are exploited by the great nations; and the very existence is threatened by those who, because they are more powerful, arrogate to themselves the right to make all the decisions and policies for peoples that are less affluent than they are. But the fact is that our peoples are not less upright and just than the great nations of the world.
>
> (Hennelly, 1997:49)

Medellín

The insights and proposals of the Second Vatican Council that seemed to promise so much for the Roman Catholic Church and people in Latin America were taken forward by the second gathering of CELAM when 600 bishops met in Medellín, Colombia in 1968. By now CELAM had developed into an increasingly strong organization that was led by committed and forward-looking bishops and social activists within the Roman Catholic Church committed to a vision of justice and social action. The direct driving organizational force behind the Medellín conference was Manuel Larraín who drew on the resources available through Vatican II and called upon key influential figures like Hélder Câmara, Gustavo Gutiérrez, Juan Luis Segundo and Eduardo Pironio. In choosing those to be heavily involved with the conference the ethos, goals and underlying theological perspective of the conference was in effect set. Medellín was in many senses the turning point in Latin American theology in terms of the development of liberation theology. There was already an emerging grass roots movement committed to the issues that eventually became firmed up into what we have come to know as liberation theology in Latin America. The documents and initiatives that emerged from Medellín were hugely influential in determining the direction in which the liberation theological movement took. It provided a platform to formally and with authority define a vision and programme of action that committed the Church to the liberation and social justice of the poor with a strong theological vision.

A key figure in the 1950s in Latin American Roman Catholicism was Dom Hélder Câmara who was active in Catholic Action. He helped set up in 1952 the National Conference of Brazilian Bishops (CNBB) and was duly elected as secretary. As he came into increasing contact with other bishops through his work he began to establish networks and see the significance that such contacts could have. He was an outspoken and popular critic of capitalism and its associated power structures.

The liberation theology of Gustavo Gutiérrez

If one text had to be identified as encapsulating the theological ground swelling and theoretical framework upon which the liberation theological movement in Latin America was founded it is Gustavo Gutiérrez's *Teología de la Liberación* (*A Theology of Liberation: History, Politics and Salvation*). This text was originally published in Lima as *Teología de la Liberación* and was translated into English in 1973 by Sister Caridad Inda and John Eaglson and published by Orbis Books. *A Theology of Liberation* was the first time that a Latin American theologian had attempted to offer systematic theological reflections on what was actually happening in Latin America in terms of social injustice, political oppression, the Church's role in these and to offer possible alternative theological visions – alternative visions, that is, from theologies of oppression. As such, Gutiérrez's text stands at the very heart of understanding the nature of Latin American liberation theology as contextual theology. As a contextual theology it is a theology that arises out of specific situations and is constructed out of the realities and needs of these situations. Tombs says of *A Theology of Liberation* that 'Gutiérrez challenged traditional theological approaches that distanced theology from everyday concerns and real life conflicts' (Tombs, 2002:121).

In the original version of *A Theology of Liberation* Gutiérrez introduces the aims of the text as:

> ... an attempt at reflection, based on the gospel and the experiences of men and women committed to the process of liberation in the oppressed and exploited land of Latin America. It is a theological reflection born of the experience of shared efforts to abolish the current unjust situation and to build a different society, freer and more human.
>
> (Gutiérrez, 1988:xiii)

In this way Gutiérrez makes explicit from the beginning of the book the basis of the theology he was developing: experience and the gospel. It is based in the experiences of oppression, it arises in its form and content from this oppression but it is based in the Christian gospel. Gutiérrez and those around him were articulating a theology which not only acknowledged the oppression that was being experienced but rejected and challenged this from a Christian standpoint. It drew on the gospel and on theoretical tools to develop a theology which incorporates an acknowledgement of these experiences of oppression and locates liberation as firmly within the Christian tradition, within the story of Christ. Gutiérrez was concerned with the role of the Church in the historical process of salvation, and as part of this the oppression of people in places such as Latin America had to be explored and addressed theologically for its meaning and for the development of a theological response. 'The Bible presents liberation – salvation – in Christ as the total gift ... Liberation can thus be approached as a single salvific process' (Gutiérrez, 1988: xiv). Justice lies at the heart of the theological vision that Gutiérrez articulates in *A Theology of Liberation*. Of interest to this study is the nature of that justice, given the context from which Gutiérrez wrote, and the ways in which Christian theology becomes the vehicle for and not an obstacle to that justice. Despite Gutiérrez's discontent with the Roman Catholic Church and with the Christian theology that emerged from the Church he still strongly believed that Christianity, theology, and indeed the Church, had a role to play in the kind of justice-seeking movement that he and other Latin American Christian theologians of the day were arguing for. His vision of justice had human dignity as a foundational element (Gutiérrez, 1988: xiv) and had ordinary human beings, not just priests or the ordained, as active agents in their own salvation history. This offered a very different view of salvation history, as one in which human beings took responsibility and acted in the here and now. Gutiérrez talks about human beings being able to 'transform themselves by conquering their liberty throughout their existence and their history' (Gutiérrez, 1988:xiv). Salvation is in process, and is not just of the future. As such it is the concern of all human beings to enact their own salvation, to participate in and shape the here and now. The Church's role in all of this is crucial but its response to oppression, to subjugation, must be of a different kind than had previously been seen in Latin America. The location of Christian witness and liberation, theologians were beginning to argue, was too often proving to be outside of the formal identified structures of the Church in Latin America. This brought questions, then, of the Church, of its role in salvation history and in the liberation that Gutiérrez and others were concerned with.

Gutiérrez includes a lengthy introduction to the revised edition of *A Theology of Liberation* which is very telling in terms of how quickly liberation theology developed to the extent that Gutiérrez needed to qualify, expand and in some cases justify the theological line taken in the original text. From publication of *Teología de la Liberación* in 1971 Lima and its subsequent translation and publication in English in 1973 to the revised edition in English in 1988 'liberation theology' had become a movement of potentially global proportions and implications. It was a term that was known, used and being developed in many different parts of the world.

So, what were the key theological components of Gutiérrez's liberation theology? Gutiérrez stresses the importance and changing nature of theological reflection as core to the Christian faith (Gutiérrez, 1988:3). In locating theological reflection both within the official life and functioning of the Church and also as beyond it, Gutiérrez was in effect repositioning Christian authority or power. Like so many liberation theologians since, Gutiérrez employs an identifiable methodology in arguing that the kind of theology that he was proposing or describing did not constitute a break from traditional or orthodox Christianity, but instead stood within a tradition. This strategy is one employed by many different types of apparently radical theologies which in the face of criticism of discontinuity with tradition make firm and often biblically based claims to continuity. So, Gutiérrez argues, for example, that the critical reflection on praxis which was becoming increasingly important in Latin American Christianity was echoed in St Augustine's *The City of God* and Paul's emphasis on faith in practice:

> According to the Bible, faith is the total human response to God, who saves through love. In this light, the understanding of the faith appears as the understanding not of the simple affirmation – almost memorization – of truths, but of a commitment, an overall attitude, a particular posture toward life.
>
> (Gutiérrez, 1988:6)

Gutiérrez gives authority to his reading of a Christianity of action, a Christianity of commitment with reference to the Second Vatican Council. He argues that the council 'has strongly affirmed the idea of a Church of service and not of power' (Gutiérrez, 1988:7). For Gutiérrez the council gave weight to the authenticity of a theology of the people and to a theology that was not overly focused on either the past or the future, but on the present. He points to *Gaudium et Spes* (the Pastoral Constitution on the Church in the Modern World) as stressing service and action and not just reflection and analysis. What is interesting about Gutiérrez's approach is that he is not arguing that commitment to action is an appropriate and acceptable Christian response in the contemporary world of the 1970s but that it is actually a necessary response. For him, each priest and each theologian has the responsibility of hearing and interpreting the signs of the times. The 'signs of the times' was a phrase that had become associated with the Second Vatican Council and with the theology and papal teachings of Pope John XXIII.

Gutiérrez acknowledges, in *A Theology of Liberation*, one of the issues that has remained a criticism and possible point of weakness for the kind of liberation theology that was emerging in Latin America in the 1970s. This criticism was that it was a theology that was drawing on Marxist ideology as the driving and shaping force behind this theology. That it was essentially political and not religious, and that its political affiliation was Marxism. Gutiérrez acknowledges the significance of Marxism for the era and context from which he was writing. Here he makes use of the emphasis on transformation through human action. Orthodoxy is not confined to credal statements or reflection. Orthopraxis is stressed and is used not in a rejection of traditional understandings of what constitutes orthodoxy but to complement and so complete faithfulness to the gospel (Gutiérrez, 1988:8). Orthopraxy was in effect, in this context, a new way of doing theology, one which involved the relocation of theological and ecclesial commitment and concern. Gutiérrez draws on the theology of Schillebeeckx, which emphasized the interdependent and crucial relationship between thought and action. Gutiérrez's aim is clear here: to move away from a sense of orthodoxy which, in his own words, amounts essentially to nothing more than 'fidelity to an obsolete tradition or a debatable interpretation' (Gutiérrez, 1988:8). Theological reflection relies not only on tradition and revelation but also on experience, on the experiences of people today and in history. Gutiérrez has a very fluid understanding here of experience and history, arguing that it is important that the Church does not attempt to close down its critical reflection on the meaning of the gospel by seeing history as complete. He makes the remarkable statement that 'theology helps safeguard society and the Church from regarding as permanent what is only temporary' (Gutiérrez, 1988:10). Such a statement stresses the contextual nature of human experience and human interpretation of the gospel. It also places great responsibility with theology for the development of liberative practices; theology must be transformative if it is to be true to the Christian gospel. Liberation theology is seen by Gutiérrez as a '*new way* to do theology' (Gutiérrez, 1988:12), and its newness is in part, in Gutiérrez's words, its openness. As a landmark theology its crucial significance for any study such as this about the contextual nature of Christian theology is its openness about its specific theological commitments and social aims. It is a theology that formally and clearly advocates a particular standpoint, but at the same time recognizes the limitations of the theology that might emerge from this reflective praxis. It is for these reasons that the liberation theology that emerged in Latin America in the late 1960s and early 1970s, and which is accessed here through Gutiérrez's text, is taken as the beginnings of contextual theology, as theology which explicitly understands and represents itself as contextual, grounded and partial. The significance given here to *A Theology of Liberation* is explained by the fact that it not only became a key theological resource for the liberation theology movement but also as symbolic of, in Gutiérrez's words, a new way of doing theology.

For Gutiérrez, at the time of writing *A Theology of Liberation*, the change evident in the world and the possibilities for change offered by theories of social change were more apparent than they might otherwise have been, because of developments in global means of communicating. In 1971 Gutiérrez argued that the patterns of relationship which lay behind the social oppression of poor people globally were due to the imposition of rule by one people on another (1988:13). The power differential between the poor and the rich meant that the imposition of such control and the constraints and oppressions which accompanied such control was hard to resist. He claimed that the response of merely imitating oppressors, of striving towards the ways of the rich, was no longer how the oppressed were responding in poor countries. He argued that a different response to an awareness of and to challenging socioeconomic inequities was increasingly being envisaged by those still trapped under the rule and control of the economically and politically powerful (1988:14). For Gutiérrez development is a crucial factor in the process of 'conscientization', and the notion of 'total social process' (1988:15) stresses the necessarily interdependent nature of development incorporating economic, political, social and cultural factors. Such development, then, has many layers and works on different levels of human experience and existence, or rather, will if it is to be genuinely total. Development cannot be on a purely economic level if it is to be total and if it is to be effective in the way Gutiérrez and others are envisaging. Gutiérrez characterizes his age using a liberative language of yearning and hope but also one of pragmatics. He argues that a 'broad and deep aspiration for liberation inflames the history of humankind in our day, liberation from all that limits or keeps human beings from self-fulfillment, liberation from all impediments to the exercise of freedom' (Gutiérrez, 1988:17–18).

In the context of being poised on the brink of radical social change Gutiérrez argues that the means by which change is sought must be carefully scrutinized to avoid simply replacing old imperialisms with new forms of imperialisms. However, Gutiérrez acknowledges that the change that is happening around the world and the change that has already happened around the world cannot be ignored. Revolution needs to be scrutinized and the means by which social change is approached must be very carefully thought through because of the depth of what is at stake, 'the possibility of enjoying a truly human existence, a free life, a dynamic liberty which is related to history as a conquest' (1988:18).

Gutiérrez clearly makes use of Marxist, and indeed other, analyses of history and of the processes by which humanity comes to find itself divided and oppressed by wealth and controlled by economies of power. He uses aspects of Marx's thought and Marxist thinking without apology or by attempting to clothe it in something more acceptable to traditionalist readers. But at the same time Gutiérrez is clear in what he means by terms such as 'liberation' and 'revolution'. Gutiérrez is also clear to acknowledge that the kind of revolution that he is envisaging does not remain in the realms of thought processes and reflection. The 'permanent cultural revolution' (1988:21) he is talking of involves struggle beyond the abstract. Gutiérrez again looks to papal documents to give authority and validation to his explanation of human history and his explanation of the concept of development. He argues that it was John XXIII in his encyclical *Mater et Magistra* who really brought discussions about human development formally into the theological arena and in particular into the discourse of the Roman Catholic Church of the time. He claims that the concept was dealt with in depth in *Pacem in Terris* and again, although with less detail, in *Gaudium et Spes* (1988:24).

The issue of the place of politics, and in particular left-wing philosophies and schools of thought such as Marxism and socialism, in Christian theology are a constant criticism levelled at the liberation theologies of Latin America, and indeed some other forms of liberation theology. The criticism arises perhaps as much because of the nature of the political leanings involved rather than actual theological and political interaction. As Tombs notes, 'Some argued that liberation theology incarnated the gospel in modern society and revitalized the life of the Church. Others attacked it for confusing faith with politics and reducing Christian theology to determinist Marxism' (Tombs, 2002:xii).

Gutiérrez stresses that recent papal documents and also the Vatican II discussions about development and liberation should be seen as a beginning (1988:23).

So, Gutiérrez is placing himself within a tradition but at the same time stresses that the Second Vatican Council and the associated papal encyclicals cannot provide a full and coherent account of the subject of liberation and human salvation history. This, then, leaves Gutiérrez open to give detailed and sustained attention to the concept of liberation, and in particular, liberation theology. Having acknowledged the recent sociopolitical theorizing and realities of revolution he then grounds the significance of this theory by appealing to the authoritative traditions of the Roman Catholic Church. He makes reference here not only to Roman Catholic theologians but to the Second Vatican Council and to papal encyclicals. As noted earlier, this location within a tradition or identifying a tradition within Christianity or within which the liberation theologian can place herself or himself becomes a characterizing feature of many different types of liberation theology. In this way the radically new and sometimes controversial nature of such theologies are often countered by the attempt to frame theology within a mainline or orthodox tradition. Gutiérrez here outlines the challenging nature of realizing human liberation through revolution. Citing Descartes, Hegel, Marx and Marcuse, Gutiérrez draws attention to the contribution of Teilhard de Chardin in envisaging human history as dynamic and changing and then moves to the core of the Roman Catholic tradition, the Second Vatican Council and papal encyclicals, to justify and support his concern for human social development. He points back to Medellín in 1968 and then presents a view of human history embedded within the traditions and teaching of the Church and recent theological developments. He does not leave this process of mapping with papal encyclicals, philosophers and theorists, but goes to the heart of the Christian tradition with the firm grounding of his own theology of liberation in the Christian Bible.

For Gutiérrez the biblical message is one of liberation. He sees its work as liberation and so sees it as effectively providing the framework for human salvation history (1988:23). Human history is about conquest, conquest in order to develop and change and liberate. The sign of the times as Gutiérrez saw it in 1971 was 'a call to commitment and interpretation' (1988:23). He argues that Christian theology has not traditionally been concerned with the collective, social aspect of development and liberation. Gutiérrez challenges this with a call to Galatians 5:1:

> 'For freedom Christ has set us free' (Gal. 5:1), St Paul tells us. He refers here to liberation from sin insofar as it represents a selfish turn in upon oneself. To sin is to refuse to love one's neighbors and, therefore, the Lord himself. Sin – a breach of friendship with God and others – is according to the Bible the ultimate cause of poverty, injustice, and the oppression in which persons live.
>
> (1988:23–24)

Gutiérrez argues that Pauline theology presents a picture of a liberating Christ, a Christ who liberates humanity to freedom. This is Christ's gift and within this freedom is the possibility of being in communion with God (1988:24). He stresses the different levels at which liberation works and so the different meanings that the word 'liberation' can be given. The term 'liberation' encapsulates the yearnings of the oppressed people (1988:24) and so for Gutiérrez this is the first level at which the term works. Second, it can be used to understand human history, to see humanity taking a degree of responsibility and determining its own path. In this sense, then, to talk of liberation, to work for liberation and to be involved with liberation amounts to participation in determining and moving the unfolding of salvation history. This is a dynamic and direct participation in human history. Humanity, argues Gutiérrez, can help determine the future. This third level at which liberation works for Gutiérrez is in terms of the role of Christ. The Bible depicts a saviour, a saviour and a liberator from sin, a sin that obscures relationships and communion with God and other humans (1988:25). Gutiérrez argues that these three levels are all expressed and can be tied to Jesus. By arguing for the interdependent nature of liberation in its different meanings and with Christ at the centre Gutiérrez secures for Christianity a clear place within both the vision and process of liberation.

Anticipating and addressing the issue of the relationship between faith and politics, Gutiérrez focuses on the demanding question of the Kingdom of God of earth and socioeconomic, political liberation. Gutiérrez stresses the earthly, temporal dimension to liberation within liberation theology (1988:29). He consistently stresses human participation in social transformation and its associated political implications. Gutiérrez argues that the radicalism evident in developing countries at the time of writing, and in Latin America in particular, involves conflict. He challenges traditional Christian understandings or theologies which stress the inner development and liberation to the exclusion or expense of any external, social factor. He is in effect arguing for a politicization of Christianity, of the aims, ethics and aspirations of Christianity. Within this there is a need to return to Christ and the Church then needs to be reconceived in the light of this. What is interesting is that Gutiérrez is not just arguing for the possibility of Christian participation in social praxis but rather:

> Participation in the process of liberation is an obligatory and privileged *locus* for Christian life and reflection. In this participation will be heard nuances of the Word of God which are imperceptible in other existential situations and without which there can be no authentic and fruitful faithfulness to the Lord.
>
> (1988:32)

Liberating praxis lies at the heart of Christianity for Gutiérrez, the Church, and all Christians are faced with the task of revisiting the Gospel and reinterpreting in the light of this. Christianity exists not as an abstract, according to Gutiérrez, but as part of the social reality of human existence. The separation of religion and the social is not possible. This reading of Christianity has consequences also for the role and significance of the Church. Its traditional exclusive hold on the sacred in terms of the location and the means for accessing salvation becomes reconsidered. If participation in social acts has theological con- sequences and consequences, in particular, for human salvation, then the tradi- tional exclusivity of the Church as the locus for salvation is challenged. Political activity can become Christian activity and so participation in salvation history. The political activity is not just any kind of political activity but political activity which is based in and works towards a vision of social justice, of equity and human rights.

Gutiérrez calls upon lay Christians to take responsibility to participate in, and in effect, create the 'New Christendom' (1988:36) that liberation theology is calling for. In this he frees the locus of power and responsibility from within the confines of the Church as it has traditionally been defined to the lay Christian. He envisages that this will be actually achieved through organization into socially active groups. The role of the ordained priest has to be reconsidered in Gutiérrez's theology. The exclusive and privileged position traditionally reserved for the priest is reassessed. The catalyst for all of this is the increasing awareness and realization of the nature of the deep and pervasive oppression that so many poor people face in the world. Lack of action, non-intervention and passivity are not options within Gutiérrez's theology of liberation. The Church (which in many ways itself becomes radically redefined) must take responsibility to address, challenge and transform injustice wherever it is found. The Church, according to Gutiérrez, cannot claim non-involvement in politics. Its involvement is there but traditionally this has been defined and justified theologically in such a way that the Church is presented as non-political. Theology, it is argued, should accordingly not concern itself with politics:

> Is the Church fulfilling a purely religious role when by its silence or friendly relationships it lends legitimacy to a dictatorial and oppressive government? We discover, then, that the policy of nonintervention in political affairs holds for certain actions which involve ecclesiastical authorities but not for others ...
>
> The dominant groups, who have always used the Church to defend their interests and maintain their privileged position, today – as they see 'sub- versive' tendencies gaining ground in the heart of the Christian community – call for a return to the purely religious and spiritual function of the Church.
>
> (1988:40–41)

Gutiérrez calls on the Church directly to use its power and influence to intervene in social issues, and to be public about its intervention. This he relates to his fundamental conviction that there is a clear relationship between human commit- ment to and involvement with issues of justice and salvation, ' ... to participate in the process of liberation is already, in a certain sense, a salvific work' (1988:46). In the context of the situation in Latin America at the time of writing *A Theology of Liberation* Gutiérrez speaks of a movement from ignorance about the reality of the oppression facing the poor people of Latin America and the shift in understanding from ignorance through partial awareness to understanding that is both structural and complete (1988:49). The dysfunctionality that has characterized some development in Latin American countries needs to be acknowledged and limitations challenged in the new order that theologians such as Gutiérrez envisage. Colonization, development and capitalist-driven economies (1988:51) have led to dependence on the structures and systems imposed by the richer countries which continue to control and determine the functioning and future of these countries. Dependence, for Gutiérrez, is key to understanding the situation of the countries of Latin America. From an understanding of Latin America as dependent, a concern with liberation then naturally arises. In fact, for Gutiérrez, a concern with liberation defines the outlook of the Latin American people.

In context Gutiérrez understands and defines liberation as involving liberation from the very countries that exert control over the development of Latin America. The means by which this will be achieved, argues Gutiérrez, will be 'a profound transformation, *a social revolution*' (1988:54). Acknowledging the significance of the Cuban revolution and the emergence of military guerrilla groups Gutiérrez argues that these events brought a reactionary response from traditionalists who continue to use violence to assert their own interests. Drawing here on the work of Freire, Gutiérrez stresses the relationship between theory and praxis and the process of conscientization (1988:57). The Church in Latin America, argues Gutiérrez, for historical reasons has been dependent on dominant and powerful political and social groups. He now argues that this relationship is weakening to the point of disengagement. This, he argues, is happening at a local level, by small groups, individuals and local churches. As some priests, religious and bishops, are politicizing themselves and engaging in social action with the explicit aim of revolutionary change. This is inevitably leading to conflict between the organized Church and those engaged in social reform and Gutiérrez refers to this as an 'identity crisis' (1988:61). The prophetic task facing the Church is not just to be critical of the established order but also to engage in constructive response to the widespread oppression and inequities. For liberation theology the Gospel is one of liberation. The message is one of justice and a move to conscientization which in this context is linked to evangelization.

One of the strongest and most powerful claims that Gutiérrez makes in *A Theology of Liberation* is the alignment of Christian identity with commitment to challenging and overturning injustice. He argues that the motivation for Christians to participate in justice-seeking activities such as challenging poverty and class-based oppression is a fundamental conviction that 'they cannot be Christians without a commitment to justice' (1988:81). He defines theology as critical reflection on historical praxis and on the Christian activity in the world today. As such, theological reflection must attempt to engage in a process of evaluation about such activity and presence today and in so doing assert and reaffirm the core Christian principles as essentially concerned with liberation.

Reaffirming the call of Vatican II and of *Gaudium et Spes* he reasserts, 'We are witnesses of the birth of a new humanism, one in which man is defined first of all by his responsibility toward his brothers and toward history' (*Gaudium et Spes*, no. 55 in Gutiérrez, 1988:81). He argues that this vision is the inspiration and motivation for the people of Latin America.

In reading Gutiérrez's theology, salvation and liberation at times seem to be interchangeable terms. He attempts to clarify the relationship between the two and infuse theologically the notion of liberation in the context of Latin American oppression and injustices. Salvation involves the overcoming of sin associated with this life (1988:84). Gutiérrez sees this as a basic, acceptable understanding of salvation. Traditionally the Church has been the location of grace, the point of access to God's grace needed to overcome or eliminate sin (1988:84). This has been increasingly challenged as grace has come to be seen not only as accessed through or residing in the institutional Church but has also been seen as accessible on a personal, individual level 'persons are saved if they open themselves to God and to others, even if they are not clearly aware that they are doing so' (1988:84). In this way Gutiérrez relocates, redefines and in some ways displaces the fundamental necessity of the institutional Church as the location and route to salvation. He also argues that salvation becomes understood not only as of another world or limited to the next life but is also of this life. It is about the transformation of the human person to fulfilling what God intended the human being to be. Sin, and the overcoming of sin, then has a social dimension. This is summed up well by Gutiérrez, ' ... salvation – the communion of human beings with God and among themselves – orients, transforms, and guides history to its fulfillment' (1988:86).

In examining salvation history Gutiérrez returns to the Bible, to Genesis, Isaiah and other biblical texts. He argues that a motif running through the Bible is the salvific acts of God through liberation, arguing that the 'liberation of Israel is a political action' (1988:88). Salvation is from oppression to a promised land, a land of freedom free from injustice. As such the Covenant encapsulates the liberative action of God. Gutiérrez describes Exodus as paradigmatic (1988:90). It serves to guide and inform human beings and societies as they oppose that which oppresses and divides them. Transformation of this life is salvific, as it is a part of the process of salvation history recorded in the biblical texts through acts such as the liberation of Israel and the ministry and death of Christ. In this, transformation participates in creation and humanity can become fulfilled by continuing the work of creation through human activity, community building, opposing oppression and exploitation (1988:91). Fulfilment and transformation are not limited to the next life or to eschatological hopes. The prophetic is happening here and now (1988:94), the future can begin, according to Gutiérrez, now:

> The full significance of God's action in history is understood only when it
> is put in its eschatological perspective; similarly, the revelation of the final
> meaning of history gives value to the present. The self-communication of

God points towards the future, and at the same time this Promise and Good News reveal humanity to itself and widen the perspective of its historical commitment here and now.

(1988:95)

Gutiérrez argues that whilst Christianity and the Christian prophets, in particular, talk of a kingdom of peace, 'peace presupposes the establishment of justice' (1988:97). Poverty, injustice, oppression are not the signs of a kingdom of peace; such things must be overcome and overcome on a human, social level, because this is how and where they function. They cannot be spoken of in purely spiritual or spiritual terms: 'The elimination of misery and exploitation is a sign of the becoming of the Kingdom' (1988:97). This raises important questions about the relationship between the Kingdom of God and human action in history (1988:100). Human action in history as liberative action is a continuation of creation and participation in salvation history. This places Christianity firmly in the here and now and very firmly with human action in history.

In liberation theology sin is not limited just to the individual nor is it seen to operate wholly on an individual or personal level. Liberation theology understands sin as structural, as evident in exploitative and oppressive actions. Sin is alienation (1988:103), but for the liberation theologian the root of this alienation is exploitation and injustice. Such is the state of sin in all of its structural forms and levels that must be challenged with 'a radical liberation, which in turn necessarily implies a political liberation' (1988:103). Christianity, then, is bound tightly to political liberation. It is through Christ that the overcoming of alienation from God can be experienced. Communion with God is the ultimate concern of liberation. Human, political liberation is tied up with overcoming alienating sin and moving into communion with God. Christianity and politics are bound together because of the state of human existence. In Christ, Gutiérrez argues, a radical liberation was seen. We encounter God in other human beings and in the ways in which human beings treat each other, 'love for God is unavoidably expressed *through* love of one's neighbor' (1988:115). For Gutiérrez there is no avoidance of human liberation for the Christian: 'To place oneself in the perspective of the Kingdom means to participate in the struggle for the liberation of those oppressed by others' (1988:116). To participate in the struggle against injustice is to convert perpetrators of injustice, but it also involves a conversion of the self. For Gutiérrez the Jesus of scripture is not a Jesus divorced from any kind of political action because Jesus was concerned with the expected and imminent 'end of the world' and the arrival of the Kingdom (1988:133). The transformation of social structures was not his primary concern. Solidarity among human beings is important because solidarity is essential for communion, which is of great concern to Christians, and communion with God is only possible in an environment of political liberation. He asserts this to the extent that 'all injustice is a breach with God' (1988:139). Gutiérrez, towards the end of *A Theology of Liberation*, calls on the Church to change. In particular this call is made in relation to the distinction between the institu-tional Church and the Church and Christians in the community (1988:141). Vatican II has enabled this process to begin with its emphasis on *aggiorna-mento* (1988:141). The Church in effect is being reconstituted at a ground level.

Gutiérrez talks not of just reform and renewal but of:

> ... a new ecclesial consciousness and a redefinition of the task of the Church in a world in which it is not only *present*, but of which it *forms a part* more than it suspected in the past.
>
> (1988:143)

In talking of an '"uncentering" of the Church' (1988:143) Gutiérrez is actually calling for a return to the early Church in which the kind of vision Gutiérrez has for the Church today was apparent. The Church as a sacrament must be functional in the world today; it must respond to injustice. It must be

> ... the visible sign of the presence of the Lord within the aspiration for liberation and the struggle for a more human and just society. Only in this way will the message of love which the Church bears be made credible and efficacious.
>
> (1988:148)

Communion with God, which lies at the heart of Gutiérrez's theology and at the heart of his understanding of Christianity, necessarily involves the end of all exploitation and oppression of people. The Church in Latin America, then, must be decisive in its positioning in relation to social injustice and the means by which this might be achieved. The Church must be rooted in the here and now. It must, in Gutiérrez's understanding, be prophetic in its challenges to injustice and oppression. As such, the Gospel itself has a political function (1988:153). The meaning of the Gospel message comes alive through action in history, liberative action. Gutiérrez is aware of the dangers of the Gospel mes-sage being too clearly and inappropriately aligned with revolutionarism. In talking of a preferential option Gutiérrez is not excluding some from 'the uni-versality of God's love' (1988:160). Christians need to be in solidarity with the poor, 'Christian poverty has meaning only as a commitment of solidarity with the poor, with those who suffer misery and injustice' (1988:172).

Gutiérrez's text was the beginning of a literary theological revolution in Latin America. Books, articles and resources were developed as tools to enable the development and realization of this new theology of liberation. Leonardo Boff's influential book *Jesus Christ Liberator* which was originally published in 1972 but translated and published in English in 1978 by Orbis Books set him firmly among the increasing group of theologians in Latin America being identified or self-identifying as liberation theologians. As did Jon Sobrino's *Christology at the Crossroad* which was published in 1977 and translated and published in English in 1978. Leonardo and Clodovis Boff developed a new approach to engaging with biblical texts which was firmly rooted in praxis, 'involving three different stages or mediations based on the see-judge-act methodology of Catholic Action' (Tombs, 2002:179). From this was then developed the notion of the hermeneutical circle in which reflection and praxis are inextricably tied together with resultant social or political action.

Ecclesial base communities

Behind these texts and meetings of bishops, priests and activists lay a solid and real commitment to social action. A grass-roots movement began to emerge and as Tombs comments this movement began to 'refashion itself as a church of the poor' (Tombs, 2002:158). Social action was the mark of this movement, centred on communities and addressing real and practical needs on an everyday basis. These Christian community groups became eventually known as ecclesial base communities (or CEBs) and are a very significant indicator in terms of what liberation theology actually amounted to in Latin America, especially in the 1970s and 1980s. As socially and politically active groups faced repression, attacks and persecution so these Christian base communities fortified against the many criticisms and rejections that they faced. They were effective because of the level at which they operated. They were in effect small groups within the regional church structures that worked with the very poor. In 1975 Paul VI's *Evangelii Nuntiandi* recognized these communities and the significance of their work and achievements. Tombs argues that at the centre of the life of the CEBs was the Bible, and group reflection on the meaning of the Bible in context (Tombs, 2002:168). From this contextual engagement with the Bible specific social action emerged as texts and passages were interpreted to motivate projects, relating to education, health, food and basic amenities (Tombs, 2002:173). In this sense, then, liberation theology was not removed from the very people that it was concerned with and wrote about. It was based in and was the inspiration for the outworkings of the gospel interpreted in liberative terms in oppressive contexts.

Liberation theology as contextual theology

There has to be an end point to the historical overview of the beginnings of liberation theology in Latin America. Here it will be the early 1970s following the publication of *A Theology of Liberation*, the Medellín Conference and the emergence of ecclesial base communities. So much more could be said here but the purpose of this chapter is to establish the context from which the first identifiable liberation theology as discernible contextual theology arose.

The price of the often radical contextual nature of liberation theology in Latin America was often very high. In 1980 Archbishop Oscar Romero was shot and killed in El Salvador as he celebrated mass. Romero lived out of his very strong commitment to liberation and his opposition to injustice. He was transformed by his experiences as Archbishop in the Roman Catholic Church but when appointed as Archbishop of San Salvador in 1977 he was seen as a traditional bishop rather than a radical or even progressive one (Smith, 1991:1). With the appointment of Romero many initially were disappointed as they saw this appointment as an opportunity for the Church to express its commitment to a more progressive social vision. However, his theology, his critical reflection and ensuing hermeneutic of reflective praxis led to this traditional figure becoming almost an embodiment of the radically contextual nature of Latin American liberation theology in the late 1970s. Earlier than Romero was Camilo Torres, who was a priest in Colombia in the 1960s and who began to organize for social reform. He organized a 'United Front' which attempted to bring together and mobilize 'peasants, slum dwellers, workers and professionals to work for social change' (Smith, 1991:16). Torres was criticized heavily by the Roman Catholic Church which resulted in him leaving the priesthood and joining the guerrilla Ejército de Liberación Nacional or ELN group which was a revolutionary, Marxist group and so took up arms to pursue the social justice he was so heavily committed to. In 1966 he was shot and killed but is widely known for his declaration, 'I took off my cassock to be more truly a priest' (cited in Smith, 1988:36).

Both Romero and Torres are more radical examples of how the contextual nature of Latin American Christian theology found expression in liberation theology. As has been seen in Gutiérrez's groundbreaking text *A Theology of Liberation* Christian liberation theology as it emerged in the 1970s bears witness to the ways in which human experiences can inform and inspire Christian theology at a most fundamental level. It also demonstrates how it is not only the content but also the form of Christian theology that is shaped by context. The Latin American experience of oppression through extreme poverty and exploitative rule became the building block for an entire theological movement that still thrives today. As has already been touched on in this chapter and as will be seen in more detail in later chapters the liberation theology of Latin America was by no means without criticism as either a Christian theology claiming its identity within the Christian tradition nor even as a contextual theology offering hope and a theological framework for the oppressed.

This chapter has focused on the emergence of liberation theology in Latin America and has identified key texts, theological events and individuals who influenced and shaped this theological revolution. As liberation theology in Latin America developed it found many different expressions within different regional and political contexts. Although there can be said to be more of a homogenous core to Latin American liberation theology than other forms of liberation theology such as black theologies and feminist theologies at the same time the diversity of Latin American liberation theologies must be recognized. So whilst this chapter has not delved into the different expressions and forms of Latin American liberation theology, because of its focus on the early development of liberation theology as contextual theology, this diversity must not be subsumed by talk of Latin American liberation theology as one thing.

In the next chapter a second type or example of explicitly contextual Christian theology will be examined. The group of theologies which have come to be known as feminist or feminist informed theologies will be explored. In feminist informed theologies the theological building block or context that informs Christian theology is gender, and in particular gender-based oppressions or experiences of injustice. There is a chronological progression here, moving on from the emergence of the liberation theologies of Latin America in the 1970s and 1980s to the emergence of other liberation theologies including those of black theologies and feminist theologies.

3 Gender matters

Feminist informed theologies

A second group of liberation theologies which are examples of Christian theologies that make a very strong claim to contextuality are feminist or feminist informed theologies. These theologies claim a strong presence in Christian communities and in academic theology in the twenty-first century. They will be examined here for the ways in which they function as contextual theologies and for the ways in which the clear and direct theological claims to contextuality, such as is often made by feminist theologians, are in fact acutely problematic. This chapter will examine the ways in which the context of gender has come to inform Christian theology through feminisms. It will also focus on how the diversity of women's lives has forced feminist informed theologies to take account of the complex and multilayered nature of oppression and to recognize that the context of any human life has many dimensions and can never be reduced to just one thing such as gender, social and economic status, race or sexuality.

So, in this chapter, feminist informed theologies will be critically interrogated for the outworkings of feminist claims to contextuality. The aim of the previous chapter with its focus on Latin American liberation theology was to examine how years of colonial rule, imperialism and oppressive social, economic and political regimes gave rise to a theological movement steeped in social consciousness and driven to challenge this oppression. Women's experiences of gender-based oppression and the rejection of gendered oppression will be examined now for the ways in which they have given shape to feminist informed contextual theologies. Gender, experienced too often in an oppressive way, is the contextual root of these theologies. We will see from their historical origins, through early and then more sophisticated developments, the ways in which feminist informed theologies make clear claims to be consciously contextual, if not radically contextual, Christian theologies. Some of the most significant and telling criticisms that have been made of feminist informed theologies focus on the very claim to be contextual. Feminist informed theologies are criticized for failing to understand human contexts in their fullest, plural and most fluid forms.

What will be argued here is that just as it is not possible to only take the category of poverty to define and understand Latin American liberation theology as a contextual theology, neither is it possible only to take the category of gender to fully understand the contextual nature of feminist informed theologies. Feminist informed theologies, just like the contexts that inform these theologies, are multilayered, diverse and ever changing according to the different experiences of women. We are moving on, then, from exploring the roots of explicitly contextual theologies in Latin American liberation theology to the outworkings of contextual theology through feminist informed theologies.

As in the previous chapter with its study of Latin American liberation theology, this chapter will give an account of feminist theologies through their historical development as liberation theologies. In this chapter the historical mapping lays the foundation for a detailed evaluation of the claims to contextuality made by feminist informed theologies. To begin with, this chapter will examine the early presence of feminisms in Christian theology to the blossoming of diverse and varied feminist informed theologies in the 1980s.

Early Christian feminist encounters

The emergence of feminisms as discernible theological perspectives shadows the rise of feminisms generally. Like the wider feminist movement, feminist theologies developed in two main waves, in the late nineteenth century and in the late 1960s and 1970s. These two waves give a historical account of the emergence of feminisms and feminist informed theologies but are distinguishable in some of their primary concerns and methodologies. A number of key nineteenth-century writings anticipate the concerns of the emerging women's movement and we glimpse in them the stirrings of feminist consciousness that was to develop into a plethora of feminisms and feminist informed theologies. These texts include Matilda Joslyn Gage's *Woman, Church and State* (1893) and Elizabeth Cady Stanton's *The Woman's Bible* (1895). Stanton and Gage, along with Susan B. Anthony, were influential figures in the nineteenth-century women's movement in North America and were involved with justice-related issues of suffrage, temperance, anti-slavery, the Equal Rights Amendment and especially women's rights. As part of their commitment to justice Stanton and Gage gave detailed attention to the causes and sites of gender-based inequalities. They were particularly critical of the role of Christianity in establishing and perpetuating such injustices. In *Woman, Church and State* Gage argued that considerable responsibility for gender-based oppression lay with the Christian Church. She also raised questions around issues of equality and hope. Priesthood, celibacy and marriage were all key issues within Gage's analysis and these have remained important for feminist informed theologies ever since. She argued that doctrinal and theological authority actually legitimized and enforced various gender-based oppressions that women were subject to. As a result women were widely regarded as inherently sinful and also as morally inferior to men. Theological authority then was used to validate and sustain a gendered hierarchical anthropology and theology. Christianity was not just incidental to gender-based oppression; it was a central causal factor.

Elizabeth Cady Stanton was another early activist in the women's movement and she was involved with planning the first women's rights convention which was held at Seneca Falls in New York in 1848. In challenging gender-based inequalities Stanton identified the Bible as a tool of oppression which she argued was used to silence and marginalize women. By focusing on biblical analysis as a way of challenging and undermining such oppression her work in this area anticipated the extensive critical feminist hermeneutics that have claimed such a shaping and highly visible presence in feminist informed theologies, especially over the last forty years. At the time this methodology employed by Cady Stanton of identifying the Bible as a tool of oppression was radical in its approach and for some this approach remains one of the most challenging aspects of the feminist Christian encounter. *The Woman's Bible* was published as a two-volume work in 1895 and 1898 and in it Stanton drew on contemporary insights of biblical scholarship. She raised questions about the role of the Bible in supporting and sustaining the gender-based oppression that women were subjected to. Stanton's project involved the detailed analysis and systematic exegesis of biblical texts from a consciously woman-identified stance:

> From the inauguration of the movement for women's emancipation the Bible has been used to hold her in the 'divinely ordained sphere', prescribed in the Old and New Testaments.
>
> (Cady Stanton, 1999:7)

According to Stanton, the Bible had been used as a tool by men to silence, control and blame women for sin and death. It is because of the comprehensive critical attention of texts such as *The Woman's Bible* and *Woman, Church and State* and because of the persistently critical thread running through these texts that they are described as evidence of feminist theologies in their earliest phase. Inevitably the creative radicalism and the methodological sophistication that has come to characterize feminist informed theologies is absent from the approaches taken in the nineteenth century but there is a clear anticipation of the key foci and approaches of Christian feminist theologies. Of particular significance was the claim that Christianity, and especially the Christian Church, was complicit in social injustices and also that biblical texts and appeals to such texts had an important role in sustaining such injustices. Christianity, the Bible and the Church were perceived as obstacles to women's liberation or justice concerns.

This first identifiable feminist Christian activity was clearly related to the emergence of the wider women's movement. Similarly, it was the second wave of feminisms that heralded the emergence of the more recent roots of what have since been identified as feminist informed theologies. Given the ethos of creativity and radical challenge in North America and Europe in the 1960s it is not surprising that this time is widely taken to mark the emergence of contemporary feminist theologies. As with earlier developments it is possible to lay down certain textual markers here. The first of these textual markers is an article by Valerie Saiving 'The human situation: a feminine view' which was published in 1960. Saiving's article is often celebrated as the beginnings of contemporary feminist theological discourse. Following the early development of critical concern of the 1890s there were of course other publications that addressed issues of religiosity and gender, but such publications were methodologically discernibly different from Saiving's work. It is the style and content of Saiving's article, along with subsequent theological engagement with the kind of issues she raised, that proved to be a definitive breakthrough in feminist theological engagement in terms of subsequent feminist Christian encounter. And this is despite the fact that at the time her article received very little recognition or acclaim.

One of the most important aspects of Saiving's analysis in 'The human situation' was her identification of the theological significance of differentiating between male and female experience (which she termed 'masculine' and 'feminine' experience). She posited as problematic the traditionally accepted generic use of the term 'men' by theologians and explored anthropological studies of the cultural influences of differences between male and female experiences, including Margaret Mead's *Male and Female* (1949) and Ruth Benedict's *Patterns of Culture* (1935). Drawing on such works Saiving located in the mother–child relationship, exclusive to women, a key formative role in establishing differentiated female and male identity. Reproductive capability was fundamental to Saiving's ideas about differences between male and female. She referred to female identity in terms of 'being' and male identity in terms of 'becoming'. She claimed that contemporary theology 'is not adequate to the universal human situation', it does not allow women to be 'both women *and* full human beings' (Saiving, in MacKinnon and McIntyre, 1980:12). From this, she argued that there is a discernible difference between female and male experiences of sin, and she specifically highlighted what she claimed was women's tendency to servitude, and dependency for identity on others.

In terms of the development of Christian feminist theologies, of significance here is Saiving's understanding of the theological implications of differentiating between male and female experiences. Saiving's analysis is based on the fundamental insight that traditionally it has largely been male experience that has informed and shaped our understanding of reality and the human situation. For her a very different understanding would emerge if female experience were part of this shaping process. This is why Carol Christ and Judith Plaskow have argued that this essay by Saiving was 'a landmark in feminist theology … ten years ahead of its time' (Christ and Plaskow in Christ and Plaskow, 1992:29). Saiving articulates here a fundamental feminist epistemological concern about the perception and naming of reality and compounds this concern with the insight that traditional namings, theological and doctrinal, are inadequate for men as well as women. Unacknowledged gendered perceptions and linguistics lead to a partial theology, and indeed anthropology, of exclusion and privilege. It is important to note here that even at this very early stage of feminist theological analysis there is the crucial recognition that traditional theologies and their underlying assumptions were detrimental and limiting not only for women but for men as well. The challenge of Saiving's work is to Christian theological formation, as her analysis focused not so much on the historical and biblical traditions of inequality but on the nature and processes of theological reflection and engagement. Specifically, the insight of Saiving's that has proved funda-mental to Christian feminist theological methodology ever since, and has in fact become almost foundational to such methodology, is the recognition of the gendered nature of experience and the striking implications that this has for Christian theology.

The early 1960s to the late 1970s was a key phase in the development of feminist theologies. The publication of texts such as Betty Friedan's *The Feminist Mystique* (1963), Germaine Greer's *The Female Eunuch* (1970) and Kate Millett's *Sexual Politics* (1970), along with the political and social activism that inspired and accompanied these feminist publications, had a substantial effect on many aspects of critical enquiry and practice, and Christian theology was by no means unaffected by this. For some, however, the feminist label, and its asso-ciated implications, were clearly problematic. Some theological studies in the 1960s explicitly resisted the label 'feminist' but seemed clearly to employ what might be termed by contemporary analysts as 'feminist' approaches and to reflect underlying feminist values. Margaret Brackenbury Crook's *Women and Religion* published in 1964 is just such an example of this. Crook rejected the label 'feminist' in description of the type of theological project with which she was concerned, claiming that

> Women have a heritage in religion to regain, develop, and carry forward. This is not a feminist movement; it concerns men as well as women and offers benefits to both.
>
> (Crook, 1964:1)

Crook talks of the 'displacement of women' (Crook, 1964:1) from full partici-pation in the traditions of Judaism, Christianity and Islam. Her aversion or rejection of the term 'feminist' in description of her work appears to be grounded in a need to stress that the kind of revisionary project she was advo-cating was the concern of both men and women, and was not limited just to women. The subtext here is clear. Feminisms, as perceived by Crook, do not extend to or include the experiences of men and so should be avoided in order to ensure an inclusive agenda. Crook's insights in *Women and Religion*, and the implications of these insights, would be appropriately characterized by many as 'feminist' despite her rejection of the term at the time of writing. This is seen, for example, in the way in which she describes women's positioning in Judaism, Christianity and Humanism:

> If a woman born and bred in any of these faiths takes a comprehensive look at the form of theology best known to her, she discovers that it is masculine in administration, in the phrasing of its doctrines, liturgies and

hymns. It is man-formulated, man-argued, and man-directed. To bring this charge against the religious leaders is not to display animosity, it is to recognize the actual state of affairs. In the Christian field, for instance, it is taken for granted that all the leading seminaries are almost entirely man-staffed, all the leading pulpits man-filled, that no woman can ever expect to become Archbishop of Canterbury or fill the Papal chair. Only rarely does a woman serve as representative in the great international assemblies of Christendom.

(Crook, 1964:5)

The publication of Saiving's 'The Human Situation' was followed by a pro-liferation of studies of Christianity and gender-based injustice. One issue that was becoming increasingly important to the whole field of women and injustice, and which came to be widely addressed in the 1960s in both North America and Europe, was that of women's access to ordained priesthood in a variety of Christian denominations. Rosemary Lauer, for example, raised the question of the theological implications of the recognition of gender-based equality and the full humanity of women in terms of ordination. Elisabeth Schüssler Fiorenza, then based in Germany, in 'Der Vergessene Partner' ('The Forgotten Partner') argued the case for a critical re-examination of the roles of women in the Church. Biblical evidence relating to questions of gender-based equality con-tinued to be an important focus of concern and Constance F. Parvey in 1969 in 'Ordain Her, Ordain Her Not' examined the relevant biblical evidence in the debate for and against women's right of access to the ordained priesthood. Questions surrounding women and the priesthood lie at the heart of the gender justice debate for many people. In the late 1960s gaining access to exclusive priestly roles was seen as absolutely fundamental to challenging male privilege and gendered hierarchies. However, from a historical perspective the reality of many women's experiences since being ordained to full priesthood in some Christian denominations has not included a realization of the hopes and expectations previously attached to overcoming this enormous barrier.

By the late 1960s and early 1970s issues of gender had a firm hold on Christian theology. Feminist values and methodologies were becoming increasingly sig-nificant as women within different geographical and Christian denominational contexts began to explore gender-based oppression and seek alternative ways on doing theology in contextual justice-seeking ways. In Europe, for example, Kari Børresen published *Subordination and Equivalence* in 1968 and Elisabeth Gössman was an influential feminist voice in Germany. In 1970, *Women's Liberation and the Church: The New Demand for Freedom in the Life of the Christian Church* which was edited by Sarah Bentley Doely was published by the Association Press in America. This was an important collection in which a number of influential and emerging theologians addressed a fundamental issue underlying the focus on gender and Christian theology, that of authority. Contributors included Norma Ramsey Jones who wrote on women and ministry, Rosemary Ruether on male domination, dualism and new humanity, and Sidney Cornelia

Callahan in 'A Christian Perspective on Feminism' raised issues of the compatibility of feminism and Christianity. Peggy Ann Way in her contribution to the collection, 'An Authority of Possibility for Women in the Church', explored the notion of ministerial authority in the light of the traditional exclusion of women from ministerial orders.

The importance of this collection is that it evidences a feminist consciousness among theologians in the 1970s and illustrates the way in which the increasingly important questions of the theological implications of feminist presence in Christianity were being addressed. Callahan's focus on the impact of feminism on Christianity is an important example of this consciousness in that it demonstrates a perceived clash between competing claims of a commitment to Christianity and a commitment to feminism. Callahan's article begins with the question of 'How can you be a feminist and a Christian at the same time?' (Callahan in Doely,1970:37). For her there is a correlation between her own commitment to Christianity and to feminism, 'Without taking Christianity seriously I would never have been prepared to accept radical feminism' (Callahan in Doely,1970:37). She draws parallels between the concerns and demands of Christianity and those of feminism. For her, most importantly, there is a shared critique and a shared vision based in justice. As both feminisms and Christianity involve critical appraisal and incorporate justice through equality and responsibility to affect change and self-empowerment (Callahan in Doely,1970:37–38). In advocating the shared convictions of feminism and Christianity in this way, Callahan stresses freedom and independence and is very much concerned with feminism as transformation. Yet even with such an analysis of the shared agendas of Christianity and feminism, Callahan still perceives there to be some kind of conflict or at least an issue of a primary authority claim between feminist and Christian commitment that needs addressing and resolving. She feels the need to make it absolutely clear that her unequivocal loyalty or commitment lies with Christianity:

> I guess in the end my feminism must be finally subordinated to the demands of Christian faith. Women's liberation is also not an ultimate value or a cause overriding all others. For me, radical feminism must also be put into a larger context and a longer race. But while radical Christianity and radical feminism share the same course they do move each other along. Or so I have found.
>
> (Callahan in Doely,1970:45)

Feminisms, in Callahan's understanding, can be best described as a specific contextual tool of Christian hope and one that essentially shares the visions and values of Christianity. Seen in this way Christianity is not in conflict with feminism. Rather, Christian commitment actually leads to the acceptance of feminist values and analysis. And the justice concerns of feminism, as perceived by Callahan, are entirely in accordance with those of Christianity. There is a sense, then, of continuity and tradition. It is writings like Callahan's 'A

Christian Perspective on Feminism' that clearly demonstrate the emergence of detailed critical analysis of the theological implications of feminist Christian encounters and, most importantly, of a Christian appeal to feminisms. This analysis, from very early on, incorporated some concern with questions of compatibility and authority. Clearly not all writers addressing issues of women and religion at this time adopted an openly feminist stance, or even utilized the term in description of their analysis. Indeed, some explicitly rejected and opposed feminist insights, and yet the theological forum had been broadened, and various issues relating to gender had been forced into the open. In a sense, the concerns had been identified and articulated, and distinct methodological insights and ways forward began to emerge.

It is with the theology and philosophy of the North American feminist Mary Daly that the first extensive and sustained critique of Christianity from an explicitly committed feminist standpoint is to be found. The impact of the work of Mary Daly in forging the identity of feminist theologies is without comparison. The issues and questions that she addressed stand as fundamental concerns to the feminist task in Christianity even today. Daly challenged the very symbols and structures of Christianity in fine detail with her analysis of them as patriarchal and oppressive to women, with substantial accumulative effect. It was with Daly's work, and especially *Beyond God the Father*, that the fundamental challenge of feminisms to Christianity was laid down. It is inseparably, both the content and form of Daly's analysis of the encounter of feminisms and Christianity that have been so influential. After attending the Second Vatican Council she wrote 'A Built-in Bias' which was published in *Commonweal* in 1965. In it she raised pertinent questions about the role of the Christian Church in effecting and sustaining gender-based injustice. Whilst Daly has written many articles and books which have consistently challenged and defied the boundaries of Christian theologies, it is her first two books that were of particular significance for the developing identity of feminist theologies. She began writing *The Church and the Second Sex* in 1965 and it was published in 1968. This book was heavily influenced by Simone de Beauvoir's *The Second Sex* and in it Daly makes the important recognition that the Christian Church, and, in particular, the Roman Catholic tradition out of which she was writing at the time, was patriarchal and oppressive to women. At this stage she argued for a reformist approach to the Roman Catholic treatment of women and to the Church as a whole. She advocated both the possibility and the need for review and reform of Christian theology in the light of feminist critique.

The Church and the Second Sex charts the historical documentation of Christianity's oppression of women. Daly saw a clear tension in this documentation between theorizing and praxis. There was incongruence between the idealization and the actual treatment of women. She traced Christianity's misogyny through Christian scripture and in particular in the writings of key theologians such as Augustine, Jerome, Tertullian, Thomas Aquinas and the nineteenth century and twentieth century, especially Leo XIII and Pius XII. Within such traditions, Daly also recognized that certain individual women had been able to attain some level of autonomy despite the extensive and systematic misogyny facing them. Daly claimed respite from what she understood as a clear tradition of misogyny with the papacy of John XXIII and with the spirit of *aggiornamento*. She cited the 1963 encyclical *Pacem in Terris* as the 'first startling breakthrough on the ideological level' (Daly, 1985:118). And whilst acknowledging the tentative and limited nature of this breakthrough, Daly clearly places groundbreaking significance in terms of issues of gender and justice with both the Second Vatican Council and in particular with the contribution of Pope John XXIII. Daly's proposals for post-conciliar advancement involved the pressing need to resist stereotypical representations of women. She drew on contemporary psychological studies and referred to the need for 'exorcism' (Daly, 1985:176) of demonic repression through stereotypes. As Daly perceived it, the task facing those concerned with such exorcism was extensive. It included addressing conceptualizing and symbolizing, god talk, social transformation and the institutional shape and ordering of the Church. Daly's commitment to this transformative task is clear. She talks of the importance of 'commitment to radical transformation of the negative, life-destroying elements of the Church as it exists today' (Daly, 1985:221) and whilst acknowledging the significance of de Beauvoir's contribution to discussions of women, Church and autonomy, she chooses not a 'philosophy of despair' but 'a theology of hope' (Daly, 1985:223), a choice which leaves her undoubtedly at this point within the traditions of Christianity.

As Daly developed her feminist critique of Christianity, and worked through the implications of accepting a radical feminist critique of Christianity, she increasingly moved away from advocating a feminist reformist approach to Christianity. In 1971 she preached a sermon at the Harvard Memorial Church and led a now famous exodus from the Church. The sermon embodied the spirit of Daly's radicalism of the time, and makes clear her rejection of traditional religion:

> We cannot really talk about belonging to institutional religion as it exists … the women's movement is an exodus community … we can affirm *now* our promise and our exodus as we walk into a future that will be our *own* future … Our time has come. We will take our own place in the sun. We will leave behind the centuries of silence and darkness. Let us affirm our faith in ourselves and our will to transcendence by rising and walking out together.
>
> (Daly, 1993:138)

Daly, who was influenced by Paul Tillich, talks of this exodus as 'a manifestation of the *Courage to Leave*' (Daly, 1993:139). In her most influential book, *Beyond God the Father*, first published in 1973, Daly charts her movement from a reformist or revisionary feminist position to an alternative post-Christian position. This stands as one of the most important feminist theological texts to date and reflects both the radicalization of Mary Daly and the wider American and European feminist awakening or consciousness. In *Beyond God the Father*, Daly rejected the possibilities of any kind of effective feminist reform for traditional religion. Instead, she called for the recognition of the death of such religions for women. There are a number of reasons why *Beyond God the Father* was, and remains today, such an important text for locating the development and identity of Christian informed feminist theologies. First, in her analysis Daly argued for the inherently gendered nature of the symbols, theology, practice, language and institutions of Christianity and then unpacked the ensuing implications of these for issues of women and justice. This analysis then served as the basis for her explicit and uncompromising rejection of the possibility and authenticity of Christian feminist theologies. Daly formulated her critique in such a way as to align the acceptance of feminisms, and all that feminisms stood for, with the rejection of Christianity. Because of this critical positioning of feminisms and traditional religion, especially Christianity, *Beyond God the Father* marks the beginnings of the sustained debate about the compatibility of Christianity and feminism.

Reforming Christianity

Daly's feminist-based critique of religion, in its radicalism, eloquence and promise, has been responded to in many different ways as Christian feminist informed theologies have developed. At the time *Beyond God the Father* was published a key voice among those advocating reform was Rosemary Radford Ruether, who was also based in North America and working out of the Roman Catholic tradition. Her contribution to the early feminist theological formations also had a distinctive influence on the shape and direction of this theology, although in a very different way to Mary Daly. Ruether's focus has been on the role of theology and religion in relation to the uncovering of systematic injustices, and the promotion of the rights of all to full humanity. In 1971, Ruether wrote:

> The building of a new world has to begin on the grass roots level, in the basic units of human relation, for this is where the history of subjugation and domination first began and where its basic imagery is still vested.
> (Ruether, 1971:183)

The situations and theoretical bases of oppression that Ruether has consistently addressed in her work since the 1960s include, the historical development of Christianity in legitimizing sexism, racism, Christian anti-Semitism, classism, militarism and the ecological crisis. For Ruether, the contexts and causes of oppressions and inequities are numerous. Her earliest theological work was concerned specifically with ecclesiology and anti-Semitism. In the late 1960s Ruether developed a critique of the institutional Church and offered proposals for a radical ecclesiology which encapsulated an alternative vision of Church and humanity. One important aspect of this radical ecclesiology as it developed was a critique of the patriarchal nature of the Church. By 1971 Ruether's theology was focusing specifically on issues of women and liberation, and throughout the 1970s the influence of her distinctive work on the increasing diversity of feminist Christian encounters was considerable. In many publications she has addressed many different aspects of what she has perceived to be the denial of full humanity of women by the Church and Christian theology. Significant writings of Ruether in this early phase of feminist theological development drew particular attention to the interdependency of various forms of oppressions and oppressive relationships. Gender-based injustice was seen as one form or type of injustice, and one that stands alongside, and often tied to, other injustices such as race, class and sexuality. For Ruether, as for many other critical thinkers, injustice was underpinned and arose out of dualistic frameworks, which split and oppose humanity based on perceived difference. Difference, then, was essentially interpreted negatively and ranked accordingly. From such analysis developed the argument that dualisms, and in particular hierarchical dualisms, needed to be challenged and replaced with a more holistic framework or understanding of humanity and the world. This more holistic, undifferentiated understanding that was advocated was understandable in its origins and intentions, but has proved hugely problematic and arguably ineffective according to its original intention. As will be seen later, blanket descriptions and representations of both women's experiences and of feminisms have betrayed the diversity and reality of women's lives. The criticism here is that the contexts of women's lives, as the fundamental resource or foundation of contextual feminist informed theologies, have not been thoroughly and genuinely incorporated into liberation theologies.

Key to the reformist feminist approach developed by Ruether in the 1970s was the strong conviction that the Christian tradition *is* a possible basis from which to develop a liberating feminist theology. For Ruether, Christian theology has justice concerns at its very heart. She argued that in both identifying and overcoming injustice Jesus specifically criticized religious and social injustice. Ruether then turned to liberation theology, as it had developed so far, and argued for the radicalization of prophetic critique (Ruether, 1976:122). In particular, she identified the fundamental task of liberation theology as overcoming alienation that Christianity has had a role in legitimizing and perpetuating. For Ruether liberation theology is not just about critique but it has a very important constructive role as well. In *New Woman, New Earth* published in 1975 Ruether identified and traced the patterns of domination and alienation which she claimed characterized Western societies. She traced the shifting patterns of women's oppression, through early tribal culture, urbanization, and industrialization to the contemporary feminist movement. The relationship of feminism to other liberation movements is crucial for Ruether and she argued for the interdependent oppressions of racism, sexism, anti-Semitism and the ecological crisis:

> Women must see that there can be no liberation for them and no solution to the ecological crisis within society whose fundamental model of relationship continues to be one of domination.
>
> (Ruether, 1975:204)

According to Ruether, because of the extensive and interrelated oppressions that face humanity the response that is needed involves a transformation of the underlying worldview. From a worldview which is characterized by patterns of alienation and domination to 'an alternative value system' (Ruether, 1975:204). The kind of worldview that Ruether envisaged is vehemently opposed to dualistic hierarchicalism and would be characterized by the development of 'a new communal social ethic' (Ruether in Christ and Plaskow, 1992:52). Ruether's feminist informed vision is unambiguously reformist in its approach and intention but nevertheless carries quite radical implications for the organization, symbols and language of Christianity:

> Perhaps the task of Christians today, as they take stock of this tradition and its defects, is not merely to vilify its inhumanity but rather to cherish the hard-won fruits of transcendence and spiritual personhood, won at a terrible price of the natural affections of men and the natural humanity of women. Without discarding these achievements, we must rather find out how to pour them back into a full-bodied Hebrew sense of creation and incarnation, as male and female, but who can now be fully personalized autonomous selves and also persons in relation to each other, not against the body, but in and through the body.
>
> (Ruether in Ruether, 1974:179)

As the 1970s advanced, identifiable fields of feminist theological engagement began to emerge. These were fields of feminist engagement which were characterized or distinguished by a range of differentiating factors, including: method, discipline area, ensuing faith commitment and denominational grouping. By 1975, in terms of discipline area, the field of biblical feminist hermeneutics in particular was a central concern and feature of feminist theologies. This, then, reflected the concerns and tendencies of both the earlier wave of feminist theology in the nineteenth century and Latin American and other liberation theology movements. The work of Elisabeth Schüssler Fiorenza contributed an enormous amount, in terms both of the formative development of the notion of 'feminist theology', and also in terms of the development of biblical feminist hermeneutics with her feminist informed reconstructionist approach to early Christian history. Like Ruether, Schüssler Fiorenza was also writing out of the Roman Catholic tradition and based in North America. Schüssler Fiorenza's early feminist theological work stressed that feminisms are characterized by a concern with the full humanity of women. Like other theologians such as Daly and Ruether, she located particular responsibility for women's oppression with Christian theology and with the associated value system and structures that embody these values (Schüssler Fiorenza, 1975:611). In the face of such an analysis of the fundamental and pervasive nature of gender-based oppression and the role of Christianity in legitimizing and so perpetuating this oppression Schüssler Fiorenza proposed substantive changes to the way in which theology should be understood and approached. She drew on contemporary critical thinking and rejected the view of theology as objective, value-free scholarship. Taking a very clear stance about the contextual nature of all human knowledge, including theology, she argued that theology is very much the product of each individual or group's experiences. It is determined in form and content by the historical and social context of the theologian. As such, theology reflects and serves the interests of a particular group or individual (Schüssler Fiorenza, 1975:616). This insight, subsequently developed and refined by feminist informed theologies, centres on the claim that theology is influenced by certain interests and so inevitably reflects these interests. Feminist theologies made very clear and explicit claims about Christian theology as contextual. This reading of Christian theology as contextual was further developed by claims and insights which were particular to this particular group of theologies. Schüssler Fiorenza, for example, having put forward the argument that all theology is contextual, develops this further with the claim that the interested, committed nature of theology has largely gone unacknowledged. Theology has been seen as objective when in fact it always reflects and serves the interests of certain groups and individuals. She argued that generally theology reflects male interests and ignores or excludes the interests and experiences of women and other marginalized groups. This exclusion of experiences, other than normative, patriarchal experiences, is hidden and denied by the way in which Christian theology is perceived. For Schüssler Fiorenza, the committed and interested nature of theology must be acknowledged, and the nature of its commitments and interests then explored and critiqued.

Feminist informed theologies with their acknowledgement of the impact of experience and circumstance on theology and with their call for all theology to recognize and explore its committed nature can be said to be consciously and explicitly contextual Christian theologies. They are contextual theologies in so far as they stress the impact of context on theology and they are specifically feminist informed contextual theologies in so far as they have a particular concern with gender and gender-based oppressions. Their reading of Christian theology as contextual theology is also potentially very radical. In that feminist informed theologies, like Latin American liberation theologies, argue that Christian theology not only has the responsibility of acknowledging its influences and shaping concerns, but it specifically has the task of reflecting the interests of the oppressed. So, it is not only contextual, but it has the task of being contextual in a particular way. It is not enough just to value experience as a key component of Christian theology; it goes further and values some experience more than other experience. According to Schüssler Fiorenza feminist theology is based firmly in a vision and commitment to 'an emancipatory ecclesial and theological praxis' (Schüssler Fiorenza, 1975:612). Only when theology is on the side of the outcast and oppressed, as she claims Jesus was, can it become fully incarnational and Christian. Christian theology, therefore, as an advocacy theology has to be rooted in emancipatory praxis and solidarity in order to be authentically Christian.

This then brings us to a central dilemma of feminist informed Christian theology. If Christian theology is inherently contextual and so inevitably addresses the concerns and reflects the experiences of those who produce it, and if women have traditionally had very little if any access to writing theology because of their lack of access to the discourses and systems of theology, then how should traditional theology be viewed and valued from a feminist point of view? Feminist informed theology has offered a range of responses to this dilemma. One is the post-Christian response of theologians such as Mary Daly, Carol Christ and Daphne Hampson who argue that the traditions and structures of Christianity are so inherently male and patriarchal that they are beyond reform. Another response has been that of the reformist approach which for varying reasons does not see the Christian tradition as beyond hope for women and sets itself the task of redressing this apparent absence. Schüssler Fiorenza's theology has directly addressed this absence of women from explicit theological formation and her work on biblical feminist hermeneutics and early church history takes forward her vision of the transformatory effects of the inclusion of women's experiences. In 'Women in the Early Christian Movement' which was included in the 1992 collection *Womanspirit Rising: A Feminist Reader in Religion*, Schüssler Fiorenza drew attention to the way in which the Bible has been used both as evidence for, and against, the subordination of women. Citing Galatians 3:28 she claimed that the Jesus movement was, in its earliest forms, inclusive:

> The new self-understanding of the early Christian movement is expressed in Galatians 3:28. In the new, Spirit-filled community of equals all distinctions of race, religion, class, and gender are abolished. All are equal and one in Jesus Christ.
>
> (Schüssler Fiorenza in Christ and Plaskow, 1992:88)

She argued that women played key roles as apostles, prophets and leaders in the early Church. In her extensive publications Schüssler Fiorenza attempts a feminist reclamation of the liberative nature of Christianity. She proposes a radical reconstructionist approach to the recovery and elaboration of women's Christian history and heritage, which she argues should serve as a lived model of inclusive Christianity, relevant for contemporary Christianity:

> Much of women's 'her-story' in early Christianity is lost. The few references which survived in the New Testament records are like the tip of an iceberg indicating what we have lost. Yet at the same time they show how great the influence of women was in the early Christian movement.
>
> (Schüssler Fiorenza in Christ and Plaskow, 1992:92)

For theologians such as Schüssler Fiorenza, the absence of women from the records and traditions of Christianity does not mean that women did not make significant contributions to the life and development of the early Christian movement. Rather, this absence is the result of patriarchal traditions which have excluded women and erased evidence of their contribution to Christianity.

In the feminist informed theology of the 1980s questions of biblical evidence and interpretation in relation to gender-based oppression emerged as a central concern. Among the most influential of the biblical scholars of the 1970s was Phyllis Trible who in *God and the Rhetoric of Sexuality* (1978) explored the ways in which biblical texts have been taken to support sexism. Informed by rhetorical criticism, Trible proposed a hermeneutics of reinterpretation of key biblical texts and language. Other writings of this time focused specifically on the Hebrew Bible (and especially the Genesis creation accounts), the Pauline passages and the gospel narratives.

Coupled with this developing feminist hermeneutics, studies of the past traditions of Christianity also emerged as important at this time. Influential theologians such as Barth and Tillich came under critical feminist scrutiny, as did key periods in Christian history, such as the early Church and the reformation. An important publication in this field that exemplifies the ways in which feminist critical engagement with historical traditions emerges as a pressing concern of feminist theologies was *Women in the Christian Tradition* (1973) by George H. Tavard. The work of Eleanor McLaughlin was also important here. In 'The Christian Past: Does it Hold a Future for Women?' first published in 1975 McLaughlin proposed certain methodological insights which she argued were necessary for a feminist revisionist approach to reclaiming Christian history. She then engaged this methodology with reference to women's religious lives of the high and late Middle Ages. For McLaughlin, the recognition of the male perspective on church history leads to a problematic resistance to a feminist valuing of Christian history:

> Understandable as this bias is against Christian tradition and the study of the Christian past, I wish to take a methodological stand beyond the anti-historicism of radical Christian feminism while at the same time rejecting the irrelevance, incompleteness, and admittedly often unconscious sexism of much of traditional church history. This alternative or revisionist approach to the Christian past seeks to set forth a history that is at once *responsible*, that is, grounded in the historicist rubric of dealing with the past on its own terms and *usable*. I mean by the search for a usable past a phrase recognized by historians who lived through the 1960s an examination of Christian history with a new set of questions that arise out of commitments to wholeness for women and for all humanity. Following from new questions, this is a history that redresses omissions and recasts interpretations.
>
> (McLaughlin in Christ and Plaskow, 1992:94–95)

The revisionist feminist approach to Christian history then was grounded in both the acknowledgement of the patriarchal nature of recorded history, and the belief in the significance of the recovery of women's Christian past.

A very important response to the feminist analysis of the patriarchal nature of the traditions, symbols and structures of Christianity in the 1970s and early 1980s was the emergence of feminist theologies based in non-traditional religiosity or spirituality. Following the general direction of Daly's rejection of

Christianity, and other traditional religions, on the basis of their irretrievably patriarchal nature, some writers moved on to the constructive task of engaging in the search for alternative bases and language for feminist theologies. One of the most influential of writers here was Carol P. Christ, who in 1975 made a self-declared move beyond traditional religion. One distinguishing feature of post-traditional feminist theologies is its focus on the language, symbols and traditions of the goddess. Naomi Goldenberg in her 1979 publication *Changing of the Gods: Feminism and the End of Traditional Religion* made clear the radical implications of committed recognition that traditional religion is patriarchal and intrinsically oppressive to women. She argued that feminist analysis and criticism of Christianity and of God is in effect bringing about the downfall of traditional religion. For Goldenberg, feminism and Christianity are irreconcilable. Christianity, with its male saviour, in her view, cannot support the feminist informed liberation of women. Many feminists turned to the symbols and traditions of the goddess in the face of the probing questions of feminist analysis.

Feminist informed theologies by 1979

By 1979 the depth and scope of feminist theological writings was substantial, and an explicit theological concern with issues of gender and religion was apparent in a variety of traditions. It is important to stress that the term 'feminist theology', even at this early time, did not solely refer to feminist critical thinking and practice within Western Christian traditions. Encounters with feminisms were apparent in a range of religious traditions and contexts. Questions of women's status and role had emerged in many different ways and with differing degrees of radicalism, for example, in relation to the traditions and practices of Judaism, Islam, Buddhism, Hinduism and Taoism. Fatima Mernissi's *Beyond the Veil*, published in 1975, signifies the critical consideration of issues of gender and justice in Islam. In Judaism, questions of feminism gained a particularly high profile, for example, focusing particularly on issues of god language, and women's inclusions in prayer quorum were addressed. The relationships between different feminist theologies are complex and criticisms of theologies as incorporating into their fundamental analysis criticisms of particular religious traditions have proved problematic in the development of feminist theologies. For example, one major issue that has emerged is that of Christian feminist anti-Semitism. Judith Plaskow emerged as a key critical voice in Jewish feminism, and along with other Jewish feminists, has argued that patterns of domination and exclusion were being enshrined in the conceptual and ethical foundations of Christian feminist theology, despite its professed liberation concerns. The underlying criticism here is that Christian feminists were placing blame for the rise of patriarchalism on Judaism. The result of this was anti-Semitic tendencies in subsequent Christian feminist theologies. This indicates something of the complexity of injustice, oppression and 'patriarchalism'.

Further very important differentials shaping feminist theologies were particular Christian heritages, denominational affinities and political and social contexts.

As early as 1979, Ada Maria Isasi-Diaz, a very influential Hispanic theologian who has been key to the development of mujerista theology, was raising fundamental critical questions about women in Latin American churches and in doing so highlighting issues of racism and exclusion alongside those of gender and exclusion. Within different Christian traditions and within different religious traditions generally, specific issues and areas of concern emerged as important, often related to the specific cultural and historical experiences of the religious tradition in question. From the variety of religious and theological contexts within which questions of feminisms have emerged, there are certain areas of concern that can be seen to be generally important and of concern to feminist theological discourses. These include issues of god language, ethics, scripture, religious language, ritual and celebration, religious organization, leadership roles, peace, ecology, motherhood, sexuality, poverty, racism and women's work.

Many of the works referred to so far here were written from North American and European contexts. The proliferation of works in these contexts has inevitably been reflected in the way in which feminist theologies are characterized and understood. However, for the nature and depth of feminist informed theologies to be fully represented recognition needs to be given to the great diversity of context, form and concern found in and among feminist informed theologies. This diversity was evident, in embryo at least, as early as 1979. A useful indicator of the dynamics and particulars of this diversity in the late 1970s is available by examining the 1979 collection *Womanspirit Rising*. Edited by Carol Christ and Judith Plaskow, this text brought together writings of women from different traditions, with different concerns and employing a range of feminist theological methods. Christ and Plaskow in the preface wrote:

> *Womanspirit Rising* brings together the positive and constructive articles on women and religion that our students have been reading in the library over the past several years. We have found that the historical, theological, and ritual pieces collected here provide a clear overview of constructive feminist writing in religion.
>
> (Christ and Plaskow in Christ and Plaskow, 1992:xiii)

Reflecting on the collection in the preface to the 1992 edition, Christ draws attention to the limitations of the diversity of voices represented at this time. Noting particularly the 'absence of voices of color, the invisibility of lesbians, and ... a failure to discuss class and educational background' (Christ and Plaskow in Christ and Plaskow, 1992:viii) all of these have since emerged as central issues in feminist discourse. However, whatever critique is made of the criteria for inclusion, the visible faces of feminist theologies at this time, are evident in *Womanspirit Rising*. The structure of the collection also suggests distinct key areas of concern for feminist informed theologians at this time, such as the theoretical underpinning of feminist theologies, feminist historical reconstruction, revision of tradition and creating new traditions, many of which were explored in relation to Christianity, goddess religion and Judaism.

From the seeds of developing feminist consciousness in the 1960s, by 1979 there had emerged a range of critical perspectives characterized by feminist informed values and methodologies. From the concerns of the 1960s, the 1970s fashioned a distinctly feminist approach to questions of religion, ethics and theology, which can be broadly described as identifying and rejecting gender-based oppression and proposing feminist informed theological responses which in theory at least were often radically contextual. The range of concerns, and the religious and social contexts that gave rise to questions of feminism in the 1970s, were vast, and it is on these revolutionary foundations that feminist theologies since the 1980s have built, dismantled, reconfigured and dismantled again the issues, practices and visions of justice of Christian theologies.

The diversification of feminist informed theologies

As feminist theological encounters rapidly expanded in the 1980s, their diverse forms and settings became increasingly apparent and decisive. With this diversity informing and challenging the identity of feminist informed theologies we see some of the theological and ideological dilemmas surrounding thoroughly con-textual theologies being played out. Diversities of culture, class, race, ethnicity, sexuality, religious commitment and existential perspective led to a multi-faceted feminist presence in Christian theology. For some, the unfolding and diversifi-cation of feminist theological perspectives was problematic, and for others lib-erating. So, despite the fact that many of the most public or visible voices of feminist informed theologies (and some would argue that this remains so today) were often largely those of North American and European women, feminist theological activity was vital and pervasive. Within this critical milieu a number of issues arose which posed difficult questions about the identity, claims, voice and future of feminist informed theologies, issues which all focused on the perceived experiential nature of theology, its claims to contextuality and the implications of such a claim for feminist informed theologies. Recognition of the problematic valuing of women's experiences is crucial not only for an understanding of the development of feminist theologies but is also crucial to any attempt to explore the identity of Christian feminist theologies, especially as explicitly contextual Christian theologies.

Context, experience and feminist informed theologies

Ever since Saiving's work in the 1960s feminist theological writings have focused in detail, and in many different ways, on the place and understanding of experience in feminist theologies. One of the fundamental insights here has been the recognition of the traditional absence of women's experiences from Chris-tian theology. Recognition of this absence, however, has not translated smoothly into inclusion in feminist theologies. Feminist theologies, like femin-isms generally, have struggled with the consequences of what has proved both a vital and problematic insight. For having proposed the importance of recovering and valuing women's experiences, and proposed the importance of genuinely contextual knowledge, questions then needed to be asked of whose experience is being referred to, and who decides on its value? Mary McClintock Fulkerson points out that 'Early criticisms from women of colour, lesbian women, and class-based feminisms noted the false universal in feminist appeals to women' (Fulkerson in Chopp and Davaney, 1997:99). Since the 1980s the claim has been extensively made that feminist informed theologies have proved as limiting and exclusive in their understanding of experience as traditional theologies. The criticism made is that the experience of a quite narrow, relatively privileged group of women is being set up as normative. So, accusations of exclusion have been made in relation to a fundamental principle of feminist theologies, calling into question or at least critically interrogating any claims that these theologies might make to contextuality.

Audre Lorde wrote in a letter to Mary Daly in 1980:

> I feel that you do celebrate differences between white women as a creative force toward change, rather than a reason for misunderstanding and separation. But you fail to recognize that, as women, these differences expose all women to various forms and degrees of patriarchal oppressions, some of which we share and some of which we do not.
>
> The oppression of women knows no ethnic nor racial boundaries, true, but that does not mean it is identical with these differences.
>
> (Lorde in Humm, 1992:139)

On one level, this criticism of exclusivism can be said to be a criticism of the failure of feminisms to recognize their particularity or contextuality, in so far as they are based in a certain group's or individual's experience. Also, it is an issue of the universal and particular relevance of feminisms for women. The problem has proved pressing because despite the fact that feminisms (and feminist informed theologies specifically) are concerned with gender inequality, they are determined in form and interests by particular contexts. So, some of the difficulties inherent in feminist informed theologies are linked to their identity as being fundamentally bound up with experience. Ellen Leonard has argued that the shift in theology, which has come to recognize and use experience as a foundation for theology, has led feminist thinkers to the realization of the need for 'a new epistemology' (Leonard, 1990:147).

Outside of the mainline Christian traditions diverse voices have emerged with strength and depth as key critical forces in feminist theologies to challenge the understanding of what constitutes women's experience. Asian feminist theologies, mujerista theologies and womanist theologies, for example, have stressed that no one group of women's experience is normative, and that feminist theologians, like all theologians, should be aware of their own commitments and influences. Some white Christian feminist theologians, recognizing the difficulties surrounding the way in which women's experience has so far been understood in feminist theologies, have attempted to address the issues of the functioning of women's experiences. Anne Carr in her editorial reflections in *Women, Work and Poverty* (1987) acknowledged that feminist theologies did indeed emerge out of the experiences of middle-class women, but argued that through self-criticism they have subjected themselves to challenging and transformative questions. Judith Plaskow and Carol Christ argued that the realization of the failure of feminism to reflect adequately the diversity of experiences found among women brings the obligation to recognize and pursue its important implications for feminist theologizing: 'To continue using the concept of women's experience under these circumstances obligates us to uncover and describe the diversity it encompasses' (Plaskow and Christ, 1989:3). This argument places an obligation with self-declared contextual theologies, such as feminist informed theologies, to remain true to the principle of contextuality, however challenging this might be.

The critical recognition being made by theologians concerning the limiting and unreflective way in which feminist informed theologies have understood experience necessitates change. For many it has become strikingly apparent that feminist informed theologies in order to fulfil their liberation theological agenda for women must remain open to transformation through self-criticism. Such openness is seen as necessary to deal with the fundamental but very challenging contention that being a woman is bound up closely with the kind of woman one is. Emily Culpepper argues that

> If we are genuinely committed to hearing the voices of women of color, this commitment will interrupt and change that basic academic enterprise the search for sources.
>
> (Culpepper, 1988:40)

This will involve celebration of diversity as a significant, distinctive quality. Unity that forsakes the reality of the diversity of experience is of no real value in terms of the vision and effectiveness of feminist theologies as contextual liberation theologies.

Since the late 1990s some of the most challenging and insightful of feminist informed theological engagement has emerged from a diversity of contexts and heritages, which leads Kwok Pui-lan to claim that 'Feminist theology has become a global movement' (Kwok Pui-lan in Parsons, 2002:23). Here, the voices of Asian, Asian-American, African-American, Hispanic/Latina and Third World women are important. From these, for example, there have emerged distinct mujerista and womanist theological perspectives, to name but two. Since Alice Walker's proposal of the term 'womanist' the term has been variously developed and elaborated by black women to locate their work and concerns as within a certain tradition. The term 'womanist' articulates the ambiguity of black feminist informed positions in powerful and convincing terms. It draws attention to the gender-aware critical perspectives of the womanist whilst at the same time stresses the particular and grounded nature of black, and indeed all, women's experiences. Delores Williams and Katie

Cannon are two womanist writers who have developed very influential womanist theological and ethical perspectives. Cannon describes well the ambiguity of womanism to both feminist theologies and black male theologies:

> Intrigued by the largely unexamined questions that have fallen through the cracks between feminist ethics and Black male theology, the womanist scholar insists on studying the distinctive consciousness of Black women within Black women's institutions, clubs, organizations, magazines and literature. Appropriating the human condition in their own contexts, Black women collectively engage in revealing the hidden power relations inherent in the present social structures. A central conviction is that theo-ethical structures are not universal, colorblind, apolitical, or otherwise neutral. Thus, the womanist ethicist tries to comprehend how Black women create their own lives, influence others, and understand themselves as a force in their own right. The womanist voice is one of deliverance from the deafening discursive silence which the society at large has used to deny the basis of shared humanity.
>
> (Cannon, 1987:171)

Ada Isasi-Díaz in *Mujerista Theology: A Theology for the Twenty-First Century* (1997) describes mujerista theology as 'liberative praxis' which arises from the situation of Latina/Hispanic women that works with a keen awareness of the limitations of European and American feminist theologies. She distinguishes between the different stages in her own development, talking of when she was 'born a feminist' and when she was 'born a mujerista' (Isasi-Díaz, 1997:40). She argues that the preferential option of mujerista theology is for Latina women and that this theology has a communal nature. However, despite this, she does not attempt to incorporate all Latina/Hispanic women into a unity. She reflects the diversity of locations or 'locus theologicus' (Isasi-Díaz,1997:64) that mujerista theologians work from and stresses the need for sensitivity to pluralism of women. It has a very strong liberation theological base, where liberation is seen as 'the criterion by which we judge what is right or wrong, what is good or bad, what is salvic or condemnatory' (Isasi-Díaz, 1997:69–70). For her, mujerista theology is grass-roots liberation theology, which is concerned with community and with embracing diversity in which 'epistemological vigilance refers to the need to avoid avoidance' (Isasi-Díaz, 1997:76).

There is now a wide acceptance that if feminist informed theologies are to stand as liberating theologies for women, then they must more fully reflect the experiences of women in their great diversity and in their specificity. Feminist theologians are stressing that experiences of economic class; race, religion, sexuality and culture are important differences among women, as are their experiences of oppression. Maura O'Neill in identifying the importance of recognizing difference in interreligious dialogue between women argues that

> The meaning of concepts such as oppression, liberation, and feminism cannot be assumed … the women who come together to dialogue must

forsake a preconceived notion of specific unifying factor to launch this discussion. One cannot assume that all of the women have either been oppressed or have seen their religion as excluding them in any way.

(O'Neill, 1990:103)

Feminist informed Christian theologies in the early 2000s

In the first decade of the second millennium the range of feminist informed Christian theologies is vast and constantly shifting, and the justice concerns and expressions of these theologies diverse. Feminist theological concerns are trans-disciplinary and specific, and are found in a variety of cultural, sexual and social contexts. The issues addressed and explored in such theologies are numerous, and studies in theory and feminist informed theologies are emerging as an essential part of this landscape. The inevitably complex and lengthy debate surrounding the limitations and possibilities of feminist theologies and issues of exclusion and priority must be constantly engaged as part of the inherent justice-centred perspective of Christian feminist theologies. The picture that has been outlined here is partial and interpreted, but what has been stressed is that more than ever, the theory, practice and theological workings of Christian informed feminist theological discourse must be subject to detailed scrutiny. The appearance of diversity, based on experience, is profoundly challenging to the notion of Christian feminist identity. And within such a diverse landscape the question of the identity of Christian feminist theologies is difficult but illuminating. Critical study of these theologies is necessarily accompanied by informed, explicit reservations. It not only must acknowledge the situated and contextual experiences of women both of oppression and of visions of justice, but also actually place these contexts at the heart of critical evaluation.

The fact that it is increasingly difficult to pin down dominant feminist theological voices bears witness to the diverse level of activity that is actually taking place in feminist informed theologies. Feminist informed Christian theological activity is evident in many Christian countries, communities and regions, as well as across the world religions. A brief snapshot here demonstrates something of the range of perspectives, concerns and approaches involved. European theologians such as Catharina Halkes, Kari Børresen, Ina Praetorius and Elisabeth Gössman are contributing towards an ever-developing picture of feminist informed activity in Europe. Latin American feminist informed theologies now incorporate a great diversity of perspectives, contexts and outlooks, which María Pilar Aquino has described as including indigenous theology, black feminist theology, holistic, and ecofeminist theology (Aquino in Russell and Shannon, 1996:116). As noted earlier, womanist theologies have developed with huge impact among African-American women in North America and influential theologians writing in this field include Katie Cannon, Emile Townes and Jacquelyn Grant. African feminist informed and womanist theologies are equally important within the global picture of feminisms and Christian theology and key theologians here include Mercy Oduyoye who stresses the challengingly prophetic aspect of feminist informed African Christian theology and Musimbi Kanyoro who is exploring and developing a feminist cultural hermeneutics. Lisa Meo describes feminist informed theologies in the Pacific region as addressing the multi-religious contexts of people's lives with a strong liberation theological concern, which, ' ... takes the message of Jesus to heart and applies it, through advocacy and empowerment, to rid women of all forms of oppression' (Meo in Russell and Shannon, 1996:110). The mujerista theology of Latina women based in North America is developing with a strong liberation theological base, and praxis-driven concerns and questions about nationalism, globalization and displacement are concerning scholars such as Ada María Isasi-Díaz. From Asian contexts a great diversity of voices, including those of Kwok Pui-lan, Hyun Kyung Chung, Virginia Fabella, Sun Ai Park and Rita Nakashima Brock, is challenging both traditional and feminist informed Christian theologies.

The level of feminist informed activity in religious contexts other than Christianity is also significant. A very important debate that has always been present since the 1970s about recognizing the importance of the diversity of religious contexts in which issues of gender and religion are being considered is still challenging feminist informed Christian theologies to examine their presuppositions and exclusionary practices and to recognize the full range of feminist informed activity in religions. Rita Gross has argued very strongly that feminist theology as it has widely been understood does not fully recognize the religious pluralism of the world in which it lives and argues that it is not paying heed to the true diversity of the world:

> One of the great discoveries of the past century and a half has been that of religious pluralism and of the fact that non-Christian religions cannot simply be labeled 'errors' but are just as sophisticated and cogent as Christianity. No reputable theology that ignores religious diversity and continues the tradition of Christian hegemony is possible in this religiously diverse world. Yet as the world becomes more aware of and sensitive to diversity of all kinds, the feminist theology movement, like much mainstream (or malestream, as some feminists would say) theological writing and education, is oblivious to the reality of religious diversity and acts as if all theology were Christian theology.
>
> (Gross, 2000:73)

She calls on those working in the area to challenge such limitations, and argues that true diversity will only be achieved when feminists from Muslim, pagan, Buddhist, Hindu, Jewish, Confucian, Taoist and indigenous perspectives are genuinely included in discussions and seen as authentic partners by Christian feminists.

Contextual descriptions which themselves only a few years ago were seen to constitute diversification and to be challenging mainstream Christian theology seem themselves to be becoming constraining categories which are beginning to break down because of contextual needs and diversity. So, just as the term 'feminist theology' has been challenged as an adequate way of describing all feminist informed Christian theology so terms such as 'mujerista', 'womanist', 'Asian' and 'Asian American' are also beginning to be disputed. Kwok Pui-lan, Seung Ai Yang and Rita Nakashima Brock in a 2005 statement about Pacific Asian North American Asian Women in Theology and Ministry (PANAAWTM) theology write:

> We recognize that both the terms 'Asian' and 'Asian American' are social and cultural constructs, arising out of particular historical stages of our political struggles. These terms have been useful for creating group identity and rallying support for political mobilization and for creating a space for our theological pursuits. They should not, however, be essentialized or homogenized so as to hinder critical reflections on diversity within our communities.
>
> (Quoted by Rita Nakashima Brock in Ruether, 2007:46)

Christian feminist theologies are diverse in terms of context, radicalism and political and social setting, and from the emergence of clear patterns of Christian feminist theological engagement it is apparent that issues of subjectivity and exclusion are key concerns. Dialogues between Jewish feminists and Christian feminists, for example, have highlighted these problems, as have dialogues between 'post-traditional' feminists and feminists working out of traditional religious contexts. Similarly, gaps in understanding and communication exist as black women, Asian women, women from developing countries, lesbian and bisexual women and other marginalized or excluded groups of women are articulating visions of justice and methodologies that are challenging some of the mainline Christian feminist voices. Stress here has to be with the contextual nature of feminisms and feminist theologies as the whole feminist informed enterprise is increasingly subject to intense critique with the deconstruction of universal notions of 'feminism', 'women', 'women's experience' and 'liberation'. Given this it is appropriate not only to speak of feminist theologies in the plural but also to move beyond the clear cut and limiting identification of particular theologies as feminist. It actually seems more helpful now to speak of 'feminist informed theologies' rather than 'feminist theologies'. This recognizes that theologies may well be informed by particular feminist insights and methodologies, or influenced in part by feminisms alongside other critical perspectives, whilst at the same time be critical of other aspects of feminisms and even reject the validity of such feminisms.

Consideration of whether feminisms exist as ongoing powerful religious and political forces in the early twenty-first century needs to give recognition to the increasing reflexivity and critical questioning of feminisms and feminist informed theologies. The state and place of feminisms in the world is, perhaps as always, uncertain. Feminisms are subject to extensive and often very negative questioning about their suitability and effectiveness in understanding and challenging gender-based difference and inequity. The history of feminisms and feminist informed theologies details a history of fierce expectation followed by limited effectiveness, and often great disappointment.

Some of the voices of discontent and dissatisfaction to be heard in recent years have argued that the initial visions of feminisms and feminist theologies seem not to have been realized in any substantial way. Such critical questioning of the effectiveness and validity of feminisms and feminist informed theologies as tools for addressing and overcoming injustice is by no means a new thing. However, this questioning has intensified to the extent that there is talk now of a discernible crisis facing feminisms and feminist informed theologies. The charges against feminisms and feminist informed theologies relate not only to ineffectiveness but relate also to the claim that they have themselves been the cause of further injustices because of their failure to recognize the true contextuality of oppression and the need for genuinely grounded contextual feminist informed theologies.

Such concerns and criticisms are seen for example in the discourses of women of colour, women of varied and fluid sexualities, and women working out of colonial and post-colonial contexts; some of who from the beginnings of the explicit second-wave feminist presence in the 1960s have argued that feminism is largely a movement and discourse of limited validity. Criticisms have been made of the location, representation and translation of women's experiences, and increasingly, experience has been shown to be an intrinsically unstable (but also potentially radically subversive and renewing) aspect of feminisms and so of feminist informed theologies. Some critics argue that the same patterns of exclusion and marginalization that have been identified in traditional theology have tainted the liberationist project of feminist informed theologies.

Feminist informed theologies in their diversity do recognize in principle that the human context is determinate of theological perspective and criteria, and that this context cannot be separated from theological perspective. The British theologian Kate Coleman demonstrates such a concern with the importance of recognizing the specificity of women's experiences in her explorations of the emergence of British womanist theology, reflecting that just as white feminisms cannot claim to represent all women so black African-American womanist theology cannot claim to speak for British women:

> As Black British women we cannot simply depend upon our insights of our African-American cousins. Our voices must also be heard if we are to achieve liberation. Thus we require that we dispense with an essentialized concept of Black womanhood and with the idea of monolithic Black identity and instead recognize that there are many and varied models of Black womanhood
>
> (Coleman, 1998:68)

Perhaps one reason why the diversity of women's experiences, the diversity of feminisms and so the diversity of feminist informed theologies have been so difficult to face up to is the realization that in recognizing both the particular and the diverse nature of the human context a challenge is in effect made to the self-identity and internal coherence of feminist discourse, in that if it is accepted that different women have different contexts, different experiences of injustice and so different justice needs, then feminisms, as tools of such justice, will by definition need to be diverse. The wider the experiences of women, the more fluid and potentially incoherent feminisms become and the more diverse and particular feminist informed contextual theologies will be. But whatever the reason behind this reluctance, recognition of the specific and particular nature of experience must be key in addressing these exclusions.

There is very little agreement about the state of play of feminisms and feminist informed theologies, especially in terms of the successes, failures and continuing relevance of feminisms. For some, feminisms have achieved what they set out to; others, however, argue that the goals of feminisms are far from being achieved, and others still talk of a backlash against feminisms, an antifeminist push that challenges and rejects the aims and methods of feminisms. Susan Faludi's *Backlash: The Undeclared War Against Women* set out clearly in 1991 what was being interpreted as a new antifeminist assault on women. Emilie Townes argues that feminist informed theologies need to recognize the extent and manifestations of the backlashes that women face, and that for black women it takes on particular forms: 'The backlash has within it a hierarchy based on race, class, and sexual orientation that has yet to be considered fully' (Townes, E.M. in Harrison *et al.*, 1994:102). Some interpret this perceived backlash as clear evidence of the continuing injustices that women face. Carter Heyward and Beverly Harrison, for example, claim that:

> Backlash has awakened many women, relieving us of the last vestiges of liberal belief that the struggle for women's liberation is well on the road to victory. Backlash confirms that the situations of women really are as bad as our deepest intuitions lead us to believe. It enables us to value the gains some women have made, some of the rights won – to be doctors, pastors, generals; to own land, homes, businesses; to name ourselves and our children; to choose whom we love, sexually and otherwise; to raise children in partnerships and communities in which new values can be fostered. But backlash also enables us to see that such gains, far from freeing women from violence, also stir men's rage and increase their resistance to what we seek in both the public and private domains of our lives.
>
> (Harrison, B.W. and Heyward, C. in Harrison *et al.*, 1994:94)

Coward offers a different perspective on the concept of backlash as articulated by Faludi, claiming that it 'threw feminism a lifeline just when it might have sunk' (Coward, 1999:10).

As well as questions about the limitations of feminist understandings of women's experiences and their associated exclusions, some of those who have previously articulated a feminist informed position and used the term 'feminist' in description of their approach, are now questioning its continuing validity.

And even asking the question as to whether it was ever really effective. Susan Faludi, Camilla Paglia, Naomi Wolf and Rosalind Coward are all influential voices in the articulation of this dissatisfaction. Rosalind Coward, for example, in *Sacred Cows: Is Feminism Relevant to the New Millennium?* argues that the success of the feminist movement has in effect changed the agenda for women. Whilst she recognizes that gender-based injustices still exist, she claims that the picture is essentially much more complex now than ever before. As a result she argues that 'Over the last few years ... I found it increasingly difficult to say I was a feminist ... I had become disenchanted with the idea of being "a feminist" in such times' (Coward, 1999:4). And yet despite such concerns she notes the reluctance among those employing feminisms to submit it to what she calls 'an audit' (Coward, 1999:7). She seems to be arguing that feminisms need a different kind of place in the world because of their successes and this leads her to the following claim, that 'Feminism no longer has to be reiterated but simply breathed' (Coward, 1999:7). What she seems to be suggesting here is the need for very different kinds of feminisms. This, however, as Coward acknowledges, will not be easy:

> ... feminism has succeeded beyond the wildest dreams of the brave women who fought its first battles. Its future in the new millennium is to face up to the problems of its success, and to see gender as just one possible reason for social and personal conflicts rather than an all-encompassing cause. But if it is going to be capable of making these changes, it will first have to let go of its sacred cows.
>
> (Coward, 1999:14)

This sense of having to move on to something else was also captured in 1999 in an article published in *Feminist Review* 'Snakes and Ladders: Reviewing Feminisms at Century's End', where the concept of snakes and ladders was offered as a metaphor for the situation facing feminisms. In this article it was argued that there was clearly a need to move beyond identity politics but at the same time there was concern with the implications of such a recognition in terms of how feminisms might go forward and how they might be the continued basis of transformatory engagement (Hall *et al.*, 1999:1).

With such concern over the state and viability of feminisms and feminist informed theologies there has been increasing talk in recent years of 'post-feminism' and the claim that we have moved beyond feminisms, or have somehow outgrown feminisms. There is still a certain lack of clarity about what 'postfeminism' actually means but clearly for some it has come to be seen as the end of feminisms. For others, 'postfeminism' constitutes a significant development in feminisms. Brookes in *Postfeminisms: Feminism, Cultural Theory and Cultural Forms* argues that postfeminisms represent

> ... feminism's 'coming of age', its maturity into a confident body of theory and politics, representing pluralism and difference and reflecting on its

position in relation to other philosophical and political movements similarly demanding change.

(Brookes, 1997:1)

She argues that postfeminism marks the moving of feminist theory into a position that she sees as 'resisting closure of definition' (Brookes, 1997:5). Such a proposal as is made by Brookes here of the place of feminist theory brings in another important issue in the destabilizing and possible reconfiguration of feminisms and feminist informed theologies. This is tied up with issues of constraints about what actually constitutes a feminist or feminist informed approach.

Feminist informed theologies as contextual theologies of liberation

Having recognized the very challenging issues related to the valuing of the diverse contexts of women's lives, and of women's experiences of oppression, questions arise concerning the viability of feminist informed theologies as contextual liberation theologies. Can the recognition of the apparent failure of feminist informed theologies as contextual theologies, as theologies which arise out of particular contexts and which are shaped by and respond to particular contexts, be incorporated and responded to within this group of theologies? Or would the changes which might be needed to genuinely and authentically respond to concerns about the constraints, if not failures, of these theologies take feminist informed theologies beyond themselves?

These are not easy questions either to ask or to answer. But what is clear is that more than ever feminisms and feminist informed theologies are diverse in form, address and context. One of the problems when talking about the failure of feminisms and questioning whether feminisms are any longer relevant is that despite the critical work that has been carried out, in some ways feminisms are still being seen as homogenous, as one thing with one aim, when clearly, for many different people, feminisms have meant many different things. Exclusions seem to be linked to processes of normalization whereby particular feminist informed critiques, visions and theologies become authoritative in and of themselves. And one of the factors that influences such tendencies is the kinds of roles that feminisms are actually given. Feminisms and feminist informed theologies clearly cannot claim to know or understand either injustice or the justice needs of women in any kind of definitive way, and when they do, they tend to exclude and to close themselves down. Problems emerge precisely when feminisms have become normative or prescriptive and become concerned with the articulation of a set vision rather than visionary. Understandings of the sites of injustice and the possibilities of justice need to remain fluid. It seems that a fuller but also consistently open picture is needed and self-reflexive feminisms and accompanying critical questioning of feminisms is entirely appropriate and in fact essential.

Recognition of the problems of feminisms have very definite implications for feminist informed theologies. Given the radically contextual approach to understanding and responding to gender-based injustice which seems to be inherent to these theologies, questions need to be asked about what this really amounts to in terms of the outworkings of such radical contextuality for feminist informed theologies. Is it the end of such theologies? In one sense, yes, because it is the end of feminist theology in its singularity but this could also mean that what we understand as feminist informed theologies as contextual theologies of liberation will be radically and continually broken down. And it is precisely the contextual nature of feminist informed theologies which leads to this renewal. How this process is viewed and evaluated, however, will vary from genuine and authentic theological creativity to unstable decentred Christian theologies.

Through such expansion, in the end, different feminist informed theologies may well bear no clear or coherent relationship to each other. The guiding factor to the engagement and validity of feminisms, feminist and womanist theologies, is contextual needs. Radically contextual theology as a response to injustice might well effectively engage feminisms as a tool of critical disclosure and move towards justice. Explorations in the contemporary viability of feminism as tools of justice seem to raise many questions and offer very few clear pathways for action and analysis. However, the questions that do emerge seem to underpin the very heart of feminist justice projects and the heart of contextual theologies. Perhaps feminisms should be seen as something much less stable and as open to multiple definitions and developments, as a movement towards critical interrogation and analysis, and not as the substantive point of reference. The 1999 publication *Is There a Future for Feminist Theology?* edited by Deborah Sawyer and Diane Collier raised some important issues in relation to the way in which feminist informed theologies in the new millennium might reconstitute themselves. Ursula King in her contribution to the collection *Feminist Theologies in Contemporary Contexts* laid down a comprehensive challenge to those engaged with feminist informed theologies:

> In spite of all that has been achieved there is still a need for feminist theologians to get out of their own isolation – whether institutionally imposed or intellectually adopted – and develop a more fully dialogical approach, not only among themselves in different parts of the world or with women of many different faith traditions, but also through reflecting from their experience of solidarity and sisterhood on some of the burning questions of our time.
>
> (King, in Sawyer and Collier, 1999:111)

At the heart of such an analysis of the continuing relevance of feminisms is the conviction that the fluidity of human contexts, culture and critical understanding means that many forms of feminisms and feminist informed theologies can no longer, if in fact they ever really did, meet the needs of many of those seeking to overcome perceived injustices surrounding issues of gender and sexualities. Also, if feminisms are to have validity or relevance at this point in the twenty-first century as tools of critical disclosure pushing towards justice-seeking practices, then a solid revisioning of feminisms, based in contextual needs and forms, is needed.

Some theologians are questioning the most challenging outworkings of the postmodern critique, whilst accepting some of its insights. For example, Schüssler Fiorenza, in responding to the issues of how feminisms and feminist informed theologies can operate in a postmodern age, challenges the post-modern doubting that authentic 'working across borders' can really happen and claims that it has been happening in feminisms. She calls on feminist informed theologies to engage likewise and despite all of the advancements made in the area in respect of attention to diversity and recognition of the problematization debate is still very critical of some of the workings of feminist informed theologies:

> The slogan 'think globally, act locally' has become a clarion call for feminist grassroots movements and theorists alike in their struggle against neoliberal capitalist globalization. However, feminist theologians and scholars in religion have not paid sufficient attention to this intellectual and political context. In my experience feminist discourses in religion tend to continue to draw exclusive boundaries between theology and religious studies, between the various subdisciplines of theology, between the West and the Rest, between Christians and members of other religions, and between the aca-demic study of religion and feminist movements in religion. Moreover, although feminists in religion have problematized race, gender, class and colonialism, very little attention has been paid to nationalism and its impact on women in religion as well as on the academic study of religion and theology.
>
> (Schüssler Fiorenza, 2002:71–72)

In many ways the kinds of criticisms that feminisms and feminist informed theologies are facing, and the kinds of responses that are being made to these critiques, seem to be pointing towards a different kind of place and use for feminisms in the contemporary world. There is a need to avoid over-simplifying and homogenizing the diverse experiences of women in order to present femin-isms and feminist informed theologies into some kind of unified and coherent system. This is a tendency that has so far often proved irresistible and highly destructive, and in many ways has stifled the promise of feminisms and feminist informed theologies to the extent that some would even contend that it has led to the end of feminisms as potentially liberative discourse or transformative social action.

Feminist informed theologies may function as contextual theologies on some levels but seem to fail to live up to the description of themselves as consciously contextual theologies on another level because of their apparent reluctance to acknowledge diversity and in particular diversities of oppression. They misread and obscure the many layers of experience that contribute towards being human and obscure the different often interrelated and interlocking forms of injustice. As such, their claims to contextuality become obscured and challenged by the outworkings of these theologies on a day-to-day basis. The outworkings of Christian theological contextuality, as seen in feminist informed theologies, are clearly problematic. In the next chapter the extent of this problem and its inherency to the very notion of contextual liberation theology will be developed in relation to a range of liberation theologies. The very contextuality which lies at the heart of these theologies brings both limitations and radical possibilities. And within this contradiction lie both the potential downfall and vitalizing base of contextual theologies.

4   Further contexts of liberation

This chapter will further explore the theological outworkings of contextuality in Christian theology by focusing on the ways in which context informs theology in a number of other liberation theologies. Through the detailed exploration of feminist informed theologies and Latin American liberation theologies in Chapters 2 and 3 an attempt was made to outline the relationships between contexts of gender and socioeconomic class, human experiences of oppression and Christian theology in contextual liberation theologies. The theologies examined in this chapter will not be examined to the same depth as those in Chapters 2 and 3 but the principle of contextuality within contextual liberation theologies will be further explored and the limitations of contextuality will be further probed by reference to a wider range of liberation theologies. Different liberation theologies will be examined for the ways in which context informs Christian theology within an identifiable group of theologies and also for some of the problems that such apparently explicit contextuality brings.

The multiplicity of liberation theologies

By the 1970s liberation theologies in various forms and guises were claiming a presence in Christian theological communities and academic settings around the world. Many readings of the Chronological development of liberation theologies place Latin American liberation theologies at the beginning of this movement followed closely by black theology in North America, feminist informed theologies in North America and Europe, followed then by the development in many different geographical and cultural locations of Christian theologies which articulate specifically contexts such as gender, colonialism, the human body, sexualities, race and ethnicity, and ecology, as the underlying shaping and motivational factor. It is the combination of the geographical or cultural location of theology with the primary oppression being addressed which gives many subgroups of liberation theologies their identities as contextual liberation theologies. So, for example, theologies such as Korean Minjung theologies, Latin American mujerista theologies, Indian Dalit theologies, Asian liberation theologies, African liberation theologies, and Palestinian liberation theologies, all give explicit theological address to grounded experiences of human oppression within particular cultural or geographical locations. Other liberation theologies place less emphasis on cultural or geographical location, but these tend to be theologies which do not articulate the geographical or cultural contexts from which they arise as problematic.

Liberation theologies have developed out of diverse human experiences of oppression, out of theological analyses of the roots and perpetuation of such oppression and out of justice-seeking responses to such oppression. The precise chronology of the development of these individual theologies and of the development of different liberation theologies in relation to each other cannot be explored here in any depth, especially as this history is contested. Instead, focus is on the ways in which different liberation theologies are informed by different contexts, and especially different contexts of oppression. From the 1970s what we have in terms of self-defined liberation theologies are a range of theologies which in different ways embraced the notion of context, human experience and liberation. As we have seen in relation to feminist informed theologies and Latin American liberation theologies the contextual base of theologies can never simply be seen monolithically. But at the same time an understanding of the primary context or oppression which is articulated as the motivational force behind specific liberation theologies is clearly very important for understanding the outworking of contextuality.

Black theologies

The group of liberation theologies known as 'black theologies' have their roots in the experiences of African-American Christians in the 1960s. These theologies are concerned fundamentally with racism and they affirm black history, culture and identity. Just as not all theology done by Christian women is feminist theology, not all theology done by black Christians is black theology. In the late 1960s in North America the black theologian, James Cone, wrote *Black Theology and Black Power*. Published in 1969 this text established itself very quickly as a groundbreaking text for both black theologies and liberation theologies as a whole. James Cone from his own experiences of theological education and through his involvement with Christian churches was concerned with the absence of African-American experience and with the racism that was endemic to American culture and society. The background against which Cone wrote in North America in the 1960s was one which had witnessed the rise of the Civil Rights Movement and the rise of the Black Power Movement. Cone argued that the black churches in North America were essentially docile or passive in the face of the race-based oppression faced by African-Americans. He argued that the theologies of the black churches have not concerned themselves with social justice as such. Rather, they have retreated into and located themselves in the inner, spiritual world of the Church. Hope is not with any kind of social transformation or change here and now, but rather, with the next world. As such, Cone argued that Christian theologies, even the Christian theologies of the black churches, were not addressing the issues and concerns of African-American

Christians, because essentially these theologies were the theologies of white Christians, with their own contextual concerns. African-American experiences were not reflected in these theologies. In the light of this, Cone raised concerns about theological education. Reflecting on his own experiences of theological education in North America, Cone argued that theological education focused mainly on white, European theologians. Such education failed to recognize the role of the white Christian churches and theologies in racism, and indeed slavery. Cone was very clear about the importance of self-consciously black contextual theologies which arise out of the experiences of African-Americans and which address some very pressing theological questions. Looking back over histories of race-based violence and oppression, including the enslavement of an estimated 15 to 20 million Africans, Cone criticizes the behaviour of white Christians towards black people in the name of religion, and specifically, in the name of Christ.

One of the most controversial aspects of black theology in North America, especially in its earliest developments, was its political associations. Just as Latin American liberation theology drew on radical social and political theory, that of Marxism, so African-American black theology drew on the social and political theories of the Black Power Movement in North America. In the late 1960s in North America the Civil Rights Movement and the Black Power Movement offered frameworks for analysing and responding to the race-based oppression that African-Americans faced. The Black Power Movement criticized the policy of integration as a far too conservative approach in the face of the extensive and endemic racism in North America. Integration only allowed for the extension of rights within an essentially white system. Something more radical was needed to go beyond simply allowing black people to integrate into a majority white system. Theologically, those involved with the Black Power Movement argued that the black churches offered no effective resources for challenging and overcoming race-based oppression. The black churches were seen not only as ineffective in this struggle but almost as an obstacle, because they channelled black energy and leadership. Cone countered criticisms of Black Power:

> I know that some religionists would consider Black Power as the Work of the Antichrist. Others would suggest that such a concept should be tolerated as an expression of Christian love to the misguided black brother. It is my thesis, however, that Black Power, even in its most radical expression, is not the antithesis of Christianity, nor is it a heretical idea to be tolerated with painful forbearance. It is, rather, Christ's central message to twentieth-century America. And unless the empirical denominational church makes a determined effort to recapture the man Jesus through a total identification with the suffering poor as expressed in Black Power, that Church will become exactly what Christ is not.
>
> (Cone, 1969:1–2)

For Cone, Black Power signifies Christ's presence in North America in the C20th. Like other liberation theologians, then, Cone not only stresses the importance of context in theology, but in particular contexts of oppression. Christ is always to be found on the side of the oppressed and for Cone, African-Americans were the oppressed people of North America in the 1960s. Black theology, as it was proposed by Cone in *Black Theology and Black Power*, was so much more than theology done by black people. Black theology is justice-seeking contextual theology from the context of race-based oppression. It has a particular social justice concern which is experiential in nature in that it arises out of the experiences of a particular group of people, and particularly out of the experiences of race-based oppression. Cone's black theology then had a specific socio-political stance which was informed by the Black Power Movement and Marxism.

In *Black Theology and Black Power* and later in texts such as *A Black Theology of Liberation* (1970), *God of the Oppressed* (1975) and *For My People: Black Theology and the Black Church* (1984) Cone developed a contextual liberation theology from the specific context of African-American race-based experience of oppression which criticized white Western theologies for failing to recognize their universalizing tendencies and for supporting and legitimizing race-based oppression. Cone's liberation theology contextualized the Christian gospel message and articulated a Christology in which Jesus identified with the poor and oppressed:

> The black theologian must reject any conception of God which stifles black self-determination by picturing God as a God of all peoples. Either God is identified with the oppressed to the point that their experience becomes God's experience, or God is a God of racism ... The blackness of God means that God has made the oppressed condition God's own condition. This is the essence of the Biblical revelation. By electing Israelite slaves as the people of God and by becoming the Oppressed One in Jesus Christ, the human race is made to understand that God is known where human beings experience humiliation and suffering ... Liberation is not an afterthought, but the very essence of divine activity.
>
> (Cone, 1970:63–64)

The challenge faced is immense: 'Being black in America has little to do with skin color. Being black means that your heart, your soul, your mind, and your body are where the dispossessed are' (Cone, 1969:151). In Cone's understanding black theology can go beyond its immediate contextual concerns and extend its vision of justice to people other than African-American people. The God of Cone's black theology is a God concerned with liberation from oppression. As a God of liberation the Christian God identifies with oppressed peoples, and in Cone's context, the oppressed people of North America were African-Americans. Cone's black liberationist theological analysis included the articulation of a Christology that for many has proved to be one of the most controversial aspects of black theologies. In his theology Cone spoke about Christ as black.

> ... the validity of any christological title in any period of history is not decided by its universality but by this: whether in the particularity of its time it points to God's universal will to liberate particular oppressed people from inhumanity. This is exactly what blackness does in the contemporary social existence of America. If we Americans, black and white, are to understand who Jesus is for us today, we must view his presence as continuous with his past and future coming which is best seen through his present blackness.
>
> (Cone, 1977:135–36)

Cone recognizes the contextual nature of his black liberation theology with its full contextual christological implications and the kinds of criticisms that this might bring. In particular, he recognizes the potential problems that his contextual christology might bring to those concerned to stress a universal Christian message. Here, Cone seems to recognize the ambiguous nature of contextuality in liberation theology, where the specific, grounded nature of theology is stressed but within a meta-framework which stresses the fundamental core of the Christian gospel as social justice orientated. Particularity in theology is crucial for Cone because all theology is particular whether it is recognized or not:

> But I contend that there is no universalism that is not particular ... My point is that God came, and continues to come, to those who are poor and helpless, for the purpose of setting them free. And since the people of color are his elected poor in America, any interpretation of God that ignores black oppression cannot be Christian theology. The 'blackness of Christ,' therefore, is not simply a statement about skin color, but rather, the transcendent affirmation that God has not ever, no not ever, left the oppressed alone in struggle. He was with them in Pharaoh's Egypt, is with them in America, Africa and Latin America, and will come in the end of time to consummate fully their human freedom.
>
> (Cone, 1977:137)

Cone's black theology sees theology in explicit and thoroughly contextual terms as a black liberation theology but the task and concern of Christian theology overall is not really seen in this way. In that, Cone, like other liberation theologians, sees Christianity at its core as having a fundamental concern with challenging and overcoming oppression. Cone, again like other liberation theologians, argues that the traditions of Christianity, and especially the biblical tradition, demonstrate the core justice concerns of Christianity. However, whilst black theology from its earliest developments demonstrated an explicit awareness of the contextuality of theology and of the grounded, contextual nature of black theology, nevertheless, according to the criticisms of womanist theologians it failed to recognize the full implications and outworkings of this contextuality and the related issue of the multidimensional nature of oppression.

Since Cone's early theology, black theologies have emerged from a wide range of contexts as contextual liberation theologies. The origins of black theologies may well lie initially in the theological responses of African-American Christians to race-based oppression but today black theologies are liberation theologies, often of the African diaspora, in considerable diversity. In Britain, theologians like Emmanuel Lartey, Robert Beckford and Anthony Reddie have contributed towards the emergence of a growing field of black theologies from an explicitly British context. In 1998 with the publication of *Jesus is Dread: Black Theology and Black Culture in Britain* Robert Beckford as a black Pentecostal Christian articulated a black contextual theology which placed the history, identity and culture of black British Christians at the centre of theology. Beckford argued that British black theology faces a number of challenges to which it must respond. Key among the challenges to be faced is social liberation. The black churches in Britain were more concerned with social welfare than social justice. Beckford argued that black theology must take black culture, and especially black popular culture or 'Black expressive cultures' (Beckford, 1998:3), very seriously. Black popular culture is a rich and contextually appropriate theological resource for black British theology because it is 'a means of expressing the concerns of black existence' (Beckford, 1998: 15). Beckford in his theological explorations proposes the notion that 'Jesus is dread' which for him is a culturally appropriate Christology for black Christians in Britain:

> ... Jesus is Dread for Black people in Britain today. Dread symbolises freedom, power and upliftment. Therefore, the Dread Christ is one who sides with all oppressed people in their struggle against all that denies them full humanity.
>
> (Beckford, 1998: 73)

One very significant contextual diversification that has brought important challenges and possibilities for black theologies are womanist theologies. Womanist theologies argue that black theologies fail to recognize the diversity within race-based oppression. Specifically, they argue that black theologies on the whole universalize black experience in so far as they reflect and draw upon the dominant male black voice and exclude the voices of women. Womanist theologians argue that all too often black theologies repeat the patriarchal bias of traditional white theologies and feminist theologies repeat the racist bias of traditional white theologies. A more thoroughly contextual theology is necessary for black women:

> Black women must do theology out of their tri-dimensional experience of racism/sexism/classism. To ignore any aspect of this experience is to deny the holistic and integrated reality of Black womanhood. When Black women say that God is on the side of the oppressed, we mean that God is in solidarity with the struggles of those on the under side of humanity.
>
> (Grant, 1989:209)

Black theologians such as Cone are responding to the criticisms of womanist theologians and including the category of gender within the matrix of oppressions that black people are subjected to. The extent to which the voices of womanist theologians will be genuinely heard by the diversity of black theologies of course remains to be seen. But male black theologians such as Beckford do give explicit recognition to the importance of recognizing diversity for black theologies and the significance of the critical questioning of womanist theologians for black theologies:

> ... womanist theology encourages a healthy suspicion towards all movements, organisations and programmes within the Black community. Womanist perspectives encourage us to ask whose needs are being met and also whose agenda is being played out.
>
> (Beckford, 1998:165)

The British political theologian, Alister Kee, in his 2006 publication *The Rise and Demise of Black Theology*, is highly critical of black theologies. Some of his criticisms relate to the scope of reference and relevance of black theologies and he is particularly critical of the claims black theologies make to contextuality. He argues that black theologies demonstrate a distinctive lack of self-criticism in respect of the specific contextual concerns that they have. For Kee black theologies fall into the category of self-described contextual theologies which fail to change or adapt as contexts change.

> Many theologies describe themselves as contextual: they arise within a certain socio-cultural context and respond to it. But frequently they are not contextual enough. Contexts change, but the theologies continue, repeating their original forms. So it is with Black theology. Its dominant form emerged in the 1960s and 1970s, an important movement which displayed courage and creativity. By the 1990s the context had entirely changed, but this contextual theology did not reposition itself. Far from exhibiting a new flourishing of creativity, commitment and imagination, it has been content to repeat the mantras of a previous period.
>
> (Kee, 2006:vii)

He is arguing that black theologies are tied to dated concerns and appeal to core concepts or 'mantras' that are no longer relevant to the context for which black theologies are still being used. He argues that North American black theologies drew closely on the biblical account of the Exodus in which God liberated the Hebrew slaves. The Exodus liberation is a very strong theme in black theologies as they seek an analogy for the enslavement and hoped for emancipation of black people everywhere. Kee rejects the validity of this analogy, arguing that the principle of contextuality must also be applied to the Bible: 'This contextual theology has not noticed that the Bible is also contextual. God does not liberate slaves. The Chosen people happened to be slaves, but God did not oppose slavery as such' (Kee, 2006:vii). For Kee, then, the

Christian God is not a liberating God per se and he points to the Bible, and Exodus 21 in particular, which outlines laws for the treatment of slaves (Kee, 2006:vii). Kee stresses that his concerns are a call to relevance for black theologies. Black theologies must genuinely become the contextual theologies of poor black people that they claim to be (Kee, 2006:ix). Such genuine contextuality, according to Kee, will involve a detailed analysis of the causes of oppression that black people face today and this will include the impact of American capitalism and civil wars in Africa rather than the traditional European colonialism (Kee, 2006:ix). Kee goes on to argue that the diversification which now characterizes black theologies has led to a distinct lack of a race-based critique. More than this he argues that black theologies have essentialized 'blackness' and that theologians such as James Cone constantly reaffirm outdated and irrelevant interpretations of black experience:

> ... Cone has reaffirmed that ontological blackness which stops the clock in the 1970s. It essentialises black experience according to the liberation discourse of modernity. He is not the first contextual theologian who fails to acknowledge when the context changes.
>
> (Kee, 2006:196)

Black theologies as contextual theologies face the same kinds of challenges as other liberation theologies in terms of the limitations of their understanding of the specific oppression they theologize out of and in relation to.

Body theologies, sexual theologies and queer theologies

Body theologies are liberation theologies which are characterized by a fundamental concern with the human body as the context or the site for experiencing the world. These theologies stress the contextual nature of all theologies and argue that each theologian is influenced by the personal and social factors influencing her or his life and that who we are as human beings is tied up fundamentally with the human body. Yet body theologies argue that for many the human body is seen as problematic as the site of human experiences, and especially as the site for experiencing God. In theological terms the body is often seen as taboo or problematic or as simply irrelevant to Christian theology. Body theologians argue that Christian theology and the Christian tradition consistently deny the human body, and especially human sexualities. Christianity, it is argued, incorporates a strong body-denying tendency and this is demonstrated by the traditions of dualism which enforce a hierarchical organization on the world which consistently places the bodily and the material in opposition to the spiritual. Dualism is seen as fundamentally destructive, an insight shared by many liberation theologians:

> Dualism, for all the different ways it is structured and all the different names it is given, means splitting the wholeness of God's creation into divisions labelled 'good' and 'bad'.
>
> (Maitland, 1983:19)

In response to such perceived negativities about the human body, body theologians are concerning themselves with a positive recovery and celebration of the human body. Body theologies take a methodological and theological stance in which the human body rather than being problematic or coincidental to human experience, especially in soteriological terms, is fundamental to this experience, and as such is to be celebrated rather than denied.

James Nelson is a North American theologian whose work in the area of Christian ethics, sexuality and spirituality led to the publication of a number of key texts in the area of body theology. These include *Embodiment: An Approach to Sexuality and Christian Theology* (1978), *The Intimate Connection: Male Sexuality, Masculine Spirituality* (1988) and *Body Theology* (1992). Nelson argues that Christianity is characterized by incarnation. For him incarnation stands at the centre of Christian practice and theology and it is apparent in and experienced in the bodiliness of every human being. He argues that human life is about relationship, about connecting with others. But when we focus on what has traditionally been seen as the spiritual we tend to move away from connecting with others and communicating with others. We move away from connection and into fragmentation. For Nelson, body theologies are a way of doing theology which take the body seriously and place great significance with it:

> Body theology is not primarily a theological description of the body. Nor is it principally an ethical prescription for how we ought to express ourselves physically. Rather, and most simply put, it is doing theology in such a way that we take our body experiences seriously as occasions of revelation.
>
> An incarnational faith boldly proclaims that Christ is alive. In other words, God continues to become embodied in our common flesh in saving, healing, liberating, justice-making ways.
>
> (Nelson, 1992:9–10)

Nelson's theology is important for the place that he gives within it to sexuality. As perhaps an obvious part of its concern body theology argues that sexuality is a fundamental and core part of human experience and of human existence. Sexuality is not inherently problematic in body theology. It is something to be celebrated as fundamental to who we are as persons.

In *Body Theology* Nelson outlines 'seven deadly sins' as seven ways in which the Christian and Jewish traditions with their negative portrayal of the human body, and especially sexuality, have influenced what Nelson termed 'our sexual alienation' (Nelson, 1992:30). Having outlined these 'seven deadly sins', Nelson proposes seven 'virtues' from within the Jewish and Christian traditions which counter these sins. What Nelson is doing then is highlighting what he sees essentially as distortions of Christianity and from within the tradition challenging these as unfaithful developments or representations. These seven sins and seven virtues summarize well some of the key concerns of body theologies. The first sin that Nelson highlights is 'spiritualistic dualism' (Nelson, 1992:30) and this is named first because it underpins the other sins he names. Spiritualistic dualism, argues Nelson, has its roots in Hellenistic and Jewish cultures and is a dualistic and hierarchical way of viewing life. It introduces a split into what should be a unity by placing the spirit or spiritual in antagonism with the temporal (Nelson, 1992:30). In this way, then, all that is material and of the body is deemed to be corrupt and sexuality is cited as particularly problematic: 'The sexual aspects of the body are the particular locus of sin' (Nelson, 1992:30). Nelson counters the sin of spiritualistic dualism in Judaism with the virtue of the belief in the 'unity and goodness of creation and with it an anthropology that proclaims the unity and goodness of the human bodyself' (Nelson, 1992:30). In the Christian tradition, by way of virtue, Nelson points to the belief in creation as good and also to the incarnation of God in Christ. For Nelson both the Jewish and the Christian traditions can be used as resources to challenge the suspicion and hostility to the human body and sexuality:

> ... the authentic core of both religious traditions affirm the unity of spirit and body, mind and matter, spirituality and sexuality. The creation-affirming Jewish faith and the incarnational Christian faith attest to the goodness of the bodyself with all its rich sexuality as part of God's invitation into our full humanness and loving communion.
>
> (Nelson, 1992:31)

The second sin named by Nelson is 'patriarchal dualism' which, according to Nelson, introduces a systematic and hierarchical split between men and women (Nelson, 1992:31). Women are deemed to be inferior and associated with the body, and men are deemed to be superior of the mind or spirit. Nelson acknowledges the depth to which the cultures and even scriptures of Judaism and Christianity are affected by patriarchal dualism but despite this argues that it can still be countered by the fundamental belief in human equality which he believes is evident in both traditions. He points to Galatians 3:28 with its affirmation of human equality, arguing that gender-based equality is the authentic Jewish and Christian heritage whilst sexism is 'religious perversion' (Nelson, 1992:32).

The third sin outlined by Nelson in *Body Theology* is 'heterosexism and homophobia' (Nelson, 1992:33). These have deeply affected the Jewish and Christian traditions with what Nelson sees as misogynistic-based interpretations of same-sex sexuality which arise from a fear of sexuality itself. Nelson argues that these deeply pervasive destructive tendencies can be challenged by the Jewish and Christian affirmations of every person in their uniqueness (Nelson, 1992:33). This leads to the fourth sin named by Nelson: 'guilt over self-love' (Nelson, 1992:34). Nelson argues that this is more a feature of the Christian than Jewish tradition but that self-denial is found in both traditions. He argues that the acceptance of the self is neither narcissistic nor selfish; rather it is the appropriate response to the scriptural instruction to 'love our neighbors as ourselves, not *instead* of ourselves' (Nelson, 1992:34). Nelson's fifth sin is 'legalistic sexual ethics' (Nelson, 1992:35) and he argues that in the area of sexuality both Judaism and Christianity have been prescriptive and legalistic regardless of context and particular situation. Nelson counters this prescriptive legalism with the virtue of love:

> Our bodyselves are intended to express the language of love. Our sexuality is God's way of calling us into communion with others through our need to reach out, to touch, to embrace – emotionally, intellectually, and physically. Since we have been created with the desire for communion, the positive moral claim upon us is that we become in fact what essentially we are: lovers, in the richest and deepest sense of that good word.
>
> (Nelson, 1992:36)

The sixth deadly sin which Nelson argues affects the traditions of Judaism and Christianity is 'sexless spirituality' (Nelson, 1992:37). Sexless spirituality has its roots, claims Nelson, in Neoplatonic divisions between the mind and body. Spirituality is divorced from the physical and centuries of body-denying tendencies promote a sexless spirituality. Nelson challenges this with the insights of incarnational theologies which are celebrating the sacramental possibilities of the human body (Nelson, 1992:38). Finally, Nelson argues that the sin of 'privatized sexuality' has confined sexuality to the intensely private realm (Nelson, 1992:38). One implication of this is that human sexuality as a result has not been subject to the same kind of tests of justice that other realms of human existence have. For Nelson there are sexual dimensions to social justice. Overall, Nelson's seven deadly sins and seven virtuous possibilities see both the limitations and possibilities of the Jewish and Christian traditions in relation to the human body, and especially sexuality:

> While Christianity and Judaism have often confounded good sexuality education and social policies, they have done so through the perversions and distortions of their own central teachings. What is more authentic to the core of both faiths can become the renewed wellspring for sexual health, sexual responsibility, and sexual justice, and for more adequate body theologies.
>
> (Nelson, 1992:40)

Body theologies stress that spirituality and religion are not inherently and fundamentally distinct from the body and human sexuality. Body theologies reject hierarchical dualisms which introduce splits between these and argue that many religious traditions do in fact celebrate human sexualities. In relation to the Christian tradition body theologies, as articulated by their proponents, are not seen to be breaking in any radical way from the tradition or to be moving away from the perceived theological roots of the tradition. As seen by Nelson's body theology they are seen as entirely consistent with the Christian story. Whilst traditions of interpretations may give a body-denying history within Christianity body theologies give a particular emphasis on celebrating the incarnational nature of Christianity. The British theologians Lisa Isherwood and Elizabeth Stuart in *Introducing Body Theology* (1998) argue that embodiment stands at the very centre of Christianity. They point out, for example, that Mary's body is both the site of revelation and of redemptive action through mothering Jesus. Jesus' own mission was one in which physical touch had a very important part. He healed through touch and it is through the body of Christ that we are saved:

> Christian Scriptures naturally have embodiment at their heart. From the moment when Mary agrees to give birth to a special child, bodies become sites of revelation and redemptive action. Jesus' mission is begun with touch, by water and by a dove. People are touched and healed, they are forgiven and healed. The dead are raised and a woman shows her love through anointing and massaging Jesus' feet. The life of Jesus as told by the evangelists is a very physical one; he was not a philosopher simply engaging the minds of people on his wanderings through the land. Here was a man who held people, threw things in anger, cursed things making them wither and cherished people back to life. Here was an incarnate/ embodied being.
>
> (Isherwood and Stuart, 1998:11)

Philip Sheldrake offers another perspective on the body, sexuality and the sacred in *Befriending Our Desires* (1994). He argues for the need to see desire as part of the spiritual journey: 'Only by attending to our desires are we able to encounter our deepest self – the image of God within us' (Sheldrake, 1994: ix). For Sheldrake, desire and sexuality are linked and this inevitably means that spirituality and sexuality are linked. Desires reflect our very deepest feelings and constitute in essence a reaching out to others. The problems often associated with desires are because of their grounded nature. They are to do with our senses. Sheldrake differentiates between desires by talking about authentic desires which originate from our deepest sense of ourselves. He argues that as people of desire we recognize through desire that we are incomplete. We are constantly open to change and desire may be taken as a metaphor for transformation. The Christian God is a god of passion but the Christian tradition has introduced a radical separation between eros love and agape love. The unity between these two needs to be restored so that we can in effect re-sacralize the erotic (Sheldrake, 1994:28). If we are able to locate eros in God then the divine might be known in human sexual experience. A distinction is drawn here between locating God in all that is erotic and the claim that genuine and loving eroticism is always an experience of God: 'God is erotic power properly understood and is the erotic power between people' (Sheldrake, 1994:29).

Sheldrake argues that as desire involves the recognition of an absence in us, of something lacking, it becomes a dynamic drive towards fulfilment. It strives to address this absence. However, for this to happen we need a genuine sense of ourselves, and we need to be open to growth. Sheldrake points out that the

Christian mystical tradition has often used the language of eroticism and of sexual love. However, he also notes that very often there is implied a transformation of sexual love into spirituality. Sexuality has been seen in opposition to spirituality and as evidence of a fallen humanity. The spiritual is all too often divorced from the sexual. Sheldrake argues that desires and the call to intimacy call on us to take risks. As we genuinely become aware of sexual desire so we come to know more about our existence on different levels. Sexual union if genuinely a gift of the self and receiving of the gift of another has a sacramental quality. It is Eucharistic, a liturgy for restoration to spiritual centredness.

Christian body theologies although by no means as extensively developed and diverse as other liberation theologies do offer some very important insights and challenges about the nature of contextuality. The reading of the human body within body theologies is largely positive, but this does not mean that the ambiguities of the body as perhaps the most fundamental context for experiencing the world are not recognized. Melanie May in *A Body Knows: A Theopoetics of Death and Resurrection* (1995) argues that whilst the body is not wholly positive, it is, nevertheless, an essential part of human experience. In introducing her own theology of the body as the context of her experiences and as the context for her own theological engagement she notes that she has 'experienced my body more as betrayer than as friend' (May, 1995:15). Whilst the human body may well be a site of pleasurable erotic experiences body theologies are also recognizing that it may equally be the site of damaging and exploitative relations and experiences. In theologies of disabilities theological understandings and constructions of wholeness and of health and perfection are all being questioned and deconstructed. *Controversies in Body Theology* (2008) edited by Marcella Althaus-Reid and Lisa Isherwood was published as part of the SCM Press series on 'Controversies in Contextual Theology'. *Controversies in Body Theology* explores some of the ways in which Christian culture slices 'the bodies of women through acts of theological dismemberment' (Althaus-Reid and Isherwood in Althaus-Reid and Isherwood, 2008:2). This collection explores some of the different ways in which religion participates in the demonization and 'slicing' of women which is fundamentally underpinned by a dualism in which the bodily is consistently negated (Althaus-Reid and Isherwood in Althaus-Reid and Isherwood, 2008:3).

Body theologies as a group of theologies are diverse in terms of their concerns and primary contexts, but within most of these theologies a number of identifying characteristics are generally found. First, the human body is not seen as fundamentally problematic as the context of human experiences. Body theologies reject the hierarchical dualism which introduces a fundamental split between the spiritual and the bodily. There is a general affirmation that human sexuality is good. Sexuality is not in itself sinful and connections between the sexual and the spiritual are stressed. There is often a concern with the need for justice inclusive of gender, sexual diversities, bodily diversity and age. Finally, there is a need for a Christian ethic which affirms the human body and sexual experience as far from being a barrier of a problem as a rich and obviously immediate resource for Christian understandings of God and of human existence. This concern with human sexuality is also found in liberation theologies which focus specifically on diverse human sexualities as the context for theology. Here, theologies have developed from the experiences of gay, lesbian, bisexual and transgendered people and specifically the alienation and oppression experienced in relation to their sexualities as different to the heterosexual norm. Theologians such as J. Michael Clark, Elizabeth Stuart, Mary Hunt and Carter Heyward have all contributed to the development of gay and lesbian theologies and so articulated theologies of resistance from the context of diverse sexualities and associated oppressions.

Queer theory has had a significant impact on approaches to understanding and re-envisaging human sexuality in Christian theology. It has moved on from the identity politics of sexuality which some argue have limited gay and lesbian theologies to a much more fluid approach. Despite what is often assumed, queer theologies and queer thinking do not limit themselves to a concern with lesbian, gay, bi or transgendered sexualities. Queer is an inclusive approach to sexualities that have been posited as outside of normative heterosexuality which has been constructed or defined in a constraining way. Reflecting on the theological employment of the term, Mary Hunt describes queer theology as 'the third stage in the evolving effort to bring the experiences of lesbian, gay, bisexual, transgendered mainstream on their own terms' (Hunt in Russell and Shannon, 1996:298). The first stage she argues can be located in the period 1972 to 1982 and is 'the homosexual stage' (Hunt in Russell and Shannon, 1996:298). This was characterized by the challenging emphasis found in the work of theologians such as Sally Gearhart and John McNeill on same-sex sexuality and theology, which often meant male experiences. From this developed what Hunt describes as the 'lesbian/gay/bisexual stage' in the years 1982 to 1992 which was concerned with the different sexualities of men and women and so opened up the category of homosexual, and within this stage HIV and AIDS developed as key concerns. Hunt describes the third stage as 'queer theology' which she places as from 1992 onwards. She recognizes the place of feminisms in queer thinking and theology and stresses the attention to difference of queer. In recent times theologians such as Robert Goss and Elizabeth Stuart are developing queer-informed Christian theologies in some fascinating and challenging directions, for example, Robert Goss's *Jesus ACTED UP: A Gay and Lesbian Manifesto* (1993) and *Queering Christ: Beyond Jesus Acted Up* (2002) Elizabeth Stuart's *Religion is a Queer Thing: A Guide to the Christian Faith for Lesbian, Gay, Bisexual and Transgendered People* (1997) and *Queer Theology: Rethinking the Western Body* (2007) edited by Gerard Loughlin.

Indecent theology

Liberation theologies because of the ways in which they have approached their contextuality have tended to stress one contextual concern such as race, gender or socioeconomic experience at the expense of other significant contextual factors. One theologian who offers a very interesting contextual liberation theology within a complex of experiences and who consciously resists the prioritizing of one concern or oppression over another is Marcella Althaus-Reid. Althaus-Reid, a Latin American theologian born in Argentina, held the Chair of Contextual Theology in the School of Divinity at Aberdeen University. Her contextual theology is of interest here for the way in which she has brought her own experiences of a number of different contextual factors, including gender, poverty and sexuality into dialogue with each other within her very radical and challenging contextual liberation theology. Althaus-Reid draws on the fields and theories of Latin American liberation theologies, feminist informed theologies, queer theologies, gender theories, postcolonial theories, Marxist studies, Continental Philosophy and queer theories and produces what she terms 'indecent theology', which is contextual theology informed by a radically interdisciplinary approach. At its most fundamental Althaus-Reid's indecent theology is a liberation theology concerned to overcome injustice as encountered and informed by Althaus-Reid's own experiences and informed reflection on those experiences. She takes a highly critical approach to the theoretical bases she draws upon and the result is a contextual theology which makes use of different justice-seeking theologies and theories without being tied unreflectively to any one theory or theology. Althaus-Reid describes her approach as follows:

> I have taken Liberation Theology as my basic theological reference because this is my theological stand, in which I have been professionally educated and from which base I worked with deprived communities both in Latin America and Britain. I still emphatically affirm the validity of Liberation Theologies as crucial in processes of social transformation and superior to idealistic North Atlantic theologies. However, Liberation Theology needs to be understood as a continuing process of recontextualisation, a permanent exercise of serious doubting in theology.
>
> (Althaus-Reid, 2000:5)

Indecent Theology: Theological Perversions in Sex, Gender and Politics, which was published in 2000, challenges Christian theology to answer the charges levelled at it from a number of critical bases, but with the underlying claim that Christianity in Latin America has functioned as an agent of constraint by compelling people, and in particular, poor women, to behave and conform according to perceived orders of decency. This amounts to a theologically justified and supported system of control that regulates behaviour and compels conformity. *Indecent Theology* is thorough in its critical base and visionary in its push towards a radical reconceptualizing of the possibilities of contextual Christian theology. The concern of *Indecent Theology* both in terms of subject and methodological shape begins and remains with the streets of Argentina and tries out new and at times obscure ideas, in an intentionally shocking and explosive dialogue between Christian theology and indecency. As a deconstructive theological project it engages in a challengingly indecent analysis of the bases of power and their theological constituents and manifestations in Latin America. The methodological mix of *Indecent Theology* is a response to the complexity of the situation that Althaus-Reid was engaging in. The situation is one in which multiple forms of oppression are at work, and so the theological critique and response necessitate a methodology that uses a variety of tools to effectively analyse and challenge this injustice. Any one specific tool of analysis and subversion employed by Althaus-Reid, be it Marxist, feminist or liberation theological, is not sufficient to address the complex reality of the context that she was concerned with. Her aim in writing the book is one of exploration of the hermeneutical circle, that questions and deconstructs liberation theologies in a process of ' ... recontextualisation, a permanent exercise of serious doubting in theology' (Althaus-Reid, 2000:5). This, then, according to Althaus-Reid is a task of recontextualizing of liberation theology. The theological basis of *Indecent Theology* is liberation theology but the context is the day-to-day lives of the people of Latin America:

> The everyday lives of people always provide us with a starting point for a process of doing a contextual theology without exclusions, in this case without the exclusion of sexuality struggling in the midst of misery.
>
> (Althaus-Reid, 2000:4)

Her focused theological address in *Indecent Theology* is to the restraints and limitations that women face in Latin America. She wants to unpack the hidden, underlying structures that support the repressive orders of decency which she sees as the root cause or factor underlying the multiple layers of oppression facing women in Latin America. So, what she does is to bring out into the open the hidden relationship between the sexual and the theological – the mutually supportive and enhancing, yet essentially masked, relationship that she claims has been at work, and which she understands as affecting the traditions of repression, particularly of women, in Latin America. As such, *Indecent Theology* can be described as a theological act of radical contextual reflection on Latin America, and the deconstruction of the orders of decency that determine, limit and repress the lives of women. The history of Christian-based decency that operates repressively in the lives both of the women lemon vendors and the women theologians in Argentina is one that involved the fragmentation of Latin American civilization through the Conquista. This, Althaus-Reid argues, in effect signalled the end of the Grand Meta Narrative of Latin America and the imposition of European Christian rule (Althaus-Reid, 2000:3).

According to Althaus-Reid, Christianity played a key part in the process of displacement which took place with the imposition of the European Grand Narrative, in that it supported the economic, social and sexual systems of exploitation (Althaus-Reid, 2000:17). The ensuing system is one in which 'Christianity in Latin America imposed a sexual economic order or usury, of usage of people in relationships' (Althaus-Reid, 2000:20) where heterosexuality

is the rule of decency and the currency of the order and the law of the regula-
tion of sexuality and indeed human lives. What is needed, in Althaus-Reid's
understanding, is a break with all of this, a theology that challenges this sexual,
economic and theological order of decency. And whilst Latin American liberation theologies have attempted to address some of the problems of Christian
imperialism, in Althaus-Reid's understanding, they have so far failed to offer
any significant challenge to this oppressive order of decency.

The problem with Latin American liberation theologies, according to
Althaus-Reid, is that whilst they have attempted to address some of the layers
of oppression they have failed to address the underlying and supporting order
of decency that underpins the decent, oppressive order (Althaus-Reid, 2000:22).
She talks of liberation theologies, such as that which is usually associated with
theologians such as Gutiérrez, as 'traditional and conventional', and criticizes
them for being a 'commercial enterprise' with the claim that as they gained
recognition and publicity in Europe they ended in 'church tourism and theological voyeurism' (Althaus-Reid, 2000:25–26). They failed to recognize that
within the category of 'poor' lay women are people of diverse sexualities. Their
concern with decency, influenced by Western theological patterns, damaged
their potential for creativity and radicalism. In effect they failed to break with
the orders of decency. They also drew on the energies and resources of women
without giving support and recognition in return. In fact, Althaus-Reid argues
that women actually came not just to be excluded but also exploited by liberation theologies through a process of idealization in which she argues women
were anonymous or, in her words, 'fetishisations, reified phenomena extra-
polated from the reality of people's lives' (Althaus-Reid, 2000:34). Instead of the
white middle-class woman idealized elsewhere the model of women that came to
be idealized was of 'the poor, ignorant but faithful Christian mother' (Althaus-
Reid, 2000:34). This model failed to take account of the desires and needs of many
women. However, whilst Althaus-Reid is not alone in articulating this concern,
what is perhaps distinct about her critique is her understanding of the extent to
which liberation theologies have excluded women and the ways in which they
have done this, through compliancy with the orders of sexual decency:

> Their model of poor women excluded our rebellions, our vocations and
> struggle to be whatever we wanted – poor but intellectual women, active in
> theological praxis, informed by serious study and reflection. The model of
> womanhood constructed by the liberationists was as deceptive in their
> benignity as the Jesuitical reduction models of Paraguay and the north of
> Argentina ... In reality, we poor Christian women were supporting that
> theological enterprise that was Liberation Theology, but were not supported
> by it in equal terms.
>
> (Althaus-Reid, 2000:34–35)

Latin American liberation theologies have failed the women of Latin America,
and Althaus-Reid bases this assessment, in part, on her own experiences. She

does not, however, propose a complete move beyond the methodological and ideological base of Latin American liberation theologies, but, in the light of such experientially based analysis, proposes to take them beyond the restrictions and decencies of their established orders.

Indecent Theology challenges heterosexist hegemonies and, using Althaus-Reid's terminology, puts Christian theology very firmly into bed with God in a sexually active way (Althaus-Reid, 2000:23). As Althaus-Reid understands it, theology is not only concerned with the sexual but it also has an inherent address, it seems, to some kind of assumed appropriate or decent behaviour: 'Theology is a sexual ideology performed in a socializing pattern: it is a sexual divinized orthodoxy (right sexual dogma) and orthopraxy (right sexual behavior); theology is a sexual action' (Althaus-Reid, 2000:87).The theologian, then, given this description of theology as a sexual act, is the performer of sexual acts. Althaus-Reid claims that when the sexual is spoken of in theological discourse it is often represented as if it is without lust; yet she claims that lust needs to be acknowledged and to be given its appropriate place in theological engagement, as the sexual without lust is an attempt to cleanse or purify it on a public level. As part of this she talks of the need to queer God. Such an act, of queering God, can only happen when theologians move away from the schizophrenic approach that has traditionally been taken by theologians, in which a split is apparently enforced between the public and the private. According to Althaus-Reid, all theologians, whatever their own sexual practices and preferences, need to come out of the closet and publicly incorporate the sexual into their theology. They need to make explicit and to acknowledge that which is already there, that which has a direct influence on the theologian's work:

> ... God cannot be Queered unless theologians have the courage to come out from their homosexual, lesbian, bisexual, transgendered, transvestite or (ideal) heterosexual closets. Out-of-the-closet theologians do not leave the personal aside, and that always implies a risk, but neither do the closeted kind. It would be delusory to believe that closeted theologians can compartmentalise their lives so easily. The difference is that the closeted theologians indulge permanently in duplicity between the realms of a public and a private theology. They build schizophrenic spiritualities, those which require to be put aside at meal times, as the late Juan Luis Segundo said. Can we keep carrying the burden of a theology which leaves us alone when having sex?
>
> (Althaus-Reid, 2000:88)

Indecent theology with its recourse to the wider range of human experiences celebrates transient sexualities. It welcomes and embraces sexual dissidency, fetishism and sadomasochism and argues that decent heterosexuality is central to exploitative hierarchical systems of power and that Christianity supports exploitative sexual configurations. Indecent theology has to undress, to deconstruct the theological enhancement and justification of repressive controlling orders of heterosexuality which Althaus-Reid sees as underlying political and economic structures. She argues that far from being absent from theology, as we might be led to believe, sexual lust is at the heart of theology in terms of the control, denial and stipulation of lust. Indeed, she goes so far as to argue that even notions such as sin and grace are bound up with sexual desire (Althaus-Reid, 2000:86). Indecent theology forces an acknowledgement of the inherently sexual nature of Christian theology. It challenges and at times forces theology to spell out the full implications of its controlling heterosexist agenda, and to face up to its imperialistic mechanisms of operation. The imperialism and orders of decency that she is talking about have essentially imposed strict limitations, the effects of which are seen especially in the lives of women. Althaus-Reid criticizes the way in which feminist informed theologies have focused on gender rather than sexual activity or sexuality in their address to the oppression of women. She argues that women's oppression is to do with more than just gender; it is also inherently and indistinguishably sexual. The purity claims of theology, then, in this way, extend also to liberation and feminist informed theologies. For example, in exploring constructions of Christology she notes that liberation theologies have attempted to represent and identify Jesus in such a way that people can identify more easily with him, but argues that indecent theology must go further than this:

> ... but an Indecent Theology must go further in its disrespect for the interpellative, normative forces of patriarchal theology. It must go beyond the positive identification with a larger Christ. It must have the right to say not only that a lesbian can identify herself with a liberator Christ but that it must sexually deconstruct Christ too. Then indecent theologians may say: 'God, the Faggot; God, the Drag Queen; God, the Lesbian; God, the heterosexual woman who does not accept the constructions of ideal heterosexuality; God, the ambivalent, not easily classified sexually'.
>
> (Althaus-Reid, 2000:85)

These theologies too have been caught up in the need for decency, hence the need for a theology of indecency.

Indecent theology, as proposed by Althaus-Reid, is a theology that accepts the feminist analysis that women, both historically and still today, have experienced widespread injustice. This is seen, for example, in her analysis of the experiences of women in Latin America, and, in particular, her analysis of her own experiences of trying to gain access to theological education. Feminist informed theology, then, in this sense, has an important contribution to make in identifying and challenging gender-based injustice. However, what is distinct about Althaus-Reid's approach is her understanding of injustice, which sees the sexual, and, in particular, the constructed order of sexual decency, as the determining and sustaining cause of this injustice. The gender-focused approach of feminist informed theologies, claims Althaus-Reid, has failed to take into account the sexual base of women's oppression, choosing to focus instead on the relatively safe category of gender. As such, feminist informed theologies also come in for criticism from Althaus-Reid and in her own uncompromising words, she challenges what she seems to read as the concern with purity of feminist informed theologies and asks some very probing questions of such theologies, in terms of their radicalism and their implications:

> Has Liberation Feminist Theology stopped eating divine phalluses? ... Does Feminist Theology have a quest for purity still, for singleness of desire and hegemonic resurrections? The quest for transcendence in Feminist Theology, even in the context of political theologies, is still a quest for an out-of-body experience of purity.
>
> If purity is a common base for Liberation Feminist Theologies, or to put it differently, if purity is to Liberation Feminist Theologies as colonial thought is to Christianity, the frame we are dealing with is indeed very limited.
>
> (Althaus-Reid, 2000:103–104)

Feminist informed theologies, in Althaus-Reid's understanding, have either not been aware of or not been prepared to address the fuller picture of injustice, as she sees it. Like Latin American and other liberation theologies, feminist informed theologies, in not recognizing or failing to acknowledge the sexual base of injustice, in effect, participate in the very orders of decency that perpetuate the injustices that women in particular are so often subject to. This, she expresses in expectedly uncompromising words of, 'The gap between a Feminist Liberation Theology and an Indecent Theology is one of sexual honesty' (Althaus-Reid, 2000:7). Given all of this, something more, in Althaus-Reid's understanding, is required. Something that is more than, or goes beyond, liberation theology, and something that is more than, or goes beyond, feminist informed theologies. In Althaus-Reid's words, 'something that will require us to take our pants off at the moment of doing theology' (Althaus-Reid, 2000:37). This something that Althaus-Reid speaks of is a theology which

> ... problematises and undresses the mythical layers of multiple oppression in Latin America, a theology which, finding its point of departure at the crossroads of Liberation Theology and Queer Thinking, will reflect on economic and theological oppression with passion and imprudence. An Indecent Theology will question the traditional Latin American field of decency and order as it permeates and supports the multiple (ecclesiological, theological, political and amatory) structures of life in my country, Argentina, and in my continent.
>
> (Althaus-Reid, 2000:2)

The repressive orders of decency, that she claims underpin the injustices of Latin American life, need to be subverted theologically because they are infused with theological authority and meaning. A further criticism that she levels at feminist informed theologies relates to the kinds of claims that it has made as being in some way universally relevant. She stresses the need to remain grounded at all times. To be contextual is absolutely fundamental to her theological understanding and approach and she argues that feminist informed theologies cannot be dislocated, theoretical theologies; they must be grounded if they are to avoid the imperialism of hegemonous feminisms:

> The problem is that in the discourse of liberation, women are already disembodied in the category of the poor woman, which is a romantic conceptualisation, a universal which fits the invention of women and the invention of the poor at the same time. In a theological materialist feminist analysis, women need to be studied in certain contexts, and not from a mere struggle of ideas about womanhood constructed in opposition to hegemonic definitions, say by reading life in opposition to the Bible, but by a process of de-abstractionism or materialist reversal.
>
> (Althaus-Reid, 2000:36)

Throughout her work Althaus-Reid is concerned with identifying and challenging injustice, and in her own grounded conceptual concerns with the women of Latin America and her analysis of the historical forms of injustice, gender is a prominent feature. In that she clearly understands gender to be a factor in the way in which injustice functions and so in the way in which injustice might be overcome. Exclusion through gender is problematic for Althaus-Reid and she attempts to uncover and deconstruct orders which support and perpetuate such exclusions. What is distinct about Althaus-Reid's approach is her persistent questioning of the limits and operating factors of exclusion. Gender is a factor of exclusion and injustice, but the fuller picture recognizes the sexual in the everyday and feminisms are accepted and incorporated into her approach in a self-reflexive way, but certainly not the full critical category and value system. She focuses in on the experiences of women in order to crack open the sexual orders of decency of Christian theology. Her address in this is not just to women, but women are primarily the subjects of her contextual focus and of her historical analysis in *Indecent Theology.*

Althaus-Reid does value feminist consciousness and theories but she identifies clear problems with the systems of feminism, with the ideology, both theological and beyond. She recognizes that feminist liberation theologies have made important contributions (Althaus-Reid, 2000:6) but argues that they have accepted or at least not challenged the decent sexual orders that restrain and control women and other marginalized groups. The economic and theological orders of control of women have an underlying sexual decency but feminists and feminist theologians have focused on patriarchal constructions of gender. From this they have relied and referred to liberal ideology that has imposed hegemonic readings of essential woman, which Althaus-Reid understands in a restraining way. They have not problematized the given realities and so have included idealist understandings of sexuality and feminist theology, and their focus has been on 'sex as gender, and very rarely on sex as "having sex"' (Althaus-Reid, 2000:87). This is hugely problematic in her understanding because 'sex as lust is an important conceptual category which is not new, but has dominated theology for centuries' (Althaus-Reid, 2000:87).

To give a very brief description of her methodology, in Althaus-Reid's approach the Christian tradition might be said to be the cultural framework of indecent encounter, the inherited, lived tradition of context and the envisaged continuing framework of the encounter. Indecent theology is not a straightforward identification with lesbian, gay, bi, queer, liberal or feminist thought and practices. *Indecent Theology* is an appropriately indecent contextual dive into radical theology. She talks of ' ... that space which is a yearning, an incompleteness, which is Indecent Theology: a process that is never finished' (Althaus-Reid, 2000:70). One of the most exciting aspects of Althaus-Reid's work is the explicit address and implications for feminist informed theologies and Latin American liberation theologies. It challenges these theologies to go somewhere discernibly different and refreshing. The question now is one of whether these liberation theologies are ready to go to such places or spaces or whether such a shift, deemed by many as necessary, would constitute an unacceptable challenge to the very identities of these theologies. In some senses, there are no hiding places for liberation theologies. In this sense, indecent theology is a moment of indecency rather than participation in any kind of constructive theological enterprise. It employs queer theory to uncover the participation of Christian theology in the repressive orders of decency. So, from Althaus-Reid in *Indecent Theology* and in other texts since such as *The Queer God* (2003) and *Another Possible World* (2007), comes not only criticisms of liberation theologies as contextual theologies in relation to the limited and fixed ways in which contexts of oppression are interpreted but also a focused challenge to narrow and static understandings of the human context through subversive and fluid theological explorations.

Promises and failures of liberation theologies as contextual theologies

No theology, regardless of its intent, can be free from critique. Liberation theologies arose as theologies of resistance and protest and incorporate a fundamental critique of traditional theology as failing to recognize the role that context has on theology and so as unreflective on their contextual, experiential base. The history of liberation theology as a contextual theology, and precisely because of its explicitly contextual nature, is wrought with not only hope, solidarity and development but also, unfortunately, with exclusion, disillusionment and fragmentation. The critiques of liberation theologies, such as we have examined here, are calling upon liberation theologies to submit themselves to the same kinds of critical interrogation. Liberation theologies cannot and must not escape the critical questions that have helped build up the tradition of contextual liberation theologies.

In many different areas and types of liberation theologies we find evidence of attempts to reconceive of liberation theology in specific contexts. SCM Press under the editorship of Marcella Althaus-Reid and Ivan Petrella is publishing a series of books called *Reclaiming Liberation Theology* and in 2006 Ivan Petrella in *The Future of Liberation Theology: An Argument and Manifesto* put forward a very strong argument for redeveloping liberation theology with challenging methodologies and consequences. Christopher Rowland's observations in *The Cambridge Companion to Liberation Theology* (1999) are worth noting here in his argument for the continuing necessity for liberation theologies:

> So the seeds of hope have been sown. Yet everywhere the situation which prompted liberation theologians to write and explore a different way of engaging in theological reflection from what had become the norm, has not improved. In many parts of the world it has become worse, and it is this continuing context which prompts a continuing need for the kind of theological engagement we find in liberation theology.
>
> (Rowland in Rowland, 1999:250)

The next chapter will focus on a group of theologies which go some way to addressing a number of the criticisms that have been made of liberation theologies, especially in relation to their contextuality. Postcolonial theologies embrace the justice-seeking agendas of other liberation theologies but promise more fluidity and diversity in their understanding of context.

5   Postcolonial theologies

This chapter will focus on postcolonial theologies as a type of liberation theology and also as a development of liberation theology. As a theology that has developed more recently than many of the liberation and justice-seeking theologies that have either been examined in depth or noted in passing so far in this study, postcolonial theologies incorporate some of the criticisms and failures of many liberation theologies to date and as such offer us a glimpse of contemporary contextual liberation theologies. As is claimed by most liberation theologies, but in particular by this group of theologies, postcolonial theologies are invigorated with contextual diversity and are constantly evolving and fluid. Before looking specifically at postcolonial theologies we need first to examine postcolonialism. Postcolonialism is a term that is used variously by different people nevertheless some sort of characterizing working definition needs to be given to it here in order to be able to understand postcolonial theologies.

Origins and background to postcolonial theory

The term 'postcolonialism' incorporates a whole set of theories, approaches and literary techniques which emerged in the 1980s as an identifiable and distinct group of methodologies concerned with understanding and analysing different power relationships and power differentials in the world and with actively seeking to challenge such inequities. Postcolonial theory perceives all inequity of power through geographical and other factors as unacceptable and in need of immediate and thorough challenge. At its most basic the distinction in power relations can be traced to a non-Western/Western binary differential determining and controlling peoples, economies and cultural systems on a global level.

The approaches and methodologies of postcolonialism are challenging and often exciting and innovative. They ask the perhaps expected questions in unexpected ways and encourage discourse to travel in unexpected directions. The result of this is an often unexpected view of the world that is fresh, often uncomfortable for those privileged according to postcolonial theory but that is always challenging and pushing for change. The roots of postcolonialism, as suggested by the word itself, lie in a rejection of the imperialistic and colonial domination of much of the world by largely European powers. The rejection of colonial rule with all of its implications was explored in part in Chapter 2 where the origins of Latin American liberation theology were traced to the increasing theologically informed and resourced resistance to the cultural, political and economic domination of indigenous peoples by those who had invaded and conquered the territories of Latin America. The same is true of many other regions around the world, including India and Africa to name just two major global communities.

In Chapter 2 we also examined how theology and Christianity in effect arrived and rode on the back of the imperial, colonizing powers in Latin America. This relationship continued on an economy of support and legitimization in which the state recognized and gave the Christian Church significant power (largely as a mechanism of control) and in return the Church supported and legitimated the state, despite atrocities and terrible poverty faced by the indigenous people of Latin America.

Postcolonialism challenges and rejects hierarchical systems of power which enable or result in some peoples within a community or country having access to power, wealth and privilege, whilst others are disenfranchised and in effect treated as non-persons or non-subjects. It was also noted in Chapter 2 that the varying historical processes by which different countries in Latin America gained measures of independence from their initial colonizers did not automatically lead to justice-infused states or countries but rather that in effect one colonizer was quite simply often replaced by another. In gaining liberation from the European colonizers the (now clearly) idealistic expectation that countries would move automatically to democratic systems of governance in which equality and justice were basic guiding factors simply did not happen. 'Foreign' oppressors were often replaced with other oppressors in relatively unstable situations in which different tribal, ethnic or political groups would be constantly challenging if not engaging in military action against each other to secure power through coups and establishing dictatorships. This pattern was by no means true of all countries and regions in the world which moved through the stages of colonization to postcolonialism but was true of many regions. Many people continued to barely survive in economic and political systems which rewarded those loyal to whichever group or individual held power and which punished and disenfranchised those who did not. Robert Young in *Postcolonialism: A Very Short Introduction* (2003) argues that the move from postcolonial status has been fraught with difficulty and has been very difficult and costly to attempt to achieve, and that globally the process of change from colonialism to postcolonialism is infinitely more complex than a straightforward throwing off of colonial rule and embracing of independence:

> When national sovereignty had finally been achieved, each state moved from colonial to autonomous, postcolonial status. However, in many ways this represented only a beginning, a relatively minor move from direct to indirect rule, a shift from colonial rule and domination to a position not so much of independence as of being in-dependence. It is striking that despite

decolonization, the major world powers did not change substantially during the course of the 20th century. For the most part, the same (ex-) imperial countries continued to dominate those countries that they had formerly ruled as colonies. The cases of Afghanistan, Cuba, Iran and Iraq make it clear that any country that has the nerve to resist its former imperial masters does so at its peril. All governments of these countries that have positioned themselves politically against western control have suffered military interventions by the west against them.

(Young, 2003:3)

Young's point is an important one about the very reasons that led the colonizers to these lands in the first place (in addition to sheer expanse of power and territorial advance) to capture and exploit the resources native to these areas. Just as the colonizers had grown to exploit and depend on the resources they drained from these lands so the indigenous people became reliant upon what little financial return they actually received for their own exported resources. So even with postcolonialization the interdependent relationship of the colonizers and the colonized was complex and not without valid reasons for maintaining some sort of collaboration. Trade and export were vital to the economies of the newly 'liberated' countries yet the very people they needed to trade with were the people they were fighting, sometimes literally, to free themselves from. As such, the nature of the colonization process meant that even following apparent independence economic survival meant dependency on the former colonizers, a situation not welcomed but in many cases impossible to resist. To survive 'independently' meant a continued dependent relationship with those who colonized and exploited these countries in the first place. The colonizers had ensured that the economic survival of those countries colonized depended on exports to the colonizers, even when so-called independence had been established.

What is postcolonial theory?

Postcolonial theory is not, despite what the term might suggest, a well-thought-out set of logical ideas which collectively and individually contribute towards the establishment of this theory. Rather, postcolonialism follows in many ways the influence that postmodernism and poststructuralism had on it and is even at its most coherent not a systematized set of theories or worldview. The writers who have emerged as the key writers of postcolonial theory through the impact that their writing has had on the development of the theory include Homi Bhabha, Edward Said and Gayatri Chakravorty Spivak. Each of these in different ways has made significant contributions to the development and clarification of what is generally understood as postcolonial theory. In many ways, then, there is no clear common thread or subject to their work, only often hints or echoes of shared visions and understandings. In short, postcolonial theory is more a set of ideas, convictions and beliefs united or held together by common factors. Kwok Pui-lan argues that the very term 'postcolonial' has not as yet even been established to the point of shared discourse, meaning that when the term is used there is not even a general shared understanding of what the term is referring to. In 2005 in *Postcolonial Imagination and Feminist Theology* Kwok Pui-lan argues that

> Although postcolonial theory has made its impact in many academic disciplines and fields of inquiry, the meaning of the term 'postcolonial' continues to be vigorously debated. Some critics have warned that the term may be applied to many peoples, nations, and territories across space and time, and hence runs the danger of glossing over vast differences if the geographical and historical particularities of individual cases are overlooked. Others have misgivings about the prefix 'post' in the temporal sense and wonder if we have really entered into the postcolonial age.
> (Kwok Pui-lan, 2005:2)

The two points made by Kwok Pui-lan here are very important. The first reminds us of what has happened previously in liberation movements – that in an attempt to establish strength through unity dominant and articulate voices are heard and so come to represent the movement or groups of people as a whole. Within this many voices which are necessarily different, have different experiences and different needs due to their very context, are not heard above the dominant voices. As such those who are often most in need of representation and in need of being heard are lost in the chaos of representation. The differences between different people then are lost. Homogenous representation of oppression whilst powerful, if it is not fully faithful to the situation, will only fall short of the aims of the original task and will in the end come back to plague the movement or the original concerns.

The second point that Kwok Pui-lan makes is actually from Edward Said, a key critic of colonialism and imperialism who died in 2003. Said established his very strong reputation through influential texts such as *Orientalism* (1979) and *Out of Place: A Memoir* (1999). Said warned that it may in fact be 'premature to speak of postcolonialism, since colonialism is not over and has simply been superseded by neocolonialism' (Said in Kwok Pui-lan, 2005:2). This replacement of colonialism with neocolonialism we saw clearly when examining the roots of Latin American liberation theology. If an oppressive dictatorial power or order is overthrown this in itself neither constitutes nor guarantees a liberated, free order. In fact, that which has replaced the old needs to be critiqued in order that its motives, practices and underlying values might be assessed and judged accordingly. Robert Young's definition adds to Said's and Kwok Pui-lan's explorations of postcolonialism and helps us to establish at least a working definition of what we mean by 'postcolonialism':

> Postcolonialism begins from its own knowledges, many of them more recently elaborated during the long course of the anti-colonial movements, and starts from the premise that those in the west, both within and outside

the academy, should take such other knowledges, other perspectives, as seriously as those of the west. Postcolonialism, or tricontinentalism, is a general name for these insurgent knowledges that come from the subaltern, the dispossessed, and seek to change the terms and values under which we all live. You can learn it anywhere if you want to. The only qualification you need to start is to make sure that you are looking at the world not from above, but from below.

(Young, 2003:20)

Nichols Harrison in 2006 in *Postcolonial Criticism: History, Theory and the Work of Fiction* adds helpfully to crafting an understanding of postcolonialism with the following words of clarity and expansion:

Postcolonial theory is not an identifiable 'type' of theory in the same (limited) sense as deconstruction, Marxism, psychoanalysis or feminism, on all which it sometimes draws: it does not have foundational thinkers playing a role comparable to that of Marx or Freud; and whereas feminism, say, is first, both conceptually and historically, a political movement and a theory of gender relations in society, postcolonial studies, as such, seems to have emerged specifically within the English-speaking academic world, particularly in literature departments. Like Marxism and feminism, though, it has evolved in response to political and historical issues of vast importance and scope, such as anticolonial militancy, and its deeper origins and many of its ends lie outside academic study.

(Harrison, 2006:9)

The origins of postcolonial theory can be traced to literary theory or more generally to the study of English literature. From this its significance to other disciplines and to understanding human life generally became apparent. The starting point of postcolonialism is colonialism and imperialism and the resultant impact on the way in which people and communities were represented and discourses developed. Whatever the perspective taken on the state of a particular country or a territory, postcolonialism is concerned with power, rule and developing independence and challenging dependency. Postcolonialism also focuses on representation, on the way in which various groups or people are represented through discourse. Postcolonial theory has focused on the power differentials at work in representation and on challenging those representations if it is deemed necessary. In short, then, the roots of postcolonial theory lie in the academic discipline of English literature, and in particular of textual and discourse analysis. However, the possibilities that it has offered as a tool and as a way to contribute to the ever-growing field of challenging colonialism and imperialism, even when on the surface imperialism and colonialism were in many cases no longer visibly in place, became apparent very quickly. Scholars from other disciplines, and very importantly non-academics, began to use the mechanisms of postcolonialism to analyse and critique different situations and different experiences.

From a theological perspective the meaning of the term 'postcolonial' can be accessed through the concise description given by the biblical scholar, R.S. Sugirtharajah. His description incorporates the complexities of what is a relatively new field of study or critical discipline without making the complexities beyond a working understanding:

> The term generates at least three meanings. First, in a historical sense, it encapsulates the social, political and cultural conditions of the current world order, bringing to the fore the cultural, political and economic facts of colonialism, and aiding recognition of the ambiguities of decolonization and the ongoing neocolonization. Secondly, as a critical discursive practice, postcolonial criticism has initiated arresting analyses of texts and societies. It provides openings for oppositional readings, uncovers suppressed voices and, more pertinently, has as its foremost concern victims and their plight. It has not only interrogated colonial domination but has also offered viable critical alternatives. Thirdly, the term implies the political and ideological stance of an interpreter who is engaged in anti-colonial and anti-globalizing theory and praxis. Applied to biblical studies, it seeks to uncover colonial designs in both biblical texts and their interpretations, and endeavours to read the text from such postcolonial concerns as identity, hybridity and diaspora. Unlike the current biblical scholarship produced, invigorated and contained by virtuous aspects of the Enlightenment and modernity, postcolonialism concentrates on the vicious aspects of modernity – colonialism and how its legacy influenced and informed the promotion of the Bible and the development of biblical interpretation.
>
> (Sugirtharajah, 2003:4)

What is very interesting about postcolonial theory is that whilst it makes use of theories and discourses of liberation at the same time it is very clear in challenging such theories and discourses as being in themselves a product of the structures and power hierarchies that they were attempting to overcome. It recognizes that the liberation and freedom that liberation theologies and liberation movements in general have been concerned with have not been fully realized, and more than that, that because they themselves have arisen out of the situation that they are attempting to overcome they are inevitably shaped, to some extent, by the oppressive, even if this comes down to a simplified vilification of the oppressor. This, postcolonial theory recognizes, is not the true spirit of freedom or liberation. It draws on the recognition that historically whilst many liberation movements and liberation theories have started out with good intentions, especially in terms of understandings of power differentials, in some cases one oppressive regime has too often been replaced following a form of liberation by what eventually develops into another oppressive regime. In such cases it is just a different group of people that are being oppressed.

In the introduction to *Postcolonial Theologies: Divinity and Empire*, a very important theological text which was published in 2004 and edited by Catherine

Keller, Michael Nausner and Mayra Rivera, the editors argue that liberation theologies have much to offer postcolonial theory and in terms of explaining the relationship between liberation theologies and postcolonial theory as it is used in Christian theology argue that such theory does not supersede liberation theologies to the point of leaving them behind. They are very clear about the location of postcolonial theory and theology:

> We persist within the force field of liberation theology. No political theology could 'supersede' and in some fundamental way transcend the historic work of liberation theology. But within our shifting and diverging contexts, where the very notion of a Christian or a poor or a black or a lesbian or a feminist or a Latina 'identity' does not move on straight tracks, we seek fresh insights into emancipation. We need – as theology has always needed, whether it admits it or not – timely theories that can better attune our faith to the new problems and potentialities of its context. The contributors to this volume find in postcolonial theory an important resource for this task.
> (Keller, Nausner and Rivera in Keller *et al.*, 2004:6)

Whilst it is clear that for Keller *et al.* various forms of liberation theologies are not seen in terms of some kind of hierarchical chain in which each one chronologically superseded and renders the last one of no use, there is nonetheless a sense of supersession and redundancy. However, what is claimed is an interdependent relationship between the various forms of liberation theology and liberation theory of which postcolonial theory is one part. Its particular significance for these authors is in part its newness, and the ways in which it offers insights and possible explanations that simply have not been seen or acknowledged before. But its building blocks are what have gone before it.

Before moving on to examine postcolonial theologies in depth a brief outline of the key characterizing features by which postcolonial theory has come to be identified and has come to play such an important role in cultural analysis and understanding will help us to first get a clearer sense of what is meant in this context by the term 'postcolonial theory'. It will also contribute towards understanding the relationship between postcolonial theologies and other theologies that are being examined in this study of contextual theology. Some of the characterizing features have already been mentioned or touched upon briefly, but reiterating their significance will help to give some sort of loose shape to a movement of thought that resists form and definition at many points. We need to bear in mind here that we are not attempting a definitive definition of postcolonial theory. Just like the trends of postmodernism and post-structuralism such a move would not only defy all that these thought patterns are resisting but such a task would also in many senses be impossible. Given that so often we are used to working with clear-cut definitions and boundaries that contain and define ideas and disciplines, such an approach is often resisted or at least dealt with uncomfortably. Postcolonial theory does not want us to feel comfortable in our detached and boundaried worlds in which cross-contamination and cross-fertilization of ideas never takes place. Such 'purity' is not the stuff of postcolonial theory, and that is why in fact it offers so much hope within and at the same time beyond and outside the traditions of defiance, cultural criticism and (in this particular context) liberation theologies that have gone before it.

(1) The origins and location of postcolonial theory

The characterizing feature of postcolonial theory to be examined first here is its origins and historical location within the development of contemporary critical theories and cultural theories, and especially within such traditions of resistance and reconfiguration. As has already been touched upon, the roots of post-colonialism are evident in its title. It is bound up with the rejection of the colonialism and imperialism that had come to dominate many parts of the world by the mid to late nineteenth century. European 'super powers' had colonized huge parts of the developing world and imposed not only political and economic control over those people colonized but also imposed cultural and religious belief systems. As such, over generations indigenous peoples who were originally colonized came to invest in the belief systems and cultural ways of their colonizers. This was often done with a hybrid rather than a pure acceptance of these belief systems and cultural traditions. So, for example, those colonized would often accept Christianity but incorporate elements of their own indigenous religious practices and beliefs into their new belief system. As such, some form of inculturation has taken place and the gospel and Christianity 'mix' or adapt with key local customs.

(2) Opposing Western power

The emergence of the kinds of liberation movements and theories that we have been focusing on such as Latin American liberation theology have often been in response to or as an alternative way of living to that proposed by the colonial structures of imperial Europe which left its mark in many places around the world in its search for political, economic and geographical dominance. Whilst many places which were once overtly ruled by Western powers are today free of such direct rule there is nonetheless often a continued dominance and colonial stranglehold on the resources of the areas once colonized. The legacy of colonialism remains in so far as the colonized peoples and lands remain bound to the colonizers, they are dependent on them for their sale of exports and remain bound up culturally and religiously with them in contours of displaced and hybrid relationships. As such, in talking of 'postcolonialism' we are not talking about the passing and leaving behind of colonialism. We are talking of a movement and theory of hope which aims towards this. It recognizes the many ways in which colonialism remains a strong global force but also recognizes the subtleties by which the colonizers have manipulated manifestations of independence.

There are pockets and larger movements of resistance which are continually challenging the varied roles of the colonizers and of resistant imperial Western powers. Such resisters argue that there is no global equity, because for one, there is no global equity of voice. Those whose voices remained silenced or whose discourses are not heard on the global platform cannot even participate in the discussion of the patterns of independence and dependence. Until such a time when representative voices from all groups and cultures can be spoken and actually heard, talk of global equity, even at the most superficial level, is wholly misrepresentative of the actualities of global power.

(3) A 'new world', a new discourse

Postcolonialism as a set of interrelated theories has developed in such a way that a new discourse which is appropriate to the language of the challenges being faced has emerged. As with so many new movements or group of theories which fundamentally challenge the status quo, existing language which is accepted as the 'norm' holds no place for giving expression to the kinds of disruptive and rejectionist vision that is embedded within this new movement. We see this clearly with the emergence of postmodernist theory, post-structuralist theory and postcolonial theory. All three have semi-invented or reclaimed, often in fact in relation to each other, words and sets of words that are used to express and capture new ways of seeing and understanding the world in which we live. In this way they are able to subvert meaning, by taking words that have often been used in a derogatory way and reused them in a positive and challenging way. As such, sometimes the language of post-colonialism, poststructuralism and postmodernism can on the surface at least be misleading, because it uses terminology which traditionally has been used in an abusive or derogatory way. A good example of this is the reclamation of the word 'queer'. 'Queer' has been used for decades as a way of deriding lesbian, gay and bisexual sexualities. It has been used to humiliate, to degrade and to assert a perversion from the societal accepted norm or at least from the societal accepted norm understood by the user of the term. With the liberation movements and the theoretical bases of poststructuralism, postmodernism and post-colonialism the reclamation of the term has been one embedded with power, so that today there are many people of diverse sexualities, of whom the terms 'gay', 'lesbian', 'bisexual', 'transgendered' and even 'heterosexual' have been often used, but who will now instead use the word 'queer' to describe their sexuality. As was explored in Chapter 4 in queer theology 'queer' is used then not as an explanation but as a statement of celebration and ownership. So instead of being a victim of a term of abuse some people have taken the term back themselves as a celebration, a bold statement of their sexuality, if it needs describing at all.

(4) Identity

A key concept which is played around with by postcolonial thinkers is identity. Important here is the work of Homi K. Bhabha. Bhabha is a postcolonial theorist who has been hugely influential in what has become to be seen as the field of postcolonialism. Born in Mumbai, India in 1949 his family were Parsis, so for Bhabha even though he was born in India he had an ambivalent identity himself as a Parsi. This sense of ambivalent identity is reinforced by Bhabha having studied and worked in England and North America. The Parsis who live in India have their roots in Persian Zoroastrianism. They have become part of Indian culture and society whilst at the same time have maintained and developed their own beliefs and practices. As such, Bhabha himself experienced the hybridity of identity from a very early age. Belonging, yet not belonging, Bhabha has argued that the Western imperialist tendency, proved through history and continuing today, is bound to its representation of the world into systematic binary oppositions. The Western way of claiming its own identity as a superior and civilized culture depends on it identifying and labelling an alternative in opposition to this. As such, the non-Western world, he argues, is seen as lesser than, as uncivilized, even savage. A key project, then, that Bhabha has set himself and others is the methodical destabilization of the binary system that underlies and maintains the Western imperial mindset which has such destructive implications for the non-Western world.

One point that has to be made by way of caution in relation to postcolonialism has been raised and reiterated by many scholars working in the field of postcolonial criticism. This is the concern that postcolonialism may in fact not be the subversive, critical tool that will genuinely challenge and reconceive of the power differential established through the processes of colonization. Rather, it may in fact be a part of the Western scheme itself, having its roots in the West and is a tool of the West's grip on critical thinking. As such, it may be more appropriate to see it as neocolonialism rather than postcolonialism. Sugirtharajah raises a second concern in relation to postcolonialism asking whether ' ... we, the native orientalists, are replicating Orientalist tendencies'; he goes on to state that, 'Like Ali Behdad, I, too, am haunted by the question whether I am a postcolonial Orientalist perpetuating the European representations of the orient within the space provided by the academy' (Sugirtharajah, 2003:32).

He concludes that ultimately the concern of the postcolonial is contextual. It is about the health, poverty and oppression of people in specific situations and with developing critical tools to challenge the discourses that underpin these. Also, he stresses the pragmatic nature of postcolonialism, arguing that challenging the oppressor with words alone has its roots in the ways of the colonizer:

> A postcolonial critic's role is not simply limited to textual dealings or literary concerns. Postcolonial hermeneutics has to be a pragmatic engagement, and engagement in which praxis is not an extra option or a subsidiary enterprise taken on in the aftermath of judicious deconstruction and reconstruction of the texts. Rather, this praxiological involvement is there from the outset of

the hermeneutical process, informing and contesting the whole procedure. If we neglect this, we may become ridiculous figures ...

(Sugirtharajah, 2003:33)

Postcolonialism and theological discourse and action

Postcolonial criticism has had a major impact on Christian theology. Although in many ways it is still a relatively new area of theological enquiry the number of texts that are being written which specifically address and advocate a postcolonial Christian theology increase by the day. This emerging and ever developing and changing theology is influenced by the works of the most noted postcolonial theorists such as Edward Said, and especially his key work *Orientalism. Orientalism* was originally published in 1978 and has come to influence many thinkers in many different fields. It is regarded by many as the founding text underlying postcolonialism. Other significant influences on Christian theology from the postcolonial and poststructuralist schools of thought include Homi Bhabha, Gayatri Chakravorty Spivak, Gilles Deleuze and Félix Guattari. Kwok Pui-lan who is emerging as one of the most exciting and influential Christian postcolonial theologians refers to the significance of Edward Said's work as issuing specifically a 'clarion call to Christian theologians and scholars in Christianity' because the West which has developed such a negative and hierarchical representation of the orient is essentially a Christian West (Kwok Pui-lan, 2005:3). Kwok Pui-lan goes on to identify what for her is the damaging contribution made by very influential Christian theologians to understandings of identity and of the other:

> While reading Said's scathing critique, I kept thinking of how the fields of biblical studies, religion, and theology have contributed to the narratives of empire, and how the great theologians I have admired were influenced or tainted by the colonialist ethos and mentality. For someone like me who has studied Christian theology and read the works of Schleiermacher, Barth, and Tillich since the age of nineteen, there are many questions to be asked and a lot of unlearning to do.
>
> (Kwok Pui-lan, 2005:4)

Kwok Pui-lan's criticisms are clearly strong and go to the heart of the Christian tradition.

Postcolonial theory and biblical studies

One of the areas of Christian theology that has been most influenced by postcolonial criticism and so from which substantial critical engagement has emerged is biblical studies. Here, the prolific work of R.S. Sugirtharajah has been very influential and prolific. Important texts here include *Troublesome*

Texts: The Bible in Colonial and Contemporary Culture (2008), *The Bible and Empire: Postcolonial Explorations* (2005), *A Postcolonial Commentary on the New Testament Writings* (with Fernando F. Segovia) (2007), *Postcolonial Reconfigurations: An Alternative Way of Reading the Bible and Doing Theology* (2003), *Postcolonial Criticism and Biblical Interpretation* (2002) and *Asian Biblical Hermeneutics and Post Colonialism: Contesting the Interpretations* (1998). Such texts bear testimony to the significance of the interplay between postcolonial criticism or theory and the Bible.

Given the amount of work that has been carried out in the area of biblical studies and postcolonialism it seems appropriate in examining the influence of postcolonial theory on Christian theology to begin with the question, what might a postcolonial theology look like? Sugirtharajah's work, although highly significant when examining biblical studies and postcolonial thinking, is by no means the only work that needs to be taken into account. There are a significant number of scholars who are increasingly focusing on the interplay between postcolonial theory and the Christian Bible. In particular, they are asking questions about the ways in which the Western colonial mindset has influenced biblical studies and how this influence might be undone and the Bible approached in a different way. Key scholars here include Fernando Segovia, Kwok Pui-lan and Wong Wai Ching. The place and significance of the Bible in the identity of Christianity is always an important part of any theology, as we have seen in the cases of Latin American liberation theology and also feminist informed theologies. The Bible remains such a powerful part of Christian identity that most radical or new theologies will engage with it in some way or another. For many groups whose oppression has been supported by or justified by the Christian tradition parts of that tradition are clearly beyond redemption when seeking to build a different kind of Christian theology, one which is liberative and concerned with equity. However, although the Bible has often been used as a tool of oppression it has consistently remained a source of hope. There are a number of reasons for this. One comes down to subjective interpretation. How one person will interpret a passage, another person may interpret in an entirely different way informed by their own context, presuppositions, an awareness of historical biblical criticism and of awareness of contemporary literary criticisms. A second reason is that whilst there are aspects of the Bible that may be read in a negative, oppressive way, at the same time there are strands, pockets or key texts which it is argued offer an entirely different perspective on the core biblical message. The Bible, then, selectively plays a significant role in challenging and undoing the damage caused by what has been perceived as the misuse of the Bible in theologies such as Latin American liberation theology, Black theology, feminist informed theologies, Minjung theology, gay and lesbian theologies, queer theologies, eco-theologies and body theologies. As such, postcolonial theology stands within a tradition in which the Bible has a key role in determining the identity of the theology and is used as a basis from which to refute the foundational ideology or theory upon which oppressive action was built. The spirit of the way in which the Bible continues to operate in this selective, liberative way in liberation theologies is captured in the following words by the Latin American liberation theologian Elsa Tamez in a text published in 2002, *The Bible in a World Context*, edited by Walter Dietrich and Ulrich Luz:

> ... to search for lights in the dark night we need a lantern that will light our feet and the path. For Christians, one of these lamps is the Bible.
>
> What is the Bible? For many of us in Latin America the Bible is a mysterious book, good and cruel at the same time. It can promote peace as well as violence. In it we find abundance and absence, as we do in our realities. It cannot be any other way. The Bible narrates diverse worlds in their own times, realities like ours, although ancient and complex to our understanding. In these worlds of the Bible we find beautiful utopias, as well as texts of terror, and we confront a God who is merciful and just, and sometimes not so merciful or just. This is what is so fascinating about the Bible: that our life, equally complex and ambiguous, is seen reflected in this book.
>
> (Tamez in Dietrich and Luz, 2002:6–7)

R.S. Sugirtharajah, as noted above, has made a significant contribution to the development of postcolonial theology through his engagement with biblical texts and postcolonial theory. His work is underpinned by the firm conviction that postcolonial criticism when engaged in conversation or when applied to biblical texts has much to offer in terms of developing biblical interpretation which is not dominated by colonial or neo-colonial methodologies and tendencies. He is concerned to identify and challenge colonial interpretations and readings of biblical texts and to offer alternative readings by employing postcolonial theory as a critical tool of deconstruction and exegesis. Sugirtharajah, drawing on the work of Samia Mehrez, makes the absolutely crucial point that in order for true and genuine postcolonialism to take place as a 'critical enterprise' (Sugirtharajah, 2002:16) it must involve commitment from both the colonizer and the colonized. The colonizer must release the shackles of power and the colonized must leave behind the relationship of dependency on the colonizer that is at the heart of colonialism. Only then, argues Sugirtharajah, can liberation begin to take place, and to take place for both parties.

Shifts towards postcolonial discourses in biblical studies

In a very important 1998 edition of *Concilium*, a leading international journal in theology which is published by SCM Press in Britain and Orbis Books in North America and highly influential in the theological academic community, we see the beginnings of the overlapping transition from feminist informed biblical studies to postcolonial informed biblical studies. In a sense such a distinction is imposed and false as the very criticisms of womanist theologians, mujerista theologians and Asian women theologians, to name just a few, had already identified the white Western universalizing tendency in feminist theology. In some of the contributions to this edition of *Concilium* we glimpse the influence and emerging significance of postcolonial criticism on biblical studies. In this edition entitled *Women's Sacred Scriptures* authors from different contexts and theological perspectives reflect on the ways in which women have approached, reclaimed, developed new hermeneutics, and generally challenged and placed selective authority with certain sacred Christian texts. It was edited by Kwok Pui-lan and Elisabeth Schüssler Fiorenza, both of whom were key and very influential theologians in 1998 and remain so over ten years later. An outline of the contents of *Women's Sacred Scriptures* gives a sense of the significant shifts that were beginning to take place in feminist biblical studies in 1998. In the first part of the text 'Women's Experience with Sacred Scriptures' the five articles focus, in different ways, on the unorthodox and challenging ways in which women have transgressed the traditional boundaries of prescribed authority in relation to Christian scriptures and the inevitably very problematic relationship that women have with restrictive and patriarchally defined 'hegemonic canons and scriptures' (Kwok Pui-lan and Schüssler Fiorenza, 1998:1). The five articles are by Ivone Gebara, Joanna Dewey, Karen L. King, Amina Wadud and Musa W. Dube Shomanah, and it is worth briefly outlining the key arguments of some of the articles to give a sense of the ways in which feminist biblical hermeneutics was beginning to shift in some of its perceptions and methodologies in 1998. This shift was one, as will become evident, from an almost universalist women's hermeneutic to one which incorporates clear elements of a postcolonial informed theological approach.

Ivone Gebara, based in Brazil, contributes to this collection with an article: 'What Scriptures are Sacred Authority? Ambiguities of the Bible in the Lives of Latin American Women'. In this article Gebara very much reflects the pre-occupations of feminist informed scholars since the 1980s, if not before, with the problem of accepting, challenging or rejecting the authority of biblical texts which seem to depict women in a derogatory manner, as inferior to men and as non-subjects. She argues that the issue of authority is a powerful and often frightening tool used to reinforce a view of women as of subordinate or inferior status to men. From this she goes on to explore key distinctions between imposed and accepted authority, noting the reciprocity of accepted authority, the regulatory power and coercion of imposed authority and perhaps most importantly, she highlights the 'illusion of religious power' and the need to challenge such an illusion (Gebara in Kwok Pui-lan and Schüssler Fiorenza, 1998:9–13). She argues that feminist informed hermeneutics offer alternative interpretations of biblical texts from those masculine hegemonic interpretations that have dominated for so long and which have done so much damage to women's lives. An interesting argument put forward by Gebara is that the women of Latin America, influenced by feminist informed biblical hermeneutics, are rejecting the patterns of martyrdom and violence in the name of liberation and accompanying utopian understandings of freedom, all of which come at a very high cost. She argues that

There is no need to turn suffering into a source of hope. We know before-hand that our conquests of autonomy and respect are stained with sorrow and tears. We do not deny the cross we carry, but we do not want to make it a symbol of our hope. Martyrs are no use to us if we go on repeating structures and actions of violence.

... Our basic task is to avoid the crosses laid on us and collectively to cure the ills that come upon us in a thousand and one ways. Our deepest desire is to be happy, to live dignified lives enjoyably.

(Gebara in Kwok Pui-lan and Schüssler Fiorenza, 1998:15)

Gebara is critical then of the essentially masculine Latin American liberation theological movement, seeing it as utopian and as unnecessarily repeating patterns of suffering, violence and martyrdom. She also criticizes male liberation theologians for what she sees as the 'abstract character of universalist masculine discourse on liberation' (Gebara in Kwok Pui-lan and Schüssler Fiorenza, 1998:15). She is challenging Latin American liberation theology to listen fully to the visions and contextual experiences of women of Latin America and to recognize the different experiences of women to men, and the contributions that these different perspectives can offer to Latin American liberation theology. As such, on one level, Gebara's article very much represents feminist informed scholarship of the 1980s and 1990s which challenged the male-dominated liberation theologies and which in a sense precedes the emergence of postcolonial theology. As such there is an almost linear development of progressive theologizing (but not surpassing and replacing in an overly simplistic and rejectionist way) which builds upon the insights of key phases and contexts of liberation theologies. For example, feminist theology initially emerged very much as a white, Western, middle-class theology, which inadvertently repeated the universalizing tendencies of its patriarchal predecessors by universalizing women's experiences as if they were one and the same, regardless of context. This was challenged by, for example, womanist, mujerista, Asian-American, Asian and African women's theologies which failed to see their own experiences reflected in the very theologies which were being said to represent their experiences. Feminist theology grew to acknowledge, and not just incorporate these theologies but to transform the nature of what was feminist theology. That is not to say that there does not remain a Western dominance in the field of feminist informed Christian theologies but the shift in what is now known as feminist theologies or feminist informed theologies is much more inclusive and diverse, and is richer and truer for this development.

In the same way, feminist biblical hermeneutics can be seen to have developed from a rejectionist approach of male-dominated biblical interpretations and understandings of authority, to one which creatively engages with biblical texts through reinterpretations, reclamations and by widening the net of Christian orthodoxy, to what we might term a postcolonial hermeneutics. In a sense, this is a movement from critique and alternative hermeneutics informed by women's experiences and contexts, which are such an important part of feminist informed theologies, to a more ambiguous awareness of the power of the reader and the author, the interpreter and the definer in developments in postcolonial theology. Gebara's rejection of what she perceives as the male utopian martyrdom outlook is informed by a feminist perspective of the different experiences and ways of knowing of women.

Joanna Dewey, a North American scholar, contributes to *Women's Sacred Scriptures* with an article on the replacement of the oral tradition in early Christianity with the written tradition. Drawing on the work of Schüssler Fiorenza she argues in 'From Oral Stories to Written Text' that this shift of authority was partially responsible for the marginalization of women in the developing Church and the grasp of patriarchalism on Christianity. Christianity, she argues, began essentially as a movement reliant on oral storytelling and witnessing and then developed into a text-based authority movement. The contextual influences and pressures on Christianity as an emerging religion within particular cultures and societies, argues Dewey, mean that 'The New Testament is not a value-neutral survey of Christianity' (Dewey in Kwok Pui-lan and Schüssler Fiorenza, 1998:27). However, like most, if not all feminist theologians, she argues that hidden or woven beneath the obscuring layers of patriarchalism lie the traditions of Christian women.

Karen L. King, another North American scholar, puts forward a strong argument about the need for a hermeneutic of suspicion when reading or studying the Bible. In 'Canonization and Marginalization: Mary of Magdala' (King in Kwok Pui-lan and Schüssler Fiorenza, 1998:29–36) she argues that this widely known figure of the Bible was a threatening presence in the authoritative scriptures of Christianity. She undermined the male-centred early Christian movement by her very presence and so, King argues, through textual analysis we see her gradual marginalization and indeed demonization. This raises significant questions about the canon and the process of canonization in terms of criteria, process and intent.

Amina Wadud in her contribution, 'In Search of a Woman's Voice in Qur'anic Hermeneutics', focuses locating the female voice within the Qur'an as well as reflecting on the female voice as a commentator on the actual text. Wadud argues that the marginality of the female voice has become the norm, the accepted state to the extent that women have become silent in relation to the Qur'an (Wadud in Kwok Pui-lan and Schüssler Fiorenza, 1998:37). Wadud weaves her own story into her study which argues for the significance of women in the Qur'an and the importance of exegesis done by the individual for the individual instead of by someone else and being given universal status. Women's voices, argues Wadud, are necessary for a balanced reading of the Qur'an.

Musa W. Dube Shomanah from Botswana moves the collection firmly in the direction of postcolonial studies. Her paper 'Scripture, Feminism and Post-colonial Contexts' opens with a quote from *Culture and Imperialism* by Edward Said and argues that feminist interpretation of the Bible has challenged the validity of the constitution and authority of the biblical canon as we know it and have at times changed it by abiding to the criteria or principle that only that which is genuinely liberative can be 'the authoritative Word of God' (Dube Shomanah in Kwok Pui-lan and Schüssler Fiorenza, 1998:47). Dube Shomanah recognizes the ambiguity of postcolonialism and goes into some depth carefully defining her understanding and use of the terms 'postcolonial', 'colonial', 'colonizer' and 'colonizing'. She places the significance of textual authority at the centre of challenging imperialism and colonialism:

> Studies in colonial and post-colonial texts find that empires are not only built or dismantled by the barrel of the cannon, but mainly by the textual practices of writing and interpretation. Colonizing foreign races and their lands involves two intertwined literary practices. First, it involves a wide range of writing processes that represent the natives and their cultures as inferior, empty and in need of European civilization. These writing processes also involve normalizing imperial relations by creating literary settings that present dominating foreign people as normal and justified.
> (Dube Shomanah in Kwok Pui-lan and Schüssler Fiorenza, 1998:48)

So, Dube Shomanah identifies just how significant texts are to the authority of the colonizer, and how potent they are when enforced authoritatively and without option. They help establish and constantly reinforce the idea that the indigenous peoples subject to colonization need the civilized practices of those who dominate them. This in turn reinforces an image of the colonized as inferior, if not savage. Within this process native or indigenous texts are duly replaced by those imposed by the colonizer. Cultures, language, tradition all begin to be delegated and in Dube Shomanah's words

> The colonized are trained to yearn for the colonizer's places, religions, languages and cultures at large.
> This is the colonization of the mind, for it alienates the colonized from their places and cultures, creating an immense identity crisis.
> (Dube Shomanah in Kwok Pui-lan and Schüssler Fiorenza, 1998:48)

The significance of texts in the colonizing process, and beyond, is clear. Given the significance of religious texts as authoritative in their own right when they are imposed as the authoritative texts of the colonizer, their significance and influence become immense. In terms of having to approach texts cautiously and with a hermeneutic of suspicion, Dube Shomanah points out the similarities of the feminist and postcolonial tasks in relation to the Bible. Both are faced with authoritative canons which have been shaped and determined by hostile contexts and influences and as a result have the task of not only challenging these canons but also have to address the problem of language and discourse. The dominant and often exclusive discourse of the oppressor, be it the colonizer or the patriarchal oppressor, is embedded with words, language and meaning designed to establish and maintain a sense of hierarchy. This not only needs to be identified and challenged but alternative language and discourses need to be developed or found to replace those which are oppressive or alienating. So here we see very clearly the ways in which there is no sharp, distinguishing line between, for example, feminist and postcolonial criticism but, in this case, a common concern and need, but also perhaps different ways of responding to these. As Dube Shomanah argues, for both feminist and postcolonial subjects, there is necessarily a process of unlearning and rewriting as part of the process of challenging that which is oppressive and alienating (Dube Shomanah in Kwok Pui-lan and Schüssler Fiorenza, 1998:49). She notes that subversion is a common tactic or strategy of both groups of subjects and also (as has been stressed throughout this study in relation to liberation theologies, whatever their context or framework) both feminist and postcolonial theory insists on the authority, authenticity and validity of its own writings, its own canon(s).

Dube Shomanah, having identified and explored some of the shared practices and strategies of feminist-informed theory and postcolonial theory in relation to textual canons, goes on to identify important differences between the two approaches. Sometimes these differences are very subtle but at the same time they are very significant distinctions. She argues that the characterizing feature of the early postcolonial resisters was one of preservation and reclamation of language and canons that had been rejected and vilified, if not lost, by the imposition of the canons of the colonizers. For her, earlier feminist resisters took a different approach, one in which they took an almost blanket approach to the rejection of traditional canons and texts as patriarchally shaped, selected and transmitted. Postcolonial resisters, on the other hand, restored and recovered their own traditions (Dube Shomanah in Kwok Pui-lan and Schüssler Fiorenza, 1998:50). This claim is perhaps a little too sweeping and generalized in its distinction and also perhaps fails to acknowledge the difference between the contexts of feminists and postcolonial subjects attempting to locate their own voices and experiences within texts. However, Dube Shomanah does identify an important difference between the methodologies developed by the two approaches. Dube Shomanah argues that there has actually been a clash between feminist and postcolonial understandings and strategies in approaching canons and the reclamation of texts:

> In short, when Western feminists advocated the devaluation of all other canons, they were heard by many post-colonial subjects as echoing the practices of the colonizer, who also derogated the canonical texts of the colonized. Two-Thirds World feminists were often urged to privilege post-colonial concerns over patriarchal oppression.
>
> (Dube Shomanah in Kwok Pui-lan and Schüssler Fiorenza, 1998:50)

Dube Shomanah points out that Kwok Pui-lan has responded to this issue by urging Western feminist theologians to remain aware of the colonial as well as patriarchal influences on the canons that they themselves are working on, so that they can avoid simply reinforcing the colonizers' influences and authority over the colonized within the texts. She is calling on feminist informed Western theologians, then, not simply to be concerned with feminist issues of identifying, challenging, rejecting, reinterpreting and widening the traditional Christian canon at the cost of other oppressive influences at work within these texts. To do so, however inadvertent and unintended, would be to collude with and reinforce the aims of the colonizer. This, then, widens the brief of Western theologians, calling on them to take on board postcolonial insights and methodologies in order to break the cycle of oppression and to step outside of the circle of collusion. As such we see here shared insights and methodologies but at the same time the later developed postcolonial theory offers and indeed impels Western feminist theologies to take on board the postcolonial insights in order to avoid colluding with the colonizing impact of the biblical texts. Dube Shomanah's article goes as far as to argue that key feminist informed biblical texts such as the two-volume *Searching the Scriptures* edited by Elisabeth Schüssler Fiorenza actually functions through its concern to recover and restore marginalized texts 'within the colonial canonical framework' (Dube Shomanah in Kwok Pui-lan and Schüssler Fiorenza, 1998:52). Dube Shomanah calls for genuine creativity in feminist informed theologies, which, for her, necessarily involves the creative engagement of Western feminist theological discourses with feminist theological discourses from a wide variety of cultural and geographical contexts.

The Latin American scholar Elsa Tamez who was born in Mexico and has had a highly influential impact on gender studies, liberation theologies and theology generally in her contribution to this collection focuses on argument that if the principle that women's experiences are an authoritative source for biblical hermeneutics is accepted then, 'it is a logical next step to state that women's lives contain divine revelation' (Tamez in Kwok Pui-lan and Schüssler Fiorenza, 1998:57). In the article, 'Women's Lives as Sacred Texts', Tamez explores women's own lives in their great complexities and differences as sacred texts.

Joan M. Martin, a North American scholar, in 'The Slave Narratives and Womanist Ethics', focuses on the African-American slave narratives and womanist responses to these. For Martin slave narratives are an important source of identity and so information about them and study of them needs not only to recognize the process and implications of enslavement for all African-Americans but also the implications and realities of patriarchalism for African-American women. Like other feminist informed writers Martin wants to reclaim these narratives as sacred texts in their own right because of the testimony, experiences and revelation that she argues they contain. Saroj Nalini Arambam Parratt, who was born in India, and Yuko Yuasa, a Japanese scholar, explore in their articles the significance of oral scripture and the performing of sacred texts, respectively. Bonna Devora Haberman, born in Canada, focuses on the praxis-based exegesis of a Jewish feminist hermeneutic. Kwok Pui-lan brings this edition of *Concilium* to a conclusion.

Whilst the articles reflect many of the now established feminist informed methodologies employed in biblical interpretation and hermeneutics we clearly see in the edition an emerging postcolonial outlook, one that is not definitive or prescriptive, but one which clearly stresses the need for both oppressor and oppressed to take part in the liberative process. This demonstrates that the distinctions in methodology or the use of terminology such as postcolonial, postmodern, feminist, etc. are not necessarily clearly demarcated but often overlap as genuine development occurs. Kwok Pui-lan notes Dube Shomanah's engagement with postcolonial perspectives, alongside feminist perspectives, and then goes on to stress the significance of postcolonial criticism for a developing liberative hermeneutic. This is a liberative hermeneutic which draws on multiple methodologies and theories including feminist and postcolonial to challenge and destabilize both Western and patriarchal hegemonic hermeneutics.

Having seen something of the shared concerns or overlap of concerns between feminist informed and postcolonial Christian theology, and the way in which postcolonial theology is calling upon liberation theologies to see the big picture rather than just one aspect of the oppression that liberation theologies attempt to oppose, it is clear that postcolonial theology marks a potential significant coming together of the concerns of various liberation theologies. At the same time postcolonial theology allows room for, if not insists upon, the contextual nature of these theologies. Turning back now to the work of R.S. Sugirtharajah and his immense contribution to the development of postcolonial theology, especially in the field of biblical studies, we can see clearly the ways in which postcolonial theory has had a direct and increasingly transformative impact on Christian theology as contextual theology. In *Postcolonial Reconfigurations: An Alternative Way of Reading the Bible and Doing Theology* (2003) Sugirtharajah challenges hegemonic Western, colonial biblical studies, their methodologies, readings and understandings with a postcolonial informed intervention. He also calls on biblical scholars to make use of postcolonial theory, claiming that so far its impact on biblical studies has been limited (Sugirtharajah, 2003:7). In outlining the benefits and relevance of postcolonial criticism Sugirtharajah claims that it does not simply reject imperialistic powers and the imposition of authoritative texts which accompanies this, but rather it is engaged and confrontational:

> ... it is an active confrontation with the dominant system of thought, its lopsidedness and inadequacies, and underlines its unsuitability for us. Hence, it is a process of cultural and discursive emancipation from all dominant structures whether they be political, linguistic or ideological.
>
> (Sugirtharajah, 2003:15)

Sugirtharajah is critical of liberation discourses which have in effect reified or made authoritative in an absolute way their own contexts and experiences. He is calling for a wider acknowledgement of the problems of power differentials and recognizes that even within the postcolonial framework there remains a relationship or connection between the colonized and colonizer. This is demonstrated by his use of Samia Mehrez's claim that in fact postcolonialism amounts to 'an "act of exorcism" for both the colonized and the colonizer' (Mehrez, 1991:258 quoted in Sugirtharajah, 2003:16). This brings us back to a conviction at the centre of postcolonial criticism that in postcolonial studies and postcolonial discourse the colonizer and the colonized are bound together. Similarly, the liberative process or the process by which the colonized can throw off the imperialist bonds necessarily involves the colonizer as well. As Sugirtharajah points out Edward Said encouraged the shared study of the experiences of both the colonized and colonizer, terming this 'contrapuntal reading' (Sugirtharajah, 2003:16). This, then, moves beyond the usual binary oppositional readings and perspectives of the two parties. Sugirtharajah points to key texts in the Bible as in need of postcolonial critique and engagement. He points, for example, to the missionary journeys which are reportedly undertaken by Paul in Acts 13–14; 15.40–18.22; 18.22–21.16. Sugirtharajah argues that passages such as these have historically been used to legitimize and back up colonial activity, the kind of which was explored in Chapter 2 in relation to the inextricable relationship between the Church and the European colonizers. Credence, authority and divine will was given to the brutal colonization of many countries and regions and this relationship sustained for many years the rule of the colonizers over indigenous people, especially once Christianity had been imposed upon them as a mark of civilization. Sugirtharajah argues that it was William Carey who first made use of the words from Matthew's gospel. Carey, a Baptist missionary in Sugirtharajah's words, ' ... resurrected the Matthaean commission as the proof text for compulsive preaching of the gospel in distant lands' (Sugirtharajah, 2003:18). Sugirtharajah, drawing on the work of Alan Kreider, argues that the early Church's activity was not heavily determined or characterized by missionary activity, as many have traditionally believed. The development of the Church was not because of evangelization and conversions through this, but rather, through martyrdom and understanding the power of faith. Carey in his commitment to missionary activity was changing the Reformation approach to such activity, according to Sugirtharajah.

Focusing on the widely perceived involvement of Paul in evangelization and missionary journeys, Sugirtharajah argues that Paul's perceived approach to missionary activity, which he argues has largely been understood to be planned, organized and methodical, actually became the model for the colonizing missionaries in the eighteenth and nineteenth centuries (Sugirtharajah, 2003:19–23). Sugirtharajah argues that a key reason for the use of a model of mission based on Acts and Paul's activities is that it supports the romanticized view of the civilized West taking Christianity to so-called heathen lands to civilize and enlighten them, for which, of course, they should be grateful. However, as Sugirtharajah points out, this ignores the by now well-established belief that there was a Christian presence in Asia, for example, long before the arrival of the Western colonizers. It is now believed that Christianity first arrived in India as early as 52 AD when St Thomas visited Kerala where he is said to have established a church and from there went on to visit other places in India and establish more churches (seven in total) before being put to death, it is believed, around 72 AD.

Sugirtharajah and other biblical scholars influenced by postcolonial theory and methodologies claim that the missionary passages that are present in the Bible and which have been interpreted in a zealous way to support a dominating colonizing relationship between Christianity and politics need to be challenged hermeneutically (Sugirtharajah, 2003:27). This is partly achieved by challenging the underlying Eurocentric interpretations and exegesis of the Bible. Instead of focusing on and stressing the links between the Hellenistic and Roman cultures, which the early Church developed within, Sugirtharajah argues that we need also to acknowledge the other cultural influences at play on Christianity at the time. For example, he tentatively puts forward the idea, with reference to the work of other scholars in the field, that Christianity may well have been influenced by its contact with Eastern beliefs and customs such as Buddhism and native Indian traditions (Sugirtharajah, 2003:30–31).

One more very interesting claim that Sugirtharajah makes is that there should remain some distance between the biblical text and the reader. By this he seems to mean that recognition must be given to the context in which the biblical texts were written and that a straightforward identification with these texts with personal human experiences needs challenging. He gives as an example the biblical story of Job and claims that for many Christians when facing some kind of personal crisis or tragedy the tendency is to liken this experience, and so derive comfort or explanation from the story of Job (Sugirtharajah, 2003:88). This, he argues, becomes stereotypical and again does not take into account context and the current, real situation being faced. He also argues that historical biblical criticism that has been important for so many scholars has in fact

> ... had a shackling and enslaving impact on women, blacks and people of other cultures.
>
>   To some of us the historical critical method is colonial, because of its insistence that a right reading is mediated through the proper use of historical-critical tools alone.
>
> (Sugirtharajah, 2003:88)

This places authority firmly with so-called proper interpretation of texts, which means the use of Western tools of critical analysis. This then does not take into account different approaches to the kind of authority given to biblical texts. The measure of authority and authenticity for Christians like Sugirtharajah is the emancipatory possibilities of a text, not its historical accuracy. Those engaged in biblical historical criticism often fail, as Sugirtharajah argues above, to remain connected in their theological work to the real world, to the context out of which they write, and so moves beyond the lives of people that it should be speaking to. However, at the same time he argues that the contextual should not be prioritized over the history of colonialism, the memories, the cultural and social damage. To speak of theology as contextual, for Sugirtharajah, is not enough. Postcolonial theology is a more appropriate description of this kind of theology, he argues, than liberation theology, contextual theology or Third

World theology, although that which lies behind these terms is not dismissed (Sugirtharajah, 2003:103).

In conclusion Sugirtharajah in his work on postcolonialism and biblical studies makes a significant contribution to an emerging field, with realistic and cautious expectations. In *Postcolonial Reconfigurations* he highlights a number of concerns about the future of postcolonial criticism – one concern relates to accessibility – that essentially postcolonial criticism is being carried out by scholars and as such is divorced from that with which it is concerned. Second, he notes the reticence of postcolonial scholars generally to discuss religion (Sugirtharajah, 2003:110–111). This second criticism, however, is understandable given the past relationship of Christianity and colonization. For many, religion, and especially Christianity in its more radically fundamentalist forms, serves to control, dictate and silence rather than being a tool of liberation and freedom.

Sugirtharajah goes even further in his criticism arguing that the Christian West is responsible for much of the political and social oppression over the last two centuries:

> Those who are familiar with history will know that the real instigators of great evils in the nineteenth and twentieth centuries – fascism, Nazism, Communism and colonialism – all came from the Christianized West. Postcolonial criticism has its roots in non-religious ideologies and frameworks – Marxism, post-structuralism and psychoanalysis. Postcolonial criticism now occupies a crucial position in academia which is mainly secular and liberal.
>
> (Sugirtharajah, 2003:111)

Sugirtharajah remains suspicious also of any form of Western missionary activity, whatever guise it comes under or whatever form it takes. He argues this in relation to the notion of the contextualization of Indian theology, which for him repeats the patterns of indigenization and inculturation. He sees all of these as Western motivated attempts to challenge and replace local cultures (Sugirtharajah, 2003:120). His criticisms extend to even the radical Indian theologies such as Dalit, tribal, Asian feminist and Buraku theologies, all of which on the surface appear to be radical, transformative but when examined by Western scholars 'reinforce all the negative aspects of Indian society' (Sugirtharajah, 2003:121). For Sugirtharajah theology is not to be found in the imitations of Western theological figureheads or in the radical movements which themselves have universalized certain aspects of their theology. Rather, it is to be found in the genuine and continually changing differences and intersections of people's lives. Encountering difference forces a re-examination of the self. He actually goes as far as to argue that theologians are meant to understand the world not change it (Sugirtharajah, 2003:125), something many liberation and other Christian theologians would strongly disagree with.

Walter Dietrich and Ulrich Luz as editors of the 2002 publication, *The Bible in a World Context: An Experiment in Contextual Hermeneutics*, echo the postcolonial claim that the Bible, in the light of postcolonial criticism and informed reflection on the experiences of those who have been colonized, becomes something different for many people around the world from what it once was. This difference is in terms of its status, its place within the community or context and its authority, the way in which it is viewed and especially the way in which it is used or employed as a tool or resource. They outline the ways in which the Bible, until recently and in many cases still today, plays a part in Christian communities and stress the different nature of the role it plays according to context. So, for example, they argue that the Protestant emphasis on the Bible as the very centre of Christianity, as the truth, is a way of understanding and using the Bible that simply has not worked. So, in this respect, they are arguing that a new way of viewing the Bible, and a new way of interpreting and making use of the Bible, is needed. This is not a reiteration of liberation theologians per se, as they make very clear in their criticisms of the way in which the Bible has been used in European liberation theologies in the preface to *The Bible in a World Context*:

> The Protestant northern and western Europe was shaped by the Bible. More than in any other area of the world the Bible was *the* 'book of books' for us. It was *the* foundation of truth, *the* source of individual piety. It was the starting point of the European liberation movement, the foundation of morals, the basis for political legitimization, and so on. That is no longer what the Bible is today. Nowadays the Bible is less read in northern and western Europe than in most other parts of the world, although it can be found everywhere indeed: standing on the shelves in everybody's home as a relic ... But it is covered in dust and long forgotten.
>
> (Dietrich and Luz, 2002:vii)

They contrast this sharply with the role of the Bible in Roman Catholic Southern Europe. With the legacy of *aggiornamento*, enforced by the Second Vatican Council (Dietrich and Luz, 2002:viii), the Bible has been very important in both Roman Catholic Southern Europe and in the Orthodox Church in Eastern Europe in the former communist regions. In North America, too, they argue the Bible is a living, everyday tool. In Africa and South Africa they refer to the Bible as 'an immeasurably valuable and powerful book, and countless people read it and listen to it' (Dietrich and Luz, 2002:viii). They stress the significance of the Bible in Asia too, and whilst noting the different contexts covered by the term Asia they argue that the Bible is read widely and very important. They raise the interesting question as to why in Japan, which they describe as perhaps the richest and most westernized of the countries of Asia, the Bible is read so widely and is so important 'among the intellectuals of Japan more intensely than in the educated classes of western Europe, despite the fact that the majority do not belong to any church' (Dietrich and Luz, 2002:ix). Their conclusions seem to centre round the notion of cultural crisis; where there is a cultural crisis then the Bible will be read and used most intensively or more intensely than might otherwise be the case. So, this must also apply to South Africa, Africa, Asia and Eastern and Southern Europe. In times of cultural crisis the Bible, they argue, becomes part of the search for identity. They stress the importance of context for reading and understanding the Bible and argue that what is needed most is '*contextual* Bible reading and *contextual* Bible hermeneutics' (Dietrich and Luz, 2002:x). This is so that the realities of human lives, and especially the differences in human lives, according to context, can be fully accounted for and understood in making use of the Bible.

Justin Upkong's paper 'Inculturation Hermeneutics: An African Approach to Biblical Interpretation' which is included in *The Bible in a World Context* offers a detailed and engaged example of the workings of biblical hermeneutics carried out from a consciously persistent contextual stance. Justin Upkong is from Nigeria and he sets out to demonstrate and develop a contextual hermeneutic of the Bible which is contradistinctive to the Western hermeneutic which he describes as '*intellectualist*' (Upkong in Dietrich and Luz, 2002:17). By this he is referring to the tendency described throughout this book associated with enlightenment thinking of seeking universal truths, of making generalized truth statements that are expounded as valid regardless of the context to which they are being applied. He argues that African approaches to the Bible are contextual but that given the diversity and changing nature of the contexts in which the people of Africa find themselves there are many different approaches and methodologies employed in African hermeneutics or readings of the Bible. The common thread, however, is their contextual nature. The approach that he develops in this paper is one of 'Inculturation Hermeneutics' (Upkong in Dietrich and Luz, 2002:18). By this he is concerned to stress the experiences and framework of reference of what he calls the ordinary person. He, like many liberation theologians before him, argues that the Bible is not an objective, neutral or disinterested text; it is not '(culturally and ideologically) an innocent text' (Upkong in Dietrich and Luz, 2002:18). As such it must be treated as being influenced by human concerns, interest and contexts and for him this then highlights the need for ' ... a critical ethical reading in terms of its stance toward other peoples and cultures in the light of basic human and biblical values of love and respect for others, justice, peace, unity, and so on' (Upkong in Dietrich and Luz, 2002:17). Following this, the Bible for Upkong must also, necessarily, be engaged with contemporary contexts, contemporary concerns, issues and experiences. So that the ordinary people that he speaks of are the subjects of interpretation of the Bible, their experiences inform the hermeneutics and it is their worldview or frame of reference that underpins biblical interpretation. Upkong offers an interesting insight into the competing authorities and claims that are made for the Bible in Africa and the solution that he offers in terms of understanding the Bible at work in the lives of African people:

> In contemporary Third World theological discourse, the Bible has often been referred to as a 'site of struggle,' and the question often arises as to 'whose Bible' (whose understanding of the Bible) is to be privileged. In a

particular sense the Bible is the site of struggle for control and legitimization between the ordinary people, the church, and the academy. In inculturation hermeneutics the primacy of the reading activity is located not among individual theologians working in isolation but among theologians working within communities of ordinary people – it is the ordinary people that are accorded the epistemological privilege. The Bible is seen as a collection of the ordinary people's experience of God in their lives and communities reflected upon and expressed in stories, prayers, and so on. For this reason, the experience of ordinary people today that share existential conditions and experiences similar to those reflected in the Bible is seen to demand a privileged position in understanding the Bible.

(Upkong in Dietrich and Luz, 2002:20–21)

One persistently interesting and important issue, as is becoming very clear here, is the relationship between liberation theologies such as feminist, black, Asian and Latin American liberation theology and what is emerging as quite critical postcolonial theologies. An interesting theologian here is Kwok Pui-lan whose theological identity seems fluid and open. Kwok Pui-lan, it seems, given her interests and approaches, can be appropriately referred to with any one of or any combination of the following descriptions: an Asian theologian based in North America, a Chinese feminist theologian, an Asian-American theologian, and a postcolonial theologian. Whilst not wanting to pin any particular label or all of these labels to Kwok Pui-lan, throughout her theological journey to the point of writing this book, perhaps most if not all could have been appropriate descriptions of her theological enterprise which she and others might well have made use of in reference to her writings. In her 2005 publication *Postcolonial Imagination and Feminist Theology* the journey that she speaks of is one in which her own identity, which is itself fraught with contradiction and conflict, is both academic and personal, if the two can ever really be disengaged. What Kwok Pui-lan does is to bring the two together in a genuinely critical discourse which does not result in the solely autobiographical angst that it is possible to genuinely discern in the text, but rather an experiment. And perhaps that's why she chooses to use the word 'imagination' in the title of the book. She sees postcolonialism as playing a crucial part in her critical theological discourse but not without being subject to examination, exploration and experimentation.

Hence, this book is interested not only in analyzing colonial discourse or in deconstructing Western dominant regimes of knowledge, but also in examining the interdependence of the cultural terrain traversed by both the colonizers and the colonized, as well as how the colonial systems of knowledge cast their impact, long after the colonizers are gone. Having gone through a lengthy period of colonial education, I am interested in exploring the steps necessary for a postcolonial intellectual to dislodge herself from habitual ways of thinking, establishing forms of inquiry, and the reward system vigilantly guarded by the neoliberal academy. By documenting my critical engagement with postcolonial thought, I hope to create a little more space to imagine that an alternative world and a different system of knowing are possible.

(Kwok Pui-lan, 2005:3)

In the context of this book this aim of Kwok Pui-lan is both fascinating and crucial for us in understanding the nature of the theological encounter with postcolonialism, and, remembering the title of her book, seeing how she brings feminist theology and postcolonial theology into conversation with one another. Its importance could be in understanding how feminist theology might develop or benefit by drawing on and making use of the tools and insights of post-colonial criticism. For these reasons, *Postcolonial Imagination and Feminist Theology* seems to be well situated as a key text in the development of the intersection between theology and postcolonial discourse, and in particular in the development of the intersection between feminist informed theologies and postcolonial thought.

Kwok rightly notes the proliferation, if it can be said to be that extensive, of biblical studies making use of postcolonial criticisms and methodologies, but notes the so far apparent less willingness or less ready venturing of other areas of Christian theology into conversation with the discourses of postcolonial criticism. She challenges this, arguing that 'This oversight is unwarranted, given the lengthy history of theology's relation with empire building, especially in the modern period' (Kwok Pui-lan, 2005:5). Despite this, she clearly recognizes the significance of postcolonialism for biblical studies and in doing this recognizes the relationship between both colonial and patriarchal power and the use of biblical texts. This, in the face of the centrally authoritative role that Christianity accords the Bible, means that the Bible must be subject to a thoroughly critical examination which draws on many different critiques, not least of these being those of postcolonialism and feminisms. As Kwok Pui-lan traces the relationship between the use and abuse of the Bible in relation to the powerful and those subject to their power, from the early Church onwards in relation specifically to the missionary movements and the theological justification behind imperialism and colonization she argues, repeating a central claim of this book, that

As colonial desire and imperialistic violence were masked and reconstituted in a blatant reversal of 'civilizing mission', the Christian church played important roles through the sending of missionaries, establishing churches and schools, and propagating ideas of cleanliness and hygiene. Christiani-zation and Westernization became almost a synonymous process in the colonial period.

(Kwok Pui-lan, 2005:17)

Despite Kwok Pui-lan's undoubted commitment to the benefits of postcolonial discourse for Christian theology she does not see it as a progressive methodo-logical and ideological move beyond theological feminisms which renders them obsolete. She believes that feminist informed theologies can benefit from post-colonial criticism and in describing what she is attempting to do in this key volume of work, she restates her belief about the multicultural and intercultural nature of feminist theologies, which she outlines in *The Cambridge Companion to Feminist Theology* (2002).

Kwok Pui-lan's work in this area, although many may disagree, is a revitalizing breath of air through paths so well trodden that their purpose seems somewhat lost. She is daring, she is imaginative and she is relentlessly hopeful without being sentimentally optimistic. In some ways, Kwok Pui-lan's *Postcolonial Imagination and Feminist Theology* is the first book that thoroughly and relentlessly engages with the details, implications and possibilities of a genuinely creative discourse between Christian theology and postcolonialism. Such a claim may well be immediately contested, but to date, no other scholar has presented us with the kind of systematic challenges that Kwok Pui-lan does. Of course, within the field of postcolonial theology it is early days, but something of the spirit of Kwok Pui-lan's investigative journey may well live on in the same vein as Mary Daly's *Beyond God the Father*, Gustavo Gutiérrez's *A Theology of Liberation*, James Cone's *Black Theology* and Marcella Althaus-Reid's *Indecent Theology*.

Within all of this Kwok Pui-lan's constant awareness of her own context stands at the centre of her work. Whilst she persistently reiterates her theological focus and concern as being one of leaning towards the possibilities of postcolonial critiques and discourses for feminist theologies, at the same time she sets out clearly her own somewhat dislocated situation:

> I recognize the privilege I have as a middle-class professor teaching at an American divinity school, with access to library resources and books that many of my Third World colleagues can only dream of. Yet I experience the daily challenge of a woman of color who must transgress constricted boundaries and negotiate new possibilities for daring to think and act differently. The book illustrates a rite of passage from one who identified herself primarily as an Asian feminist theologian in the past to one who increasingly embraces her diasporic existence.
>
> (Kwok Pui-lan, 2005:25)

So, what are the key points that Kwok Pui-lan would like Christian theologies, and with her own context in mind, feminist informed theologies, to hear and engage with from postcolonial criticism and discourses? And what, given Kwok Pui-lan's clear commitment to being constantly attentive to context, in all of its aspects, do postcolonial criticism and discourses have to offer as tools for contextual ways of doing theology? Where might postcolonial tools take contextual theology? To summarize is of course difficult, is open to claims of misreading and is always limiting. But given the significance of her work, the task of bringing together the key implications of Kwok Pui-lan's theologizing here is called for. First of all Kwok Pui-lan calls upon and begins the process of imagining just what a Christian theology might actually look like for the postcolonial-informed Christian outside of the restraining boundaries of the legacies if not still existing imperialistic chains of Eurocentric theology. She stresses the relative infancy of 'women's articulation of their experiences of colonization' (Kwok Pui-lan, 2005:30), but argues that they are now beginning to have the opportunity to represent and speak for themselves in ways which will be heard. They may be in line with the Western measure stick of scholarship in terms of academic discourses but they are their own ways, and she gives examples such as poetry, dance and storytelling, all of which, incidentally, have been used by feminist informed theologies in their disillusionment with and alienation from traditional theological discourses. This leads to the inevitable question of women's heritage and which in one way or another brings women into conflict with the Church. She argues the need for women to forthrightly claim their subjectivity as part of the process of reclaiming their own heritage (Kwok Pui-lan, 2005:34). Drawing especially on the work of womanist theologians and women in postcolonial Asian contexts, Kwok Pui-lan stresses the importance of imagination, historical imagination: 'The historical imagination aims not only to reconstruct the past, but also to release the past so that the present is liveable' (Kwok Pui-lan, 2005:37). It is here that we begin to see the clear influence of postcolonial thinking on Kwok Pui-lan's Christian theology, and especially her feminist informed theology. Kwok Pui-lan is critical of French feminist theorists for their stringent Eurocentric academic '*jouissance*' (Kwok Pui-lan, 2005:37). Writing from her own diasporic context Kwok Pui-lan stresses the importance of dialogical imagination, and not just imagination in and of itself. Such dialogical imagination demands, necessitates careful and deliberate attention to the different contextual ways of theological engagement.

Kwok Pui-lan recognizes the multilayered nature of oppressions, like many before her, and writing from her own context explores the possibilities that postcolonial criticism might hold for the ever lively and disputed area of gender and Christian theology. She puts forward a strong argument that it is only in recognizing the multilayered, interdependent and interlocked oppressions such as gender, race and class, that progress can truly be made to begin to develop a theology that does not privilege one particular area or issue over another, or a theology that ignores and plays down the significance of any such area. The interesting point that she raises here relates to tradition, that ever problematic element of Christianity for many innovative and liberation theologies. Tradition is problematic for such theologies because such theologies seem to go against the grain of the so-called established orthodox tradition, when in fact what they are, are contextual interpretations and constructions: 'In order to reterrotorize Europe and to place Christian history in proper perspective, we must develop an international and multicultural understanding of Christian tradition' (Kwok Pui-lan, 2005:67). This means including indigenous resources and involves the full participation of those who have been subject to the processes of colonization in participating, 'shaping and expanding the Christian tradition' (Kwok Pui-lan, 2005:69).

Central to her argument is the claim that whilst the majority of the colonizers were male, women too, whether directly or indirectly, were also colonizers. As a result, and also as a challenge to the essentializing readings of women's experience and women's epistemology, Kwok argues that she is not advocating the replacement of male ways of doing things with female ones in postcolonial theologies, but rather that all multilayered, interrelated and inextricable factors of gender, sexuality, race, religion, age and the colonial context need to be taken into account in developing postcolonial theological discourses and practices (Kwok Pui-lan, 2005:73). Furthermore, those involved with such theological enterprises must be constantly vigilant and constantly critique their own discourses.

As a contextual theologian Kwok Pui-lan goes on in the second part of her study to focus specifically on the implications of postcolonialism for feminist informed theology, reflected in the title she gives to Chapter 5, 'Postcolonial Feminist Theology: What is it? How to Do it?' (Kwok Pui-lan, 2005:125). She offers here a clear example of what is at the heart of the theological post-colonial enterprise, both in relation to postcolonial feminist theology and other postcolonial theologies. She constantly questions and disrupts the flow of theo-logical activity in a critical questioning that holds always in mind questions about subjectivity, voices and power. Then she faces up to the implications of the answers that emerge, which may not always be entirely welcome and are not always easily, if at all, slotted into the constructed framework. In fact, any framework here may need shifting, if not dismantling, regardless of what has gone before and regardless of what great achievements have been made and great strides forward:

> In assessing the relation between theology and empire, postcolonial feminist theologians need not reinvent the wheel or create theology ex nihilo. Although they are not bound by the Western tradition, they will be ill advised to dismiss it if they want to speak to a larger audience to push for theological and institutional changes. The Western theological tradition is not monolithic, nor are its interpretation and organization fixed. A post-colonial feminist perspective will help open the theological texts to new inquiries and negotiations.
>
> (Kwok Pui-lan, 2005:145)

Kwok Pui-lan also focuses on the experiences of feminist informed theologies from the Third World and especially on the socio-political situations of such women and their own analyses of these. She also draws attention, quite appropriately, to the pragmatism of such women in the face of the apparent promise of a new or different kind of liberation theology, especially given their experiences of previous liberation theologies – liberation theologies which she argues have not only failed to recognize them as subjects but have really offered no theological forms of liberation as such. As Kwok Pui-lan notes, the political theologies of Third World feminist theologians are multi-form and contextual (Kwok Pui-lan, 2005:166).

In the remaining chapters of the book Kwok Pui-lan addresses some key questions about gender, Western understanding of culture and issues of the identity of Christianity, which inevitably arise from a study such as this. Because it has travelled so far in its questioning of Eurocentric Christianity as Christianity, Kwok's focus on the identity of Christianity has important implications for any study that focuses on the implications of a consciously and often radical contextual reading of Christian theology.

Postcolonial theology from the colonies

One further very interesting book in the area of postcolonial theology which needs mentioning here is *Postcolonial Theologies: Divinity and Empire* which was published in 2004 and edited by Catherine Keller, Michael Nausner and Mayra Rivera. One of the interesting features of this text is that some, if not most, of the contributors to the text are not themselves writing out of what might be defined as a postcolonial context or do not have a heritage as being directly subject to the ravages of colonization. This is readily recognized by the editors in their preface to the text and demonstrates that postcolonial theory and methodologies are being used by a wide range of theologians, and not only those theologians or communities who either have a colonial past or find themselves in a neo-colonial or postcolonial situation. This echoes, for example, male theologians who took on board the insights of feminist theologies and themselves claimed to engage in feminist theology. This caused some reaction among women feminist theologians and the question inevitably arose as to whether a man could genuinely engage in feminist theology, and, along the same lines, similar questions arose as whether a white person could engage in black theology and whether a heterosexual person could engage in lesbian, gay or bisexual theology. There are of course a multitude of answers to such questions. Those theologians in contexts such as Africa, India, South Africa, and Latin America readily call on the colonizer to join them in developing a genuine postcolonial theology. Part of this is meant, it seems, to be a call to those still holding the bastions of power to recognize their role and let go of this role but in a genuine vein of postcolonialism. The editors of *Postcolonial Theologies* argue that in fact even though many of the contributors are not the subjects of colonialism or a colonial or neo-colonial heritage, they are all making use of postcolonial theory in their various theologies. They do, however, add something to the description of their enterprise which whilst on the one hand might be said to be a very positive affirmation of the importance and possibilities of postcolonial theory and theology but on the other hand comes perilously close to making universal claims for its significance:

> Moreover, our title suggests that even some of us who are situated amidst the privileged colors or classes of a 'neo-colonial' or 'imperial' United States may claim to do a 'postcolonial theology'. Furthermore, few of us in this volume represent a literally postcolonial political context (such as

Asian, Latin American and African nations). Yet all of us make use of 'postcolonial theory'. It is a theory that we believe offers a particular gift for religious thought. It deserves consideration as one among many strategies, a discourse added to other traditions of liberation. But we use postcolonial theory in ways that commit us to something more than theory – that is, to an engaged and engaging theology, a work of resistance to the layered, ongoing, and novel colonizations of the planet. This book offers itself as a resource not just for scholars of religion and theology, but for seminarians, pastors, and all who recognize in religion a power of social transformation; indeed, for all who feel the lure to an ever more embracing, more radically relational, more truly planetary theopolitics.

(Keller *et al.*, 2004:xi)

This last phrase 'truly planetary theopolitics' in description of a genuinely contextual theological perspective and written in the context of postcolonial awareness seems to be open to question if to be not directly open to challenge. Can a contextual theology claim to be planetary theopolitics? This question will no doubt remain unanswered here but what we can do is point again to the genuine and persistent conflict that seems to be at work between claims to be contextual and the need to make some kind of universal truth claims or advocating a superior or right way of doing theology, or theopolitics in this case. This conflict is a genuine conflict that is partly associated with the nature of religion, and partly associated with the nature of the particular theologies that have been the focus of this study. That is, theologies which are in opposition to and which arise out of oppressive situations; theologies which reflect the experiences, lives and histories of people who have been subjugated and oppressed by the colonizing processes.

Postcolonial theology as contextual theology

Postcolonial theology can make very strong claims in respect of its nature as contextual theology. It arises out of multiple awarenesses which themselves have given rise to consciously contextual theologies of many different types. Whilst keeping a sense of the diversity that are postcolonial theologies, postcolonial theology can nevertheless be characterized as incorporating a strong sense of multiple Christian identities and of human subjectivity, as rejecting a hegemonous Christian voice as representative of global Christianity and as challenging, universalizing tendencies in Christian scholarship. Postcolonial theologies are subversive of even their own positions and approaches and are concerned to continually question and critically interrogate. Historically the roots of postcolonial theology lie with a rejection of colonialism, colonial rule and the remnants of the colonizer/colonized relationship, even after supposed decolonization. Change and subversion lie at the heart of postcolonial theological approaches. However, postcolonial theory, argue its proponents, speaks to all regardless of context and experience. It is not only of use to those in colonial, decolonized or neo-colonial situations. It calls on all people to examine, subvert and undermine all systems of dominance which wash over the realities of people's lives and subjectivity. All power differentials, whatever their origin and whatever systems underpin and perpetuate them, need to be challenged. Both the colonizer and the colonized need to hear postcolonial voices. Postcolonial theologies value difference through contextual experience. Although postcolonial theologies stress the importance of memory, there is a very strong emphasis on the contexts of human lives as the starting place and the arena of theological activity and engagement. In this way, then, postcolonial theologies are contextual theologies. Time will tell whether the theoretical bases of postcolonialism are lived out in full in Christian theological form, but what postcolonial theologies have that other liberation theologies so often do not have is the key principle of subverting and reinventing themselves so as not to become formalised in any overly static way. The forms that postcolonial Christianity might take are in some ways down to the imagination. What we have so far are examples of postcolonial theologies and of postcolonial ways of doing Christian theology, pockets and glimpses of postcolonial, contextual theology.

6 Contextuality in critical perspective

Liberation theologies are theologies which have developed in response to experiences of social, political and economic injustice. The types of injustice that have given rise to liberation theologies are wide ranging and the geographical and cultural contexts from which they have emerged are diverse. Liberation theologies are explicitly contextual theologies in that they consciously articulate the personal, social and political contexts of the theologian or theological community as key if not primary motivating and shaping factors. The contexts that inform the theological task in liberation theologies are specifically contexts of oppression. The contexts of oppression and struggle from which liberation theologies have developed include poverty, colonialism, sexism, homophobia and militarism. The social justice concerns of liberation theologies are infused with theological significance and as practical contextual theologies they are radically committed to praxis on some level. This praxis is focused in some way or other on overcoming injustice.

Whilst there is clearly great diversity among liberation theologies, for example, in terms of specific justice concerns and methodologies, there is nevertheless a shared conviction that Christianity is a religion which is inherently concerned with justice. For liberation theologians the justice-seeking theologies that they develop then are not distortions or radical departures from the core principles of Christianity but rather reflect the fundamental concerns of Christianity. Stephen Bevans argues that for praxis-orientated contextual theologies, such as liberation theologies, a commitment to social justice is the appropriate Christian response to God:

> True Christianity, it becomes clear, must work against oppressive structures not just by seeking to change certain features, but by seeking to supplant them completely. Liberation and transformation, not just gradual development or friendly persuasion, is the only way that men and women can fulfil their call to be genuine children of God. As practitioners of the praxis model began to reread the Bible and Christian tradition, they began to discover many forgotten things about Christianity and its roots in Hebrew religion: that the Bible itself is a product of struggles for human freedom; that Jesus' message is a message not primarily of doctrines but of structure-shaking

attitudes and behaviour; that sin must be opposed not by compromise but by radical reordering of one's life. Social change – and the social location of the poor and the oppressed – began to be seen as a privileged source of theology. Commitment to social change in terms of Christian principles and from the perspective of the poor and marginalized led not only to social transformation but to a deeper and more challenging knowledge of God as such.

(Bevans, 2002:71)

As has been seen in relation to Latin American liberation theologies, black theologies, feminist informed theologies, body theologies, sexual and queer theologies, contextuality in liberation theologies brings a theological commitment not only to explicitly embed theology in the social, cultural, sexual, bodily context of the theologian or the theological community but also to prioritize or privilege the contexts of the oppressed. Liberation theologies are concerned to stress the dynamic role of context in all theologies but they are often more concerned with some contexts than others. Different types of explicit contextual theologies other than liberation theologies share this theological commitment to embed theology in context but not to the prioritizing of contexts of oppression. This is a distinguishing feature of the contextuality of liberation theologies. Bevans, in relation to his sevenfold classification of contextual theologies, presents a matrix of ways in which contextuality is found in Christian theologies. This ranges from the theological emphasis on the translation of the Christian gospel or message in specific contexts, to synthesis or inculturation, to the radically contextual countercultural model. Whilst the study of liberation theologies in this book is by no means exhaustive as a study of the diversity of liberation theologies it has explored some of the outworkings of contextuality in liberation theologies. And whilst different liberation theologies clearly understand context in different ways and engage and incorporate key contextual factors into theology in different ways, a number of things can be said about liberation theologies as explicitly contextual theologies.

The rest of this chapter will outline key features of the contextuality of liberation theologies:

(1) Liberation theologies as contextual theologies are characterized by the fundamental conviction that *all* theology, regardless of theological perspective or motivation, is contextual.
(2) They are committed to the theological principle of the privilege or priority of the oppressed.
(3) They often share a problematic tendency towards narrow understandings of context.
(4) They are being challenged to address the tendency towards narrow understandings of context with its attendant exclusions and move towards fluidity and reflexivity.
(5) For each of these liberation theologies questions of tradition and identity arise in relation to contextuality.

All theology is contextual

As noted throughout this study liberation theologies place particular theological and methodological significance with recognizing the situated, contextual nature of all theology. The impact of context on theology is not simply confined to those theologies which explicitly articulate and develop theologies which are sensitive and responsive to context. According to liberation theologies, *all* theologies, regardless of whether they articulate any contextual awareness, are influenced and shaped by the context of the theologian or the theological community. Given the influence of context on theology all theologies need to acknowledge the specific contextual influences at work on them and as a result of this engage on some level with associated questions of relevance beyond the immediate theological, social and cultural context. Theologies need to recognize that they are situated and specific. They are influenced by specific human concerns and contexts. They are not objective or 'true' and as such are not automatically relevant and appropriate for all people in all contexts. History bears witness to the imperializing and exclusive tendencies of theologies, especially Western theologies, which assume this universal relevance.

Walter Dietrich and Ulrich Luz in the preface to *The Bible in a World Context: An Experiment in Contextual Hermeneutics* (2002), a book which they jointly edited, put forward a very convincing argument about the need for contextual theology, and in particular, contextual hermeneutics:

> When our own ways of understanding no longer work, it is essential to listen to others and learn from them. It seems to us that Western biblical scholarship suffers most from being 'without context.' It is carried out abstractly and therefore leads to abstract results and truths, which are not related to any context. 'Abstract' is not only understood in the usual sense as being opposed to 'concrete'. 'Abstract' also means: unattached to the life and reading of 'ordinary' people, far away from their questions, developed in the ivory tower of the university. 'Abstract' means: detached from the present and from its problems, concerned only with the reconstruction of a past with all its problems. Finally, another way of scholarly, 'abstract' reading that is disconnected from the real concerns of present-day readers is to flee into an imaginary 'text world' – imaginary, because it is entirely created by scholars. 'Abstract' in the widest sense means: without context. All this does not contribute to understanding, which is related to our own context.
>
> (Dietrich and Luz, 2002:ix–x)

As has been seen, however, despite the importance of this call to contextual recognition, liberation theologies themselves have too often failed to fully respond to this call.

Preference in theology

Liberation theologies not only argue that all theologies are influenced by context but they also prioritize some contexts over others. This principle of liberation theologies is the preferential option for the poor. Gustavo Gutiérrez in the expanded introduction to the revised 1988 edition of *A Theology of Liberation* outlined his understanding of the theological implications of the preferential option for the poor. Gutiérrez pointed to the documents that emerged from Medellín and the papal encyclicals and statements of John XXIII and John Paul II and the stress found there on preference for the poor (Gutiérrez, 1988:xxv–xxvii). He argued that the preferential option for the poor is a concern of liberation theology which has been widely accepted within 'the universal church' (Gutiérrez, 1988:xxv). For Gutiérrez the preferential option for the poor is a commitment to the poor which echoes or reflects God's own commitments as seen through the biblical texts:

> The entire Bible, beginning with the story of Cain and Abel, mirrors God's predilection for the weak and abused of human history. This preference brings out the gratuitous or unmerited character of god's love. The same revelation is given in the evangelical Beatitudes, for they tell us with the utmost simplicity that God's predilection for the poor, the hungry, and the suffering is based on God's unmerited goodness to us.
>
> The ultimate reason for commitment to the poor and oppressed is not to be found in the social analysis we use, or in human compassion, or in any direct experience we ourselves may have of poverty. These are all doubtless valid motives that play an important part in our commitment. As Christians, however, our commitment is grounded, in the final analysis, in the God of our faith. It is a theocentric, prophetic option that has its roots in the unmerited love of God and is demanded by this love.
>
> (Gutiérrez, 1988:xxvii)

Gutiérrez makes clear that the poor and oppressed should not be given preference because they are in some way superior to others; rather, they should be given preference 'because God is God, in whose eyes "the last are first"' (Gutiérrez, 1988:xxviii). So, for Gutiérrez the preferential option for the poor does not arise simply because of contextual circumstance; rather, it is a fundamental Christian ethic based in an understanding of God's own concerns.

William O'Neill, S.J. argues that in Jon Sobrino's theology God has a 'partiality' for the oppressed (O'Neill in Pope, 2008:33). God's purpose can be known in history, in this life, and by participating in social justice-seeking action in effect we participate in salvation history. Ada María Isasi-Díaz spells out the imperative for solidarity with the poor and oppressed in her mujerista theology. She argues that the Christian religion brings an ethical imperative for solidarity with our neighbours:

> The paradigmatic shift I am proposing calls for solidarity as the appropriate present-day expression of the gospel mandate that we love our neighbor. This commandment, which encapsulates the gospel message, is the goal of Christianity. I believe salvation depends on love of neighbor,

and because love of neighbor today should be expressed through solidarity, solidarity can and should be considered the *sine qua non* of salvation. This means that we have to be very clear about who 'our neighbor' is. Our neighbor, according to Matthew 25, is the least of our sisters and brothers. Neighbors are the poor, the oppressed, for whom we must have a preferential option. This we cannot have apart from being in solidarity with them.

(Isasi-Díaz, 1997:88)

For Isasi-Díaz the imperative to stand in solidarity with the poor and oppressed is to participate in the realization of the '"kin-dom" of God' (Isasi-Díaz, 1997:89). Salvation history for Isasi-Díaz is the ongoing process of liberation in which alienation is overcome. Liberation theologies also see very important hermeneutical implications in the option for the poor. Elizabeth Stuart in *Religion is a Queer Thing* (1997) highlights this epistemological privilege: 'the people today who correspond most closely to those with whom Christ identified himself ... have a privileged insight into God's presence and revelation in the world today' (Stuart in Stuart, 1997:24).

Narrow understandings of context

Contextual theologies of liberation have had a tendency to interpret and represent context in a narrow way. Womanist and mujerista theologians, for example, illustrate that liberation theologies' own limited understanding of oppression, and especially of the multilayered nature of oppression, has had devastating implications for those that even these apparently radical and subversive theologies seem to have ignored. In effect, despite the importance given to recognizing the diversity of human experience and the importance of reflectivity and explicit contextuality in theology, liberation theologies have themselves failed to live up to the challenge that they have laid down to theology in general. They have repeated some of the same mistakes and even created new exclusions in their theologies. Katie Cannon in 1987 articulated the challenge that exclusions within black and feminist liberation theologies through a narrow understanding of contexts of oppression bring for womanists:

Intrigued by the largely unexamined questions that have fallen through the cracks between feminist ethics and Black male theology, the womanist scholar insists on studying the distinctive consciousness of Black women within Black women's institutions, clubs, organizations, magazines and literature. Appropriating the human condition in their own contexts, Black women collectively engage in revealing the hidden power relations inherent in the present social structures. A central conviction is that theo-ethical structures are not universal, colorblind, apolitical, or otherwise neutral. Thus, the womanist ethicist tries to comprehend how Black women create their own lives, influence others, and understand themselves as a force in their own right. The womanist voice is one of deliverance from the deafening discursive silence which the society at large has used to deny the basis of shared humanity.

(Cannon, 1987:171)

Womanist theologians criticize black theologies for articulating black experience monolithically and criticize feminist informed theologies for articulating women's experience as homogenous categories. These theologies have failed to recognize the ongoing impact of hierarchies of oppression because of their concern to present a unified liberation theology. In feminist informed theologies, for example, oppressions on the basis of race, economics, sexuality, geographical and contextual location have often been subsumed by the prioritizing of gender-based oppressions. Jacquelyn Grant spells out clearly her criticisms of feminist informed theology: 'Feminist theology is inadequate for two reasons: it is *White* and *racist*' (Grant, 1989:195).

Fluidity and reflexivity: The challenge to liberation theologies

These narrow and partial understandings of context, and especially of contexts of oppression, do not necessarily lead to the closing down of the possibilities of liberation theologies as effective contextual theologies. If the voices of concern and criticism about the exclusions of liberation theologies are genuinely heard then it is possible that they may lead to more fluid and genuinely reflexive contextual theologies which respond to changes in context and changes in understandings. However, the challenge is not an easy one to accept for it will entail the critique of some of the very core principles and theological components of liberation theologies. The reinvention of liberation theologies, however, is always a possibility. We see glimpses of these possibilities in a number of ways. We see it in the critiques of liberation theologians themselves as they search for new meaningful ways of responding to the evershifting contexts and concerns of oppression. Leonardo Boff spells out clearly the challenges ahead for liberation theologians:

> If our theologies do not help us dream and lead people to live it, we will not have fulfilled the mission the Creator reserved for us in the community of beings, that of the good master and not the Satan of the Earth, nor will we have listened to or followed the One who said 'I have come to bring life, and life abundant'. Sisters and brothers, let us grow up, in the conscience of our responsibility, knowing that no concern is more important than to care for the common home we have, and to achieve that the whole family may live united in this common home with care for the common home we have, and to achieve that the whole human family may live united in this common home with care, solidarity, fraternity, compassion and reverence, which produce a single happiness for the short time we have received to spend on this small planet.
>
> (Boff in Althaus-Reid *et al.*, 2007:9)

The call to change is being influenced by a number of factors. One of these factors is from within the context of theology itself. Because those for whom liberation theology claims to speak have challenged and have even rejected the effectiveness of these theologies. A second factor is the changing circumstances in which those liberation theologies find themselves. In Latin America, for example, although in many ways some of the most pressing concerns that gave rise to theologies of liberation in the first place still exist, the political, social and even religious contexts are changing. The collapse of socialism and rise of capitalism, as Daniel Bell in *Liberation Theology After the End of History* argues, place new challenges before the liberation theologian:

> Latin American liberationist thought is in crisis it has run up against the end of history, the triumph of savage capitalism. It has become entangled in the infinite undulations of the ascendant capitalist order.
>
> Liberation theology is in crisis. This crisis need not be fatal, however, for the wound that precipitated it is self-inflicted and its remedy may be at hand. Liberationist thought is in crisis, not because the capitalist juggernaut really is irresistible, as Fukuyama would have us believe, but because the liberationists have succumbed to the capitalist order by accepting the order's discipline. In particular, they have embraced the modern vision of politics as statecraft.
>
> (Bell, 2001:43–44)

Latin American liberation theologies in the twenty-first century are beginning to reinvent themselves as a new generation of liberation theologians emerge. The contexts of Latin American liberation theologies have changed because of changed political, socioeconomic conditions. Change is both desirable and inevitable for liberation theologies, but that does not mean that these changes mark the end of liberation theologies nor does it necessarily constitute the decline of liberation theologies. Ivan Petrella over the last few years has written and contributed to a number of texts, all concerned in some way with the future of liberation theologies in Latin America. Texts such as *Beyond Liberation Theology: A Polemic* (2008), *The Future of Liberation Theology: An Argument and Manifesto* (2006), *Latin American Liberation Theology: The Next Generation* (2005) and *Another Possible World* (2007) argue that the new generation of Latin American liberation theologians face some of the old challenges but also some new ones. Petrella calls on liberation theology to recover the intrinsic link between liberative thoughts and the means of achieving these. He argues that liberation theologians should be concerning themselves with the practicalities of realizing liberation. He argues that liberation theologies have lost their focus on the historical project with the effect that liberation theologies now exist in the realm of discussion instead of action.

The future of liberation theology is thus tied to recovering a central notion from its past. The current situation takes us back to an original assumption of liberation theology, that historical projects are needed to make real a material and social liberation as well as truly to understand what is at stake in ideals such as the preferential for the preferential option for the poor and liberation. This is the way that the emptying and cooption of the language of liberation can be avoided. The notion of a historical project, however, has fallen far into the backdrop of current liberation theology.

(Petrella in Petrella, 2005:152)

Petrella has concerns about the description of liberation theologies as contextual theologies, seeing in this description another way to 'take the edge off their critique' (Petrella, 2008:132) and seeing it reducing liberation theologies to 'the category of a particular theology in dialogue with other strands of modern theology' (Petrella, 2008:133). This, argues Petrella, ignores the fundamental difference of liberation theologies as theological enterprises. This does not mean that Petrella sees liberation theologies as non-contextual nor does he see them as beyond dialogue. Rather, for Petrella, they very much have a context, but for him this context has limits to its particularity:

> Liberation theologies are born from the struggles of the poor and the oppressed, struggles that were translated into an epistemological break with the whole of the Western, wealthy, white, and male theological tradition; they are not one theological school among others in the canon ... They sought and seek a new understanding of theology itself. The basis of that new understanding is the attempt to do theology from the perspective of the oppressed majority of humankind. Here lies the famous epistemological break: liberation theologies – whether Latin American, black, womanist, African, feminist, queer etc. – realize that theology has traditionally been done from the standpoint of privilege ... By grounding themselves in the perspective of the oppressed, therefore, liberation theologies are grounded in the broadest context available today and come as close as possible to being the first truly global theologies. All theologies are particular and local, but liberation theologies, in their particularity, are as universal as theology can today ever be.
>
> (Petrella, 2008:134–135)

Petrella's reluctance to see liberation theologies as contextual theologies seems to be linked to concern over the meaning of 'contextual theologies' and also linked to his concern about what kinds of claims can be made for liberation theologies beyond the local. This takes us to a key issue in the study of contextual theology – that of the relationship of the local and the particular to the universal.

Contextuality, tradition and identity

A key issue at the heart of the debate about contextual theology is that of identity and tradition and the relationship between the particular and the universal. This issue may take the form of many questions, such as: what is the relationship between radically different theologies which seem to bear no relationship to each other? Where is the Christian tradition in these theologies which are so radically different from what has gone before and which are so radically different from each other? Given their radicalism, especially their radicalism in relation to elements of Christianity, what is discernibly Christian about these theologies so that we might even speak of them as Christian?

This study is not a study of the Christian identity of liberation theologies of contextual theologies; however, some acknowledgement of the contested place of tradition in liberation theologies is needed here. Stephen Pattison writing about theological reflection argues that

> The fact is there is no formal norm. There are all sorts of ways of doing theology which are so different that it sometimes seems that the only thing that unites them is a common claim to be talking about God and religious experience. Theologies work at many different levels and with very different aims, methods and concerns.
>
> The moral for the student is that if theologians are so very different in their approaches and cannot agree on what theology is, there can be no one right way of doing theology and perhaps one's own way is as good as anyone else's it has its own validity and usefulness within one's own situation.
>
> (Pattison in Woodward and Pattison, 2000:37–38)

This approach, however, may not sit well for all. It suggests of relativism in theology and ties the validity and relevance of a theology completely to its context. It argues that as theology arises out of a specific context so the only significance and relevance of that theology is within that specific context. This reading of theology as relative does not sit well with any kind of understanding of Christianity as a religion with inherent and core truths. Pattison's own motivation in offering such a description of theology as above is important. He was concerned in 'Some Straw for Bricks: A Basic Introduction to Theological Reflection', the article from which the quote is taken, to enable the student of theology to begin to navigate the many Christian theologies. The issue of tradition in contextual theology is important, and no less so in liberation theologies. Sigurd Bergmann himself grapples with the role of tradition in contextual theology, claiming that often in contextual theology tradition has been overlooked in the concern with other aspects of theology. He argues that because of contextual theology's concerns with the here and now, with specific historical liberation concerns, 'Urgent problems have led to base groups and theologians first reflecting upon the contemporary situation' (Bergmann, 2003:49). This, he argues, has given critics of liberation theology the opportunity 'to voice disagreement from an alleged traditional interpretation of Christianity' (Bergmann, 2003:49). Bergmann, urges contextual theologies to reflect upon tradition as part of their theological task. He calls for a reading of tradition which recognizes the normative, imperial Western Christianity but which also recognizes the array of Christian traditions from different contexts (Bergmann, 2003:52). Bergmann rejects both David Tracy's correlation hermeneutical model for interpreting tradition as well as Robert Schreiter's argument for local theologies. For him Tracy's model focuses on the establishing of a critical correlation between a specific situation and an interpretation of the Christian tradition. Bergmann's concerns relate to the uncritical assumptions about a core, unchanging tradition in Tracy's theology (Bergmann, 2003:53). Schreiter's understanding of tradition is also at least partly problematic for Bergmann. He interprets Schreiter's understanding of tradition in *Constructing Local Theologies* essentially as a series of local theologies in specific cultural contexts. Theology and culture influence each other. Tradition it seems is a local concept and it operates within a context in which each local theology both participates in and shapes tradition.

> According to Schreiter's we cannot look on tradition as a criterion of truth for Christian assertions of faith. Each theology arises within a culturally conditioned situation, and each tradition is a result of the handing over of local theologies. With this point of view, it is not possible to elevate the interpretation of one local theology as a norm over the other. The conception of what constitutes the entirety of the tradition remains open. That which characterizes the collective series of local theologies remains a constant challenge in interpretation to each local theology. The local theology must create catholicity in dialogue with the past generation's theology for the sake of coming generations.
>
> (Bergmann, 2003:56)

This is not the only possible reading of the approach of contextual liberation theologies to tradition. Many different liberation theologies locate within Christianity a tradition of justice or a tradition of liberation which they argue is the authentic or genuine Christian tradition. This tradition will differ according to the specific contextual theology and the specific biblical and other sources used to evidence its existence. It is a tradition which claims to have both ancient roots and also continuing relevance today. Jacquelyn Grant in *White Women's Christ and Black Women's Jesus* (1989) argues that liberation theologies are characterized by the following convictions:

> (1) Human condition results from the conscious (or unconscious) ethical decisions of human beings; (2) The divine reality is on the side of the oppressed poor, the outcast, the wretched, the downtrodden; and (3) Therefore the gospel reveals that the primary intention of God in the incarnation is one of liberation.
>
> (Grant, 1989:1)

It is Grant's last two points that are so important here. Liberation theologies make very clear and strong claims to 'orthodoxy' through their theologies of

God, through their Christologies, through their biblical hermeneutics and through their understanding of human salvation history. The God of Christian liberation theologies is a God whose preferential concern is for the poor and oppressed because that is the nature of God as love. Jesus through his ministry and through his life and death demonstrated this preferential concern of God for the poor and oppressed. For liberation theologians then Christians have an obligation, which is in itself an opportunity to stand beside the poor and oppressed.

This tradition of justice, which liberation theologies variously interpret and locate at the very heart of Christianity, is interpreted in different ways and identified and recovered using different tools, particular to specific liberation theologies. We see something of this way in which this functions in the feminist informed liberation theology of Carter Heyward who describes herself as a traditionalist. Heyward argues for a very strong tradition between her own experiences and those of the earliest Christians, arguing for a continuity between the life and teachings of Jesus and contemporary events among women in the Church (Heyward, 1984:8):

> The theological norm is the primary hermeneutical principle ... the theo-logical norm operative for me is right-relation or the love of one's neighbor as oneself. In the Old and New Testaments this is referred to as the 'second commandment' ...
>
> (Heyward, 1982:15)

Through the development of her theology of mutual relation, and the central place within this that she gives to the Christian figure and symbol of Jesus, she is able to bring the often radical insights and critiques of feminisms to Chris-tianity whilst at the same time claim a clear relationship to the perceived Christian tradition. She renames or reconfigures a justice-seeking Christianity in which there is a very definite continuity between Christ and feminist informed theology. In *The Redemption of God* she rejects the description of her theolo-gical approach as 'a faulty hermeneutic given zealous voice by one confused woman', claiming instead that it is ' ... a recurrent voice of orthodox Chris-tians' (Heyward, 1982:xvii). It is the location of this liberative or justice-seeking principle as essential Christianity and the subsequent identification of liberation theologies with this liberative tradition which enables liberation theologians to speak of themselves as traditional or even orthodox.

This placing of liberation theologies within the authentic liberating tradition of Christianity is seen even more clearly in the feminist informed theology of Elisabeth Schüssler Fiorenza. The hermeneutic of suspicion, central to her approach, challenges the traditional authority of biblical texts. This is under-pinned by the claim that as biblical texts have been used as tools to oppress and silence women they need now to be subjected to rigorous critical scrutiny before they can be accorded any kind of function or authority in the lives of women and men. Her theology is based on a reading of Christianity, or at least of authentic Christianity, as inherently justice seeking or liberative. Christian theology for Schüssler Fiorenza is not only contextual and specific but has a particular commitment as an advocacy theology: 'Only when theology is on the side of the outcast and oppressed, as Jesus was, can it become incarnational and Christian. Christian theology, therefore, has to be rooted in emanicipatory praxis and solidarity' (Schüssler Fiorenza, 1975:616). Schüssler Fiorenza appeals to an understanding of an original or authentic Christian message of equality that she argues has been marginalized and silenced by the patriarchal movements of recorded history and societal and religious development. She points back in historical terms to an original justice-based Christian vision and praxis free from oppressive tendencies. Her feminist reconstructionist model aims to liberate the egalitarian impulses of the early Christian movement and engage them constructively in contemporary contexts. She claims historical credence for her reading or interpretation of Christianity as justice seeking, arguing that the historical processes by which the initial or original Christian message was recorded, transmitted and developed were influenced by kyriarchal concerns and interests. As a result this means that the egalitarian Christian experience has largely been erased or marginalized to the extent that a radical approach of recovery or reconstruction is needed to piece together this largely lost tradition.

The radicalism of feminisms in such readings, critiques and reconstructions of Christianity are not only justified but necessary given the distorting historical processes of the transmission and development of Christianity. The egalitarian vision or discipleship of equals that Schüssler Fiorenza places at the centre of Christian history and at the centre of the Christian experience is incorporated and maintained by feminist visions and values. The discipleship of equals in Schüssler Fiorenza's theology is understood in the following way:

> The praxis and vision of Jesus and his movement is best understood as an inner-Jewish renewal movement that presented an *alternative* option to the dominant patriarchal structures rather than an oppositional formation rejecting the values and praxis of Judaism.
>
> (Schüssler Fiorenza, 1983:105)

From this *ekklesia* of women places women's experiences and feminist informed analysis and praxis at the centre of Christian theology. It stresses the historical continuity of the discipleship of equals and contemporary feminist informed Christian theology. It is in this way that Schüssler Fiorenza can be seen to incorporate the radical insights of feminisms into theology whilst at the same time still claim a direct relationship to the perceived Christian tradition. The authority that she places with the experiences of women and feminist informed analysis determines or guides the theological process.

Tradition remains a very complex question to ask of liberation theologies, especially given their emphasis on context. At the same time, however, most if not all of these theologies do talk of tradition and articulate themselves as standing within the 'authentic' tradition of Christianity. Many liberation theologies turn to the biblical tradition and identify a liberating core or liberating principles in the search for the authentic Christian gospel, the true Church, the essence of Christianity. For Elisabeth Schüssler Fiorenza this is the discipleship of equals; for Rosemary Radford Ruether it is the prophetic messianic tradition; for body theologians such as James Nelson it is the embodied nature of the Christian gospel, the incarnation of God through Christ in human form; for black theologians such as James Cone it is the biblical tradition of God's concern with oppressed and delivery from oppression; for Latin American theologians such as Gutiérrez it is God's preferential option for the poor that is at the heart of the Christian gospel.

Conclusion

This book has clearly focused more on what is contextual about Christian contextual liberation theologies rather than what is Christian about contextual liberation theologies. There has inevitably been some overlap of these distinct but intricately related questions but the main concern has been to explore the forms, guiding principles and limits of contextuality in liberation theologies. Liberation theologies have been shown to be Christian theologies which are characterized by a criticism of traditional theology as being too often the theology of privilege. Liberation theologies articulate theologies out of contexts of oppression and aim to engage theology in opposing oppression. Liberation theologies are particularly critical of the ways in which theology fails to acknowledge the importance of the context(s) of the theologian and the theological community. They call for reflective and responsive theologies which articulate clearly the contextual factors that motivate and shape them. However, this stress on context had proved to be quite problematic for liberation theologies, as R.S. Sugirtharajah argues:

> Generic and pan-Asian, pan-Latin American and pan-African theologies of the 1960s have given way to localized-identity and issue-specific theologies. The result has been the emergence of feminist, Dalit, Burakumin and tribal theological discourses. These theological articulations are largely attempts to grapple with subaltern status and to recover identity and authenticity. In this process communities have been reimagined, and reconceptualized. Metanarratives such as that of unity in diversity have been celebrated but then discredited. Paradoxically, identity-based theologies are in danger of reifying their own subjecthood and contexts. What began as a startlingly original discourse is now rife with theological clichés, and as a result the discourse both undermines and plays into its own stereotypes. Identities and contests change. Once this happens, to keep on parroting uncritically the old catchphrases is to run the risk of turning these once emancipator concepts into ossified absolutes and paper-tiger triumphalism.
>
> (Sugirtharajah, 2003:3)

Here, the developments and increasing presence of postcoloni
become of particular interest. Not just as challenging and innovat
theologies in their own right, but as contemporary theologies whicl
much still in their infancy, have the benefits of a more sophisticaᵤₑᵤ ₐₙᵤ ᵤᵣₑᵤ
and tested use of poststructuralist thinking in theology. They are developing
new ways of doing theology, learning from the criticisms that have been levelled
at other liberation theologies so far. It may be tempting to describe postcolonial
theologies as the next generation of contextual theologies of liberation, but this
oversimplifies the chronological and theological relationship between liberation
theologies, and they are more than this. But they do have much to offer contemporary Christian theologies whose agenda is characterized by a concern
with both the contextual and also with justice.

This book has explored the place of contextuality in Christian theology by
looking at just one group of Christian theologies. From this it has identified key
issues facing theologies which make explicit the place of the human context in
their theologies. The study of other types of Christian theologies will yield a
different set of data about the contextual nature of Christian theology and will
give rise to a different set of questions.

Bibliography

Abeysekara, A. (2004), 'Identity for and against itself: Religion, criticism and pluralization', *Journal of the American Academy of Religion*, 72(4), pp.973–1001.

Althaus-Reid, M. (2000), *Indecent Theology: Theological Perversions in Sex, Gender and Politics*, London and New York: Routledge.

—— (2003), *The Queer God*, London and New York: Routledge.

Althaus-Reid, M. and Isherwood, L. (eds) (2008), *Controversies in Body Theology*, London: SCM.

Althaus-Reid, M., Petrella, I. and Susin, L.C. (eds) (2007), *Another Possible World*, London: SCM Press.

Bakewell, P. (2004), *A History of Latin America: c. 1450 to the Present* (Second Edition), Oxford: Blackwell Publishing.

Ballard, P. and Pritchard, J. (2006), *Practical Theology in Action: Christian Thinking in the Service of Church and Society*, London: SPCK.

Beckford, R. (1998), *Jesus is Dread: Black Theology and Black Culture in Britain*, London: Darton, Longman & Todd.

Bell, D.M. Jr. (2001), *Liberation Theology After the End of History: The Refusal to Cease Suffering*, London and New York: Routledge.

Benedict, R. (1935), *Patterns of Culture*, London: Routledge & Kegan Paul.

Bergmann, S. (2003), *God in Context: A Survey of Contextual Theology*, Aldershot: Ashgate.

Bevans, S.B. (2002), *Models of Contextual Theology* (Revised and Expanded Edition), Maryknoll: Orbis Books.

Bhabha, H.K. (2006), *The Location of Culture*, London and New York: Routledge.

Boff, L. (1978), *Jesus Christ Liberator: Critical Christiology of our Time*, Maryknoll, NY: Orbis Books.

—— (1979), *Liberating Grace*, New York: Orbis Books.

Bonino, J.M. (1975), *Doing Theology in a Revolutionary Situation*, Philadelphia: Fortress Press.

Børresen, K. (1968), *Subordination and Equivalence*, Oslo: Oslo University Press.

Bosch, D.J. (1991), *Transforming Mission: Paradigm Shifts in Theology of Mission*, Maryknoll: American Society of Missiology Studies, no.16.

Brookes, A. (1997), *Postfeminisms: Feminism, Cultural Theory and Cultural Forms*, London: Routledge.

Cady Stanton, E. (1999), *The Woman's Bible*, New York: Prometheus Books.

Cannon, K.G. (1987), 'Hitting a straight lick with a crooked stick: the womanist dilemma in the development of a Black liberation ethic', *Annual of the Society of Christian Ethics*, pp.165–177.

Carr, A. (ed.) (1987), *Women, Work and Poverty*, Carr, A. and Schüssler Fiorenza, E. (eds), *Women, Work and Poverty ('Concilium')*, Edinburgh: T & T Clark.

Chopp, R. and Davaney, S.G. (eds) (1997), *Horizons in Feminist Theology: Identity, Tradition and Norms*, Minneapolis: Fortress Press.

Christ, C. (1977), 'The new feminist theology: a review of the literature', *Religious Studies Review*, 3(4), pp.203–212.

Christ, C. and Plaskow, J. (eds) (1992), *Womanspirit Rising: A Feminist Reader in Religion*, San Francisco: Harper SanFrancisco.

Chung, P.S., Kärkkäinen, V. and Kyoung-Jae, K. (eds) (2007), *Asian Contextual Theology for the Third Millennium: A Theology of Minjung in Fourth-Eye Formation*, Princeton Theological Monograph Series 70, Eugene: Wipf and Stock Publishers.

Cobb, K. (2005), *The Blackwell Guide to Theology and Popular Culture*, Oxford: Blackwell Publishing.

Coleman, K. (1998), 'Black theology and black liberation: a womanist perspective', *Black Theology*, 1, pp.59–69.

Cone, J. (1969), *Black Theology and Black Power*, New York: The Seasbury Press.

—— (1970), *A Black Theology of Liberation*, Philadelphia: J. P. Lippincott.

—— (1975: 1977), *God of the Opressed*, London: SPCK.

—— (1984), *For My People: Black Theology and the Black Church*, Maryknoll: Orbis Books.

Cooper, T. (2007), *Controversies in Political Theology: Development or Liberation?*, London: SCM Press.

Coward, R. (1999), *Sacred Cows: Is Feminism Relevant to the New Millennium?* London: HarperCollins Publishers.

Crook, M.B. (1964), *Women and Religion*, Boston: Beacon Press.

Cruz, E.R. (2004), 'The future of the New World that was supposed to be', *Dialog: A Journal of Theology*, 43(1), pp.34–36.

Culpepper, E. (1988), 'New tools for theology: writings by women of color', *Journal of Feminist Studies in Religion*, 4, pp.39–50.

Daly, M. (1965), 'A built in bias', *Commnweal*, 81, pp.308–311.

—— (1984), *Gyn/Ecology: The Metaethics of Radical Feminism*, London: The Women's Press.

—— (1985) [1968], *The Church and the Second Sex*, Boston: Beacon Press.

—— (1986) [1973], *Beyond God the Father: Towards a Philosophy of Women's Liberation*, London: The Women's Press.

—— (1988), *Webster's First New Intergalactic Wickedary of the English Language*, London: The Women's Press.

—— (1993), *Outercourse: The Be-Dazzling Voyage*, London: The Women's Press.

Davaney, S.G. (1987), 'Problems with feminist theory: historicity and the search for sure foundations', Cooey, P.M., Farmer, S.A. and Ross, M.E. (eds), *Embodied Love: Sensuality and Relationship as Feminist Values*, San Francisco: Harper & Row.

De Beauvoir, S. (1981), *The Second Sex*, Harmondsworth: Penguin Books.

Dennis, M., Golden, R. and Wright, S. (2007), *Oscar Romero: Reflections on His Life and Writings*, Maryknoll: Orbis Books.

Dietrich, W. and Luz, U. (eds) (2002), *The Bible in a World Context: An Experiment in Contextual Hermeneutics*, Grand Rapids, Michigan/Cambridge, UK: William B. Eerdmans Publishing Company.

Doely, S.B. (ed.) (1970), *Women's Liberation and the Church: The New Demand for Freedom in the Life of the Christian Church*, New York: Association Press.

Doetis Roberts, Sr., J. (1976), 'Contextual theology: Liberation and indigenization', *Christian Century*, 28, pp.64–68.

Dussel, E. (ed.) (1992), *The Church in Latin America 1492–1992*, Kent: Burns & Oates.

Eller, C. (1993), *Living in the Lap of the Goddess: The Feminist Spirituality Movement in America*, New York: Crossroad.

Ellingsen, M. (2005), *The Richness of Augustine: His Contextual and Pastoral Theology*, Louisville: Westminster/John Knox Press.

Faludi, S. (1991), *Backlash: The Undeclared War Against Women*, London: Chatto & Windus.

Freire, P. (1995), *Pedagogy of Hope*, London, New York: Continuum International Publishing Group.

—— (1996) [1970], *Pedagogy of the Oppressed* (translated by Myra Bergman Ramos), London: Penguin Books.

Friedan, B. (1963), *The Feminine Mystique*, London: WW Norton & Co.

Gage, M.J. (1980) [1893], *Woman, Church and State*, Watertown: Persephone Press.

Gibellini, R. (1987), *The Liberation Theology Debate*, London: SCM Press.

Gilbert, A. (1990), *Latin America*, New York: Routledge.

Gill, R. (1975), *The Social Context of Theology: A Methodological Enquiry by Robin Gill*, London and Oxford: Mowbrays.

Goldenberg, N. (1979), *Changing of the Gods: Feminism and the End of Traditional Religion*, Boston: Beacon Press.

Goss, R. (1983), *Jesus Acted Up: A Gay and Lesbian Manifesto*, San Francisco: Harper-SanFrancisco.

—— (2007), *Queering Christ: Beyond Jesus Acted Up*, Eugene: Resources Publications.

Graham, E., Walton, H. and Ward, F. (2005), *Theological Reflection: Methods*, London: SCM Press.

Grant, J. (1989), *White Women's Christ and Black Women's Jesus: Feminist Christology and Womanist Response*, Atlanta: Scholars Press.

Greer, G. (1970), *The Female Eunuch*, New York: McGraw-Hill Book Company.

Gross, R.M. (2000), 'Feminist theology: religiously diverse neighborhood or Christian ghetto?', *Journal of Feminist Studies in Religion*, 16(2), 73–78.

Gutiérrez, G. (1988) [1971], *A Theology of Liberation: History, Politics and Salvation* (Revised Version), London: SCM.

Hall, C., O Sullivan, S., Phoenix, A., Storr, M., Thomas, L. and Whitehead, A. (1999), 'Snakes and ladders: reviewing feminisms at century's end', *Feminist Review*, 61, 1–3.

Hampson, D. (1990), *Theology and Feminism*, Oxford: Basil Blackwell.

Harrison, B.W., Heyward, C., Hunt, M.C., Townes, E.M., Starhawk Barstow, A.L. and Cooey, P. (1994), 'Roundtable discussion: backlash', *Journal of Feminist Studies in Religion*, 10(1), pp.91–111.

Harrison, N. (2006), *Postcolonial Criticism: History, Theory and the Work of Fiction*, Cambridge: Polity Press.

Hennelly, A.T. (ed.) (1997), *Liberation Theology: A Documentary History, Edited with Introductions, Commentary and Translations by Alfred T. Hennelly, S.J.* (Fourth Edition), New York: Orbis Books.

Hewitt, M.A. (1995), *Critical Theory of Religion: A Feminist Analysis*, Minneapolis: Fortress Press.

Heyward, C. (1982), *The Redemption of God: A Theology of Mutual Redemption*, Washington DC: University Press of America.

—— (1984), *Our Passion for Justice: Images of Power, Sexuality and Liberation*, New York: Pilgrim Press.

Hoagland, S.L. and Frye, M. (eds) (2000), *Feminist Interpretations of Mary Daly*, Pennsylvania: The Pennsylvanian State University Press.

Humm, M. (ed.) (1992), *Feminisms: A Reader*, London: Harvester Wheatsheaf.

Isasi-Díaz, A.M. (1979), 'Silent women will never be heard', *Missiology*, 7(3), pp. 295–301.

—— (1997), *Mujerista Theology: A Theology for the Twenty-First Century*, New York: Maryknoll.

Isasi-Díaz, A.M. and Segovia, F.F. (eds) (1996), *Hispanic Latino Theology: Challenge and Promise*, Minneapolis: Fortress Press.

Isherwood, L. and Stuart, E. (1998), *Introducing Body Theology*, Sheffield: Sheffield Academic Press.

Jantzen, G.M. (1998), *Becoming Divine: Towards a Feminist Philosophy of Religion*, Manchester: Manchester University Press.

Kee, A. (2006), *The Rise and Demise of Black Theology*, Aldershot: Ashgate.

Keller, C., Nausner, M. and Rivera, M. (eds) (2004), *Postcolonial Theologies: Divinity and Empire*, St Louis: Chalice Press.

King, U. (1993), *Women and Spirituality: Voices of Protest and Promise* (Second Edition), London: Macmillan Press.

Leech, K. (1981), *The Social God*, London: Sheldon Press.

Leonard, E. (1990), 'Experience as a source for theology: a Canadian and feminist perspective', *Studies in Religion/Sciences Religieuses*, 19(2), pp.143–162.

Linzey, A. and Wexley, P. (eds) (1991), *Fundamentalism and Tolerance: An Agenda for Theology and Society*, London: Bellew Publishing.

Lonergan, B. (1990), *Method in Theology*, Toronto: University of Toronto Press.

MacKinnon, H. and McIntyre, M. (eds) (1980), *Readings in Ecology & Feminist Theology*, Kansas City: Sheed & Ward.

McFarlane, A. and Posada-Carbó, E. (1999), *Independence and Revolution in Spanish America: Perspectives and Problems*, London: Institute of Latin American Studies.

Maitland, S. (1983), *A Map of the New Country: Women and Christianity*, London: Routledge & Kegan Paul.

Marks, D.C. (2002), *Shaping a Theological Mind: Theological Context and Methodology*, Aldershot: Ashgate.

May, M. (1995), *A Body Knows: A Theopoetics of Death and Resurrection*, New York: Continuum International Publishing Group.

Mead, M. (1949), *Male and Female: A Study of the Sexes in a Changing World*, New York: William Morrow & Co.

Mehrez, S. (1991), 'The subversive poetics of racial bilingualism: Postcolonial Francophone North African literature', Dominick LaCapra (ed.), *The Bounds of Race: Perspectives on Hegemony and Resistance*, Ithaca: Cornell University Press, pp.255–277.

Menon, K.D. (2005), 'Religious pluralism and interfaith dialogue: A view from India', *CrossCurrents*, Spring, pp.37–40.

Mernissi, F. (1975), *Beyond the Veil: Male–Female Dynamics in a Modern Muslim Society*, Cambridge, Massachusetts: Schenkman.

Milbank, J. (2006), *Theology and Social Theory: Beyond Secular Reason* (Second Edition), Oxford: Blackwell Publishing.

Millett, K. (1977) [1970], *Sexual Politics*, London: Virago.

Nelson, J. (1978), *Embodiment: An Approach to Sexuality and Christian Theology*, Minneapolis: Augsburg Fortress Publishers.

—— (1988: 1991), *The Intimate Connection: Male Sexuality, Masculine Spirituality*, Grand Rapids: William B. Eerdmans Publishing Company.

—— (1992), *Body Theology*, Louisville: Westminster/John Knox Press.

O'Neill, M. (1990), *Women Speaking, Women Listening: Women in Interreligious Dialogue*, Maryknoll: Orbis Books.

Parsons, S. (2002), *The Ethics of Gender*, Oxford: Blackwell.

Parvey, C. (1969), 'Ordain her, ordain her not', *Dialog*, 8(3), pp.203–208.

Pattison, S., with Woodward, J. (1994), *A Vision of Pastoral Theology*, Edinburgh: Contact Pastoral.

Petrella, I. (ed.) (2005), *Latin American Liberation Theology: The Next Generation*, Maryknoll: Orbis Books.

Petrella, I. (2006), *The Future of Liberation Theology: An Argument and Manifesto*, London: SCM Press.

—— (2008), *Beyond Liberation Theology: A Polemic*, London: SCM Press.

Piedra, A.M. (1985), 'Some observations on liberation theology', *World Affairs*, 148(3), pp.151–158.

Plaskow, J. and Christ, C.P. (1989), *Weaving the Visions: New Patterns of Spirituality*, San Francisco: Harper & Row.

Pope, S.J. (ed.) (2008), *Hope and Solidarity: Jon Sobrino's Challenge to Christian Theology*, Maryknoll: Orbis Books.

Prior, M. (1997), *The Bible and Colonialism: A Moral Critique*, Sheffield: Sheffield Academic Press.

Pui-lan, K. (2000), *Introducing Feminist Theology*, Sheffield: Sheffield Academic Press.

—— (2005), *Postcolonial Imagination and Feminist Theology*, London: SCM Press.

Pui-lan, K. and Schüssler Fiorenza, E. (eds) (1998), *Women's Sacred Scriptures (Concilium*, 1998(3)), London: SCM Press.

Rowland, C. (ed.) (1999), *The Cambridge Companion to Liberation Theology*, Cambridge: Cambridge University Press.

Ruether, R.R. (1971), 'Male chauvinist theology and the anger of women', *Cross Currents*, pp.173–85.

—— (ed.) (1974), *Religion and Sexism: Images of Woman in the Jewish and Christian Traditions*, New York: Simon & Schuster.

—— (1975), *New Woman, New Earth: Sexist Ideologies and Human Liberation*, New York: The Seabury Press.

—— (1976) 'What is the task of theology?', *Christianity and Crisis*, 36, pp.121–125.

—— (ed.) (2007), *Feminist Theologies: Legacy and Prospect*, Minneapolis: Augsburg Fortress Publishers.

Russell, L. and Shannon, J. (eds) (1996), *Dictionary of Feminist Theologies*, London: Mowbray.

Said, E. (1979), *Orientalism*, New York: Vintage Books.

—— (2000), *Out of Place: A Memoir*, New York: Vintage Books.

Saiving, V. (1960), 'The human situation: a feminine view', *Journal of Religion*, 40(2), pp.100–112.

Sawyer, D. and Collier, D.M. (eds) (1999), *Is There a Future for Feminist Theology?*, Sheffield: Sheffield Academic Press.

Schreiter, R.J. (1985: 2007), *Constructing Local Theologies*, Maryknoll: Orbis Books.

Schüssler Fiorenza, E. (1975), 'Feminist theology as a critical theology of Liberation', *Theological Studies*, 36(4), pp.605–626.

—— (1983), *In Memory of Her: A Feminist Theological Reconstruction of Christian Origins*, London: SCM Press Ltd.

Schüssler Fiorenza, E. (ed.) (1993), *Searching the Scriptures, Volume One: A Feminist Introduction*, New York: Crossroad.

Schüssler Fiorenza, E. (ed.) (1994), *Searching the Scriptures, Vol.2: A Feminist Commentary*, New York: Crossroad.

Schüssler Fiorenza, E. (2002), 'Thinking and working across borders: The Feminist Liberation Theologians, Activists, and Scholars in Religion Network', *Journal of Feminist Studies in Religion*, 18(1), pp. 71–74.

Segal, L. (1987), *Is the Future Female? Troubled Thoughts on Contemporary Feminism*, London: Virago.

Segovia, F.F. (2000), *Interpreting Beyond the Borders*, The Bible and Postcolonialism, 3, Sheffield: Sheffield Academic Press.

—— (2000), *Decolonizing Biblical Studies: A View from the Margins*, Maryknoll: Orbis Books.

Segovia, F.F. and Sugirtharajah, R.S. (eds) (2007), *A Postcolonial Commentary on the New Testament Writings*, London and New York: T. & T. Clark Publishers.

Sheldrake, P. (1994), *Befriending Our Desires*, Notre Dame, Ind.: Ave Maria Press.

Smith, C. (1991), *The Emergence of Liberation Theology: Radical Religion and Social Movement Theory*, Chicago and London: The University of Chicago Press.

Sobrino, J. (1978: 2002), *Christology at the Crossroads: A Latin American Approach*, Eugene: Wipf and Stock Publishers.

Stuart, E. (ed.) (1997), *Religion is a Queer Thing: A Guide to the Christian Faith for Lesbian, Gay, Bisexual and Transgendered People*, London and Washington: Cassell.

Suchocki, M. (1980), 'The challenge of Mary Daly', *Encounter*, 41, pp.307–317.

Sugirtharajah, R.S. (1998), *Asian Biblical Hermeneutics and Post Colonialism: Contesting the Interpretations*, Sheffield: Sheffield Academic Press.

—— (2002), *Postcolonial Criticism and Biblical Interpretation*, Oxford: Oxford University Press.

—— (2003), *Postcolonial Reconfigurations: An Alternative Way of Reading the Bible and Doing Theology*, St Louis: Chalice Press.

—— (2005), 'Scripture, scholarship, empire: Putting the discipline in its place', *The Expository Times*, 2005, pp.2–11.

—— (2008), *Troublesome Texts: The Bible in Colonial and Contemporary Culture*, Sheffield: Sheffield Phoenix Press.

Tavard, G. (1973), *Women in the Christian Tradition*, London/Notre Dame: University of Notre Dame Press.

Thistlethwaite, S.B. and Engel, M.P. (1998), *Life Every Voice: Constructing Christian Theologies from the Underside*, Maryknoll: Orbis Books.

Todorov, T. (1999), *The Conquest of America: The Question of the Other*, Norman: University of Oklahoma Press.

Tombs, D. (2002), *Latin American Liberation Theology*, Boston: Brill Academic Publishers.

Trible, P. (1978), *God and the Rhetoric of Sexuality*, Philadelphia: Fortress Press.

Volf, M. (2003), 'Liberation theology after the end of history: an exchange', *Modern Theology*, 19(2), pp.261–269.

Vuola, E. (2002), *Limits of Liberation: Feminist Theology and the Ethics of Poverty and Reproduction*, New York, London: Sheffield Academic Press, A Continuum Imprint.

Woodward, J. and Pattison, S. (eds) (2000), *The Blackwell Reader in Pastoral and Practical Theology*, Oxford: Blackwell Publishing.

Young, R.J.C. (2003), *Postcolonialism: A Very Short Introduction*, Oxford: Oxford University Press.

Index